3⁰⁰

Vic Braden's

Tennis for the Future

Vic Braden's

Tennis for the Future

by Vic Braden and Bill Bruns

A Sports Illustrated Book

Little, Brown and Company   Boston • Toronto

Seventh Printing

T06/77

Unless otherwise noted, the photographs in this book were taken by Vic and Melody Braden.

Special photography by John G. Zimmerman

Instructional charts and drawings by Moe Lebovitz

Thanks to the following people who agreed to appear in the photographs for this book: Odartey Annan, Troy Davis, Mike Hearl, David Kramer, Russ Larsen, Cathy Ley, Mary Ley, Richard Ley, Marita McKee, Mike Markillie, Pamela Muesse, Rick Stephens, John Stewart, Ike Tyler, Don Usher, Tom Warfel, and Fred Wilson.

Library of Congress Cataloging in Publication Data

Braden, Vic.
  Vic Braden's Tennis for the future.

  "A Sports Illustrated book."
  1. Tennis. I. Bruns, Bill, joint author. II. Title. III. Title: Tennis for the future.
GV995.B686   796.34'22   77-5603
ISBN 0-316-10510-4

*Sports Illustrated Books
are published by
Little, Brown and Company
in association with
Sports Illustrated Magazine*

MV

Designed by Chris Benders

*Published simultaneously in Canada
by Little, Brown & Company (Canada) Limited*

PRINTED IN THE UNITED STATES OF AMERICA

Acknowledgments

It only takes a little time to thank a few of the people who have done some big things for me:

The people who gave me a start — Lawrence Alto, Hap and Agnes Funk, Fielding Tambling.

The man who taught me most of what I know about tennis — Jack Kramer.

The people who gave me a break when I needed it — Greg Harney; Lamar Hunt; Al Hill, Jr.; Mike Davies; Bob Briner; Eddie Toler; and George MacCall.

The photographers who continue to teach me — John Zimmerman, Phil Bath, and Russ Adams.

The brilliant physicists/computer scientists who aid our exciting tennis research efforts — Dr. Pat Keating and Dr. Gideon Ariel.

The man who put my thoughts into words — Bill Bruns.

The company that built my tennis college at Coto de Caza — the Great Southwest Corporation, and especially Bruce Juell, Vic Palmieri, Nelson Rising, and Bob Wilhelm.

The man who finally taught me that income must exceed expenses — Charles Silverberg.

And finally — my parents, my three brothers, my three sisters, my five children, and my beautiful wife Melody.

— VIC BRADEN

Contents

Vic Braden's

Tennis for the Future

Introduction

TENNIS SEEMS INNOCENTLY simple to those who are outside the fence looking in. There are no sand traps to worry about, or moguls, or blitzing linebackers, or 7-10 splits. The court looks so huge and the net seems so low that people tend to think, "Heck, this game's a piece of cake."

Yet those of you who have played tennis, and who have tried to improve, know how difficult it is to advance beyond the stage where you're just happy to get the ball back over the net without any special "sauce" or a particular strategy. Even professional athletes from other sports admit that tennis can be downright humbling. They can't understand how they can be strong, fast, and coordinated — yet miss the ball. Or that a ten-year-old kid can yo-yo them around the court and show no mercy, except to say afterwards, "Gee, mister, you're getting better."

The truth of the matter is that you can laugh your guts out in tennis from the first day you pick up a racket, but once you try to keep the ball inside the boundaries — under pressure — this game can also produce a great amount of stress. The court starts to shrink, the "low" net seems to catch your best forehand drives, and there's no place to hide your ego if you hit the ball into the next county, miss it completely, trip over a crack on the court, or smash an overhead into the net as your opponent prays on the other side. Plus, you're out there with very few clothes on; if you lose, you lose half-naked. Students often tell me they wish they could wear a football helmet or a long robe so they could hide from their mistakes.

Basically, a good tennis player can be defined as one who is able to hit a target area while under stress. But that's the problem. Stress does strange things to people. The longest service toss I've ever witnessed went over the back fence, 12 feet up and 21 feet back. In singles I see people run to the net and get so mixed up that instead of hitting the ball they yell, "Yours." Others will run nicely to hit a volley — but catch the ball instead of swinging at it. Then there are those players who simply freeze up when their opponent prepares to return a shot. They're so afraid to make the wrong decision that they just stand there poised in their ready position thinking, "Is it going to be to my backhand or to my forehand? . . . Son-of-a-gun, it was to my backhand."

The goal of this book, therefore, is to help you handle this stress and perform well under pressure by helping you develop *the right strokes, a confidence in these strokes, and a no-frills approach to strategy.* Your basic swing on each stroke is my main concern because that's what tennis boils down to: do you have the weapons? You can have unbelievable anticipation, fancy footwork, and a brilliant mind, but if you have a crummy swing when you get to the ball, you're not going to win. Conversely, you can have slow reactions, lousy footwork, and get caught late, yet still make a good hit if you can effect a perfect swing. So work hard to develop proper strokes and, if we have to, we'll call a cab to get you to the ball in time.

Lefthanders, there's a place for you here, too. You may think that tennis is tougher for you to learn, but remember: your stroke patterns are identical to those used by righthanders, but in reverse. In other words, your forehand is exactly the same as a righthander's backhand, and your backhand is the same as his forehand. Physical laws dictate where the ball goes and these laws remain the same no matter which side you swing from. Still, I have great empathy for lefthanders because I know they are always being discriminated against in instruction.

When I first started coaching, I got an early lesson in how easy it is to forget that not every player is righthanded. There was a young boy in my group who was a natural athlete — but a crummy tennis player. He was hitting righthanded and he really had me baffled, so finally I said, "Gil, I can't understand it. You have all the moves, you look terrific, but you can't hit the ball at all. I must be doing something wrong."

"Yeh, man," he said. "You let me hit lefthanded and I'm terrific." I had directed the entire lesson to righthanders and he was simply doing what I asked him to do.

Not only will good strokes help you relax as you play, so will a sense of humor. I want you to have fun as we go along because I've always felt that learning to play a better game of tennis can co-exist with laughter if you will base your self-critique not upon how many matches you win or lose but upon your own self-improvement. When I see a student at my tennis college who can laugh at his mistakes, I know he's going to go home an improved player. He's having more fun and he's apt to try some of the new things that can help his game. The uptight people only get worse.

Levels of proficiency take a long time to achieve, but your enjoyment can be immediate. Thus I try to be as entertaining as I can, while realizing that a coach can't humor people into playing good tennis — you and I eventually have to get down to nitty-gritty details about technique in order to make any real headway. Therefore a second objective of this book is to help make you self-reliant out on the court, no matter what your level of play. I want you to understand *how* to execute a particular stroke, *why* you want to swing that way, and *where* you want to try to hit particular shots. Not until tennis technique and strategy make sense to you will you have the confidence and willingness to develop the right strokes or to change your swing to overcome specific weaknesses.

A qualified professional can get you started on the right road, but after that, the answers to this game are *in your head*, not locked up with a local pro, to be dispensed in 30-minute lessons. That's what's beautiful about this game. *You* can teach yourself good sound strokes and *you* can learn to detect errors in that technique. Independent thinkers, not dependent thinkers, make the biggest gains in tennis, so quit looking outside the gate for help — the solutions to developing sound strokes aren't far-out theories, they're inside you.

In order to help you help yourself improve at a faster rate — with or without the aid of a teaching pro — I present self-evaluative drills and check-points throughout the book that will enable you to analyze your own strokes during a match, while rallying with a friend, or while swinging your racket in the living room. I'll give you ideas for a do-it-yourself tennis lab, so that you can practice perfect strokes at home, while strengthening the muscles you need to make these strokes effective. With court space at an increasing premium, and few people willing to use such time simply to practice, you'll be way ahead of your rivals if you can learn to coach yourself, even while waiting for a court.

If you are already working with a qualified teaching pro, this book should increase the value of your lessons, and enrich your relationship with that pro. If you read this book and then take lessons, you will know exactly what the pro is trying to tell you about your game and what he is trying to achieve. You should even be able to detect unqualified pros.

This book is not for you, however, if you are shopping around for a revolutionary approach, trick shots, gimmicks, or a get-rich-quick theory that will "unlock" the secrets of the game. I don't believe that any pro — myself included — has a unique theory on how to play better tennis. All good strokes are supported by sound physical laws, not a pro's theory, and these laws reduce tennis strokes to a common denominator: people can approach

Common tennis theories and techniques are constantly being researched at the Vic Braden Tennis College. Here, a special ball-projection machine is used to study the effects of ball rotation and other in-flight characteristics.

the ball in any kind of unique fashion they want, but to produce identical results on two different shots, the ball must be hit exactly the same way both times.

The pro's job is to make you understand the forces that are at work when the racket contacts the ball, and to help you develop a swing to accommodate them. Unfortunately, most people try to fight reality by clinging to their same old swing and making "adjustments" with their racket face. These adjustments are the reason they keep finishing second in a field of two.

The techniques I emphasize in this book will go against the grain of certain tennis instruction and well-established myths. Yet nothing I teach violates physical laws, to the best of my knowledge. People have told me that I have "an interesting system," and they often ask if there's a pro in their area who teaches it. I have to tell them that I simply base my approach on the basic physical laws which dictate the action of the racket, its impact on the ball, and the movement of the body. In addition, we're all governed by the realities of the court and the net.

For example, tennis is a *lifting* game. The net is a high barrier — much higher than most people envision — and this means that you must try to produce topspin on your forehand and backhand *if* you want to hit the ball hard and still bring it down deep in your opponent's court. *No matter what your ability or your strength — or what you've been told — you can learn to hit topspin.* It doesn't take a strong arm or a powerful wrist, but it does require the ability to get low with your racket and your body so that you can contact the ball with a vertical racket face that is moving from low to high.

I place a lot of emphasis in my teaching on the all-around virtues of topspin because I want you to play this game right. With topspin — as opposed to underspin or anything hit on a horizontal plane — you can hit the ball harder, with greater safety, short or deep; thus you can beat an opponent who camps at the baseline or one who likes to rush the net. You cannot hit hard swinging on the horizontal unless you have unbelievable accuracy, and without speed on the ball you severely limit your opportunities against good players.

Everything in this book has been tested in special research or experiments at my tennis college or through my association with the great players in the game over the last 30 years. Despite that, I know that if what I say doesn't make sense, you won't try it. So sit back periodically and think about what I'm saying. If my rationale for a certain stroke sounds far out, then put me to the test out on the court. If you're thinking, "I don't need to work on my forehand — it's terrific," see if you can hit a target area (a three-foot radius around your intended target) while under stress.

Try the following test. Since the goal on forehands, when both players are at the baseline, is to land the ball within five feet of your opponent's baseline, lay a piece of rope from one singles sideline to the other, five feet inside the baseline. Then stand at the baseline and have a friend start hitting balls to your forehand. Play against yourself and see if you can win by giving yourself a point when your shot lands inside the target area, a point against you when it doesn't. Even by yourself, when you bounce the ball and hit a forehand, you'll have a hard time winning one game in a set.

Similarly, you may have the weirdest-looking serve in the world, but it's your own creation and it works in Pismo Beach, so you're not about to give it up despite what I might say. That's fine by me. I never insist that people change their crazy strokes, only that they put them to the test. If you can serve with a windmill motion and still hit the ball into your opponent's backhand corner 8 out of 10 times, I won't laugh — I'll just want to know your secret. But if you have a cannonball serve that only goes in once every other April, then think about changing your swing and your concept of the serve. You can take an individual approach in this game, but you can't fight physical laws if you expect to play well.

Just be fair with yourself. Learn to have fun with this game because you can't do all the things on the court you think you can do, nor is there much room in which to do them. *When you really study your game, and learn which shots you actually "own," that's when you begin to place less emphasis on strategy and fancy shots, and much more attention to working on your strokes.*

A final warning about this book: If you've finally grown tired of losing to the same people week after week, year after year, and you want to gain a little respect for your tennis game, you might be thinking, "I'll read Vic's book, schedule a match with Bertha next Tuesday, and blow her off the court with my new strokes." I wish I could promise you that kind of quick success, but as I'll discuss further in Chapter One, when you start tinkering with your tennis game you often regress before improving. Instead of losing to Bertha 6-3, 6-3 as you usually do, you may lose 6-0, 6-0 for a couple of weeks, and I can hear you telling friends, "I just read Vic Braden's book, tried out the new concepts, and now I couldn't even beat my grandmother." Obviously I don't need that kind of endorsement.

So try to give what I say a chance. I'm confident I can help you make

Remember, tennis is less complicated — but not any easier — than you think. When playing from the baseline (top), you'll beat almost anybody that you play if you can learn to consistently hit down the center into a five-foot radius at your opponent's baseline.

some pretty sizable gains if you will put these theories to the test with an open mind and a willingness to make key changes in your swing. Remember, tennis is a game you can play from age three to ninety — and good strokes will last a lifetime.

Chapter One

Common Myths and Key Fundamentals

I F YOU'RE LIKE many tennis players, the chances are good that you can't control the shots you brag about in the locker room, nor are you likely to master those shots you see the pros try to hit — sharply angled cross-court drives, topspin lobs, underspin drop shots, service returns at your opponent's feet. So let's be honest. Cut out the fancy thinking and just concentrate on mastering the basic fundamentals. *Learn to hit the same old boring shot and you'll beat most of the people who now beat you.*

If you can learn to hit the ball deep and down the middle — and keep it in play — that's all the strategy you'll need to know to beat 99 percent of the players in the world. Trying to play this way may sound a little dull — "I want to do something *big* out there" — but believe me, you'll never get bored with winning. I've never heard anyone complain, "Nuts, I won again."

Before I delve into specific stroke production, I feel it's important to provide an overview of the game that will help make my approach to these strokes — and strategy — more meaningful. First, I will explore some of the physiological and psychological reasons why people don't improve. Second, I will try to refute entrenched myths that keep people from playing better tennis. And third, I will present the fundamentals that I regard as crucial to a sound tennis game.

Learning Blocks

Parents often ask me how competitive they should be when they play tennis against their children. I tell them, "Beat their brains out because in two or three years they'll be murdering you and you'll want to have something nice to remember." Most youngsters who get hooked on tennis are not afraid to make changes that will improve their games. But adults are thinking, "Gee, I've only got about 30 years left — maybe I'd better not mess around with my swing." They work desperately *not to look bad* by sticking with what is comfortable, rather than pushing through that awkward, frustrating period of making corrections that will eventually help them look good *and* win.

Thus, when you begin to work on a different grip or a new stroke, you will learn to play a much better game of tennis if you can remember one thing: *try to feel good about feeling crummy* because the crummy feeling that accompanies new and accurate strokes is going to make you famous.

No matter how uniquely you may swing, making changes in that swing is always painful because you must break muscle-memory patterns; you're going against what has become comfortable for you to do and what is ingrained, even if you've only played the game five or six months. We have people at the tennis college who give us 185 moves on their forehand, but when we try to make one basic correction that cuts off 110 extraneous moves, they say, "Boy, that is really awkward." Yet that uncomfortable feeling that accompanies the correct swing is what you must adopt if you hope to correct a bad habit. Even a slight grip change requires a whole new set of muscles. A person will come to the tennis college who has played for 25 years, but when we alter his grip an eighth of an inch he gets blisters.

Believe me, I know how grooved a habit can become. When I was giving lessons at the Toledo Tennis Club, one of my adult students had a bad habit of stepping forward with the wrong foot as he swung. I had only been teaching about a year but I figured I knew it all. So I nailed an old tennis shoe to a piece of wood, and pounded through eight-inch spikes to anchor it into the clay court. Then I had the fellow put his back foot in the shoe and take a swing. I wanted him to get the sensation of leaving that foot stationary as he stepped forward with the other. Well, he took one swing and yanked the board right out of the clay court. He also pulled every ligament in his right leg. He was in a cast for a long time and it just about ruined his tennis game. But both of us learned how strong muscle-memory really is. Fortunately he didn't sue me.

Interference by your ego is another hindrance to effecting important changes in your swing. When the pro starts tinkering with what you feel is comfortable, the natural tendency is to think there's something wrong in his method rather than in your swing. Furthermore, every good teaching pro has heard the complaint, "Jeez, I was better before I took lessons." Very often this is true. No matter what the sport, when you are trying to make corrections, there's always a force trying to bring you back to your old comfort levels. Dr. Joe Sheehan, the UCLA psychologist and speech therapist whose research work related to stutterers, has termed this phenomenon the Approach-Avoidance Conflict: you want to do something the new way but you want to maintain some of the old, and thus you get caught in the middle, vacillating between the two. This can be murder on your tennis game.

For instance, people will spend a week at the tennis college and try hard to solve basic problems in their swing. But when they return home to play their old rival, they may lose 6–0, 6–0, whereas before they lost 6–3, 6–3. It's only natural for them to think, "Boy, I can't wait to get back to my old form and lose 6–3, 6–3." Their ego takes such a beating over the next couple of weeks that unless they have patience and really work hard at grooving these new stroking sensations, they will soon retreat to their same old comfortable swing. The reason they get worse before they get better is that by working on new things, they no longer have a good handle on their old game nor do they have control of their new, and thus they have very spotty performances.

What it really comes down to is this: *if the pain you are suffering in losing to people is greater than the pain of making changes, then you'll try like heck to make the changes.* You'll experiment, you'll have an open mind, you'll concentrate, you won't try to avoid your weaknesses as you polish your strengths — and you'll have a much better future in this game than the average person. Believe me, most people tend to stay the same once they reach a certain level of performance, and you'll be amazed at how quickly you move up to higher playing levels if you can hang in there long enough to get the kinesthetic feeling for your new strokes.

Another deterrent to acquiring good strokes is the myth in tennis that you should "Do what feels natural," since everything that's right feels comfortable. On the contrary, my experience with thousands of students has been that *nearly everything that's natural in tennis turns out to be less desirable.* I can't think of any change in your swing, or even your grip, that will feel natural to begin with. In fact, if I ask a relative beginner to try something new, and he or she does it right on the first or second try, I'm absolutely shocked, for I've only seen this happen two or three times in a 30-year career of coaching. (This doesn't mean, however, that you can't take a much more relaxed attitude toward a game that's unnatural.)

The reason tennis is such a difficult game to master is that it's natural to roll your wrist over on the forehand instead of keeping it fixed; it's natural to swing on a horizontal plane rather than from low to high; it's natural to play people instead of the ball; it's natural to watch your opponent's shot and to try to confirm your decision about which direction the ball is going rather than react instinctively the instant the ball leaves his racket. If tennis were a natural game, we would have far more people swinging correctly, right from the beginning. Instead, people are flocking to teaching pros because the accurate movements in tennis, in my opinion, are not natural; they have to be learned, and muscle-memory patterns have to be broken down.

Of course, this doesn't mean that if you're unnatural in the beginning you will be awkward in the end. You can learn to play the game with fluid, easy strokes when at first you were stiff and uncomfortable. Yet when somebody tells me immediately after the first trial, "Hey, I tried your stroke — it's fantastic," I know that person probably hasn't really made a change, because if it feels good, it's usually what that person has been doing all along. That's why good pros won't teach "comfort." They won't keep telling you, "If it feels good, keep doing it," unless what you're doing is correct.

Myths and Misconceptions

Nearly everybody brings to the tennis court a great many incorrect impressions about how the game is played — and how well they play. But don't think lightly of these impressions, for they have everything to do with your attitude about the game, your future progress, and even the internal battle with your subconscious.

Believing the Court Is Gigantic

When you stand on the baseline, it's only natural to envision the court as a gigantic expanse, with plenty of leeway for your wrap-around follow-through. Instead, you should try to visualize playing on a long, narrow sidewalk with a follow-through that takes your racket out toward your target. Stand on the right baseline/sideline corner and see for yourself how little you can vary your follow-through when hitting from the baseline. Point your racket down the singles sideline to a righthander's backhand corner, and then to his forehand corner, and you have moved the direction of your

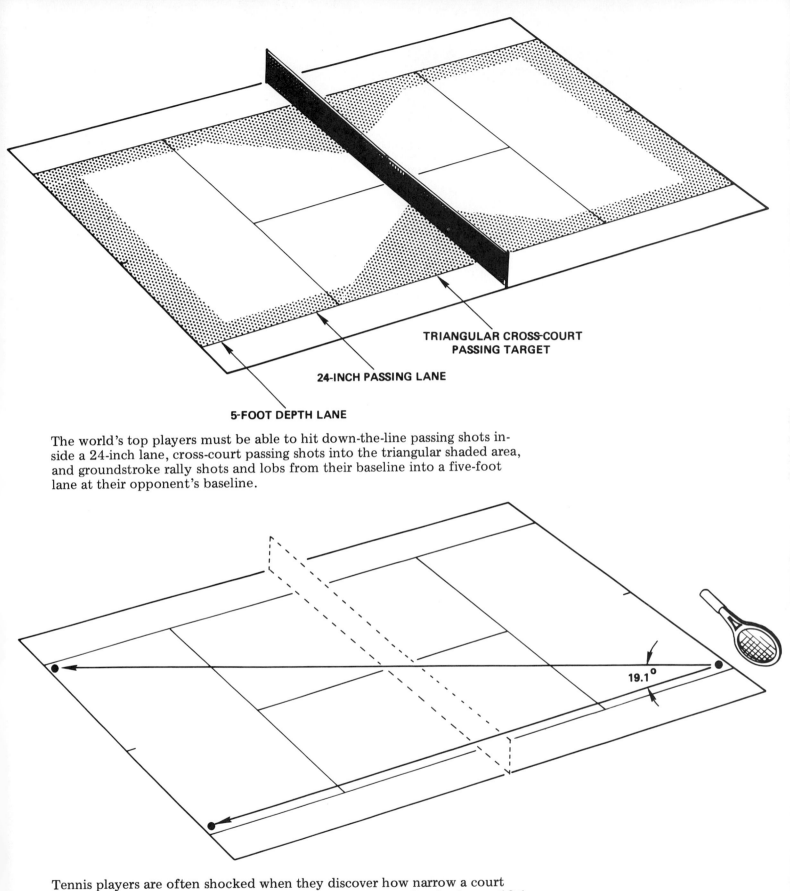

TRIANGULAR CROSS-COURT PASSING TARGET

24-INCH PASSING LANE

5-FOOT DEPTH LANE

The world's top players must be able to hit down-the-line passing shots inside a 24-inch lane, cross-court passing shots into the triangular shaded area, and groundstroke rally shots and lobs from their baseline into a five-foot lane at their opponent's baseline.

19.1°

Tennis players are often shocked when they discover how narrow a court actually is. A hitter's racket face, at a baseline corner, need only change 19.1 degrees at the ball-racket impact point to run an opponent from one baseline corner to the opposite baseline corner.

If you're 5'6" tall and you stand with your toes touching the baseline, this is what you see when looking through (and above) the net.

A solid net helps convince the 5'6" player that he or she had better have respect for that high barrier which stops so many shots.

This is the baseline view for a six-foot player. Did you six-footers ever realize that from your own baseline you have to look *under* the net tape to see a shot land in your opponent's court?

follow-through only 19.1 degrees. From the center stripe, pointing from corner to corner, you still have just 19.6 degrees to play with.

Unfortunately, even though the follow-through for a shot down the line (passing shot) must virtually resemble the follow-through for a cross-court drive, this isn't the way most people swing. When they get their opponent in one corner they think, "Now I've got him!" and they proceed to take a 180-degree swing that pulls the ball 10 feet wide. I try to tell them, "You seldom get a chance to play your opponent on the next court."

The Concept of the "Low" Net

People love to talk about the low net. Yet you always see them going up to the net and retrieving their last shot with the cry, "One more inch, Bertha, and I would have killed you." What they don't understand is that in terms of hitting a tennis ball on a horizontal plane, the net is actually very high. When you stand at the baseline you must be at least 6'7" tall in order to look over the net and see your opponent's baseline. This means that 99 percent of us never really see our opponent's court when playing from the baseline; we spend our lives looking through those little squares in the net in order to see the ball land.

Therefore, to play this game correctly you must think about *lifting* the ball up over a high barrier. Picture a volleyball net rather than a tennis net, and concentrate on elevating your shots — with a degree of topspin — so that the ball lands deep in your opponent's court rather than always catching the tape. (See Chapter Two for a detailed description of topspin.) I've found that an interesting thing happens, psychologically, when you put up a solid net. People suddenly start bending their knees and elevating the ball because they can't even see their opponent's feet, let alone the court. But when you put up the regular net again, they say, "That's better," and they go back to their old horizontal swing. Pretty soon they start taking that 39-foot trip to the net to pick up the ball.

The Fallacy of Believing in "Net-Skimmers"

Players who continue to visualize a low net simply reinforce one of the most prevalent myths destroying good tennis everywhere: the concept that tennis balls should be hit on a horizontal plane, with hard, line-drive shots

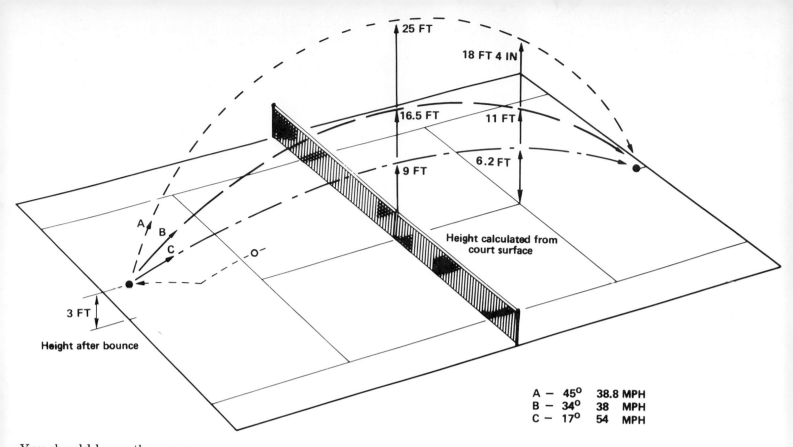

25 FT

18 FT 4 IN

16.5 FT   11 FT

9 FT   6.2 FT

Height calculated from court surface

A
B
C

O

3 FT

Height after bounce

A — 45°   38.8 MPH
B — 34°   38   MPH
C — 17°   54   MPH

You should know the approximate ball speed and elevation that will produce the desired results in match play. This chart shows ball speeds and elevations when hitting mild topspin shots from a three-foot height at the baseline.

the ideal. Interestingly, the pros have an entirely different approach. They know that tennis is not just a driving game, but a lifting game; that to hit the ball hard and still make it come down inside their opponent's court, they must develop an ability to hit topspin while elevating the ball four to six feet over the net when both players are at the baseline. The pros also know that balls hit on a horizontal plane also begin to drop sooner than balls hit at the same speed but elevated with topspin.

Thus I'm always amused by the paradox illustrated by the average player who says, "I can't wait to play like a pro and hit those nice low net-skimmers," and the pro who goes into the locker room after a match and moans, "Jeez, I'm playing so crummy. My ball's going so close to the net it's a joke."

The Theory of the Fallible Racket

I've always stressed the point that a tennis ball is really your pal, not your enemy: most tennis balls are round and they go exactly where you hit them. Unfortunately, if you take the ball on as a pal your ego needs an out, and so your racket becomes the target for all your frustrations and excuses. Tell me it's not true that often when you hit a truly lousy shot your first instinct is to blame your racket? You pluck the strings or give it the knee test, while muttering, "That doggone guy really sold me a lemon." Sporting goods dealers have told me that people actually come in and complain, "I'm returning this racket because it has no backhands in it at all."

Let's be realistic. Even at the pro level, it doesn't matter whether you use wood or metal, gut or nylon — the racket will go well beyond your ability level. I've seen Bobby Riggs beat a good player with a broom, and if there's that much resiliency in straw, then gut or nylon is not your problem. In fact, all the great players I've known have only talked about their inability to effect the right stroke pattern. They've never said, "I failed to win the tournament because I had a crummy racket." Sure a $120 racket may give you a little extra juice and make you feel good, but it's not going to help you win matches if you continue to swing improperly. Almost any racket will do what you ask of it if you place it in the right position at the right time. Yet most people place the racket in the wrong position at impact and expect it to produce a winning shot.

"I'm Not Smart Enough to Play Good Tennis"

In talking about the intricacies of technique and tactics for the more advanced player, I sometimes unintentionally scare people off. They start thinking, "I'm not smart enough to do all that. I just want to stay at the baseline and try to get a suntan." Thus I always try to assure my students that it doesn't require any exceptional intellect to grasp the basic concepts that can help them beat 95 percent of the tennis population.

I once gave a battery of personality and psychological tests to 20 successful tournament players, hoping I could isolate some of the psychological variables that help make a champion. I thought, for instance, that tennis demanded a lot of high-level intellectual functioning and that the top players were really smarter than we normals. But when my test results came in, IQs ranged from 88 to 144 — from educable mentally retarded to gifted. So I start with the assumption that nearly all the readers of this book are in that range, and that you have the ability to understand the most complex, but logical, theory ever promulgated about the game of tennis.

In my view, sophisticated theories about technique and strategy normally have little relevance in tennis. The game ultimately comes down to the basic question: *do you have the weapons?* If you are at the baseline and the ball is hit to your backhand and your opponent rushes the net, you normally have only four options — lob over his head, drive a passing shot down the line, hit the ball cross-court, or try to give him a new navel. You don't need a Ph.D. in tennis to know that whatever option you choose, the real question is: can you hit a backhand?

Furthermore, physical laws dictate where the ball goes, not your IQ or a coach's "unique" approach. To hit the ball hard and make it land in a particular zone with a certain speed, you must hit with the same speed and ball rotation as everyone else, whether you are Rod Laver or Bertha Finkenbaum. If the racket is placed perfectly and contacts the ball properly, then the ball is going to be on target regardless of your IQ. Better to have quick reactions and an ability to coordinate body movements. For you can be the smartest person in your club, but if you're at the net and the ball is screaming at you 100 miles an hour, you can forget your swing, your name, everything.

"Okay, Then, I'm Too Uncoordinated"

One of the most common fears in tennis is the feeling by some people that they can't play the game, or they'll never be very good, because they don't have the coordination or an athletic background. Thus I tell all my students, "If you can walk to the drinking fountain without falling over, you have the physical ability to play this game pretty well." I'm always honest about the difficulty everybody will encounter with this game, but I point out that enjoyment and "success" certainly don't need to be measured by how many matches you win or lose. Taking part in a physical activity and striving to improve your strokes — that's what counts. The list of the relatively uncoordinated people who have become fine players simply because they had the desire and the hunger to learn to play the game properly is endless.

Adults are always coming to the tennis college who claim they have no athletic ability whatsoever, and who give us the impression they're going to buy an ice cream cone and stick it against their forehead on the way to their mouth. But when they get out on the court they are terrifically coordinated and they have tons of fun. When we talk to them about this we usually discover that ever since high school they have been suffering from a delusion that they were athletic failures. "I never made the high school team," they will say, almost apologetically. But they've been comparing themselves with the super jocks — the upper two percent of the population — when they should have compared themselves to the average person.

It's tragic to see people who live in mortal fear of looking bad athletically, who think that nobody can have fun playing with them, or that they have to hit the ball well in order to really enjoy the game. I try to tell these people,

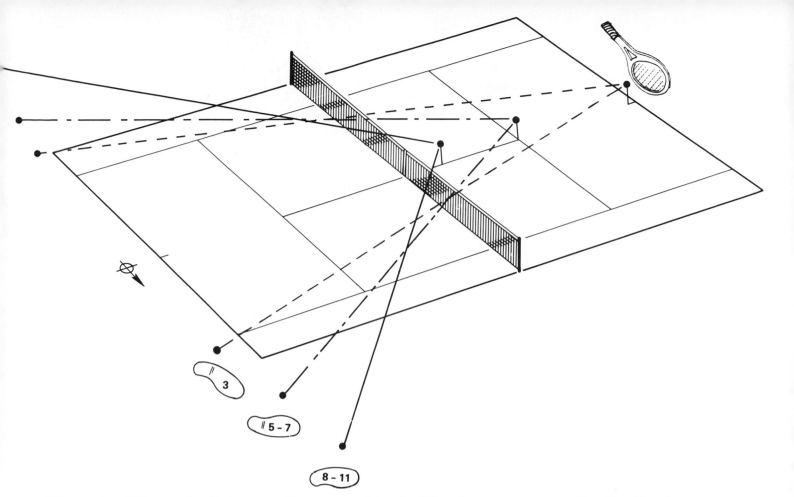

"So you lose? So you don't play as well as you want to play? So what — you're still running around, you're getting some sun, you're meeting new people, you're having fun. That's what the game is all about."

Fundamental Considerations

The following are some basic precepts of the game that never change, no matter what kind of shot you are hitting or what the circumstances, whether it be the first round at Forest Hills or the finals in Pismo Beach. I like to think of it as "non-technical technique."

Keep the Ball Deep

The main goal in good tennis is simple: *don't hit the first short ball.* Keep all of your shots deep and in play and you will be famous by Friday. By pinning your opponent behind the baseline you (a) give yourself more time to react to his return shot, (b) prevent him from moving in to do his in-fighting near the net, and (c) reduce the angle at which he can hit. For example, the most he can run you, hitting from the baseline, is normally three steps to your left or three to your right. If your shot lands short, near the service line, he can stretch you five to seven steps with his next shot. And if

You'll seldom have to run more than three steps laterally to retrieve your opponent's shot if you can force him to hit from behind his baseline. If you hit short shots and allow your opponent to hit from midcourt, you may have to run laterally as many as five to seven steps. Be ready to run all the way to the fence if you allow your opponent to hit while close to the net.

he is volleying at the net, he can move you eight to eleven steps, right off the court.

That's why you always hear the good players say, "Keep the ball deep," and why Jimmy Connors and Chris Evert are always reaching the finals and semi-finals. They get such great depth on their shots that it's difficult to penetrate and gain the net. In fact, after one of his victories at Forest Hills, Connors' first response to newsmen was, "I was hitting the ball with a lot of depth." And Harold Solomon commented, after losing to Connors, "I hit too many short balls."

Give Your Opponent One More Chance to Take Gas

A lot of people, especially men, envision tennis as a game where they can push people around. This isn't to say you can't run your opponent from one side of the court to the other, up and back, with an assortment of calculated shots. But the reality in tennis is that you beat yourself or the other person loses to you. As Jack Kramer always liked to say, "Tennis is giving your opponent one more chance to take gas." And Chrissie Evert told me that her dad always said, "Let your opponent make the mistakes."

In beginning and intermediate tennis, errors outnumber placements 20 or 30 to 1. Even in the pros, forced and unforced errors end the point much more often than outright winners. In fact, in all my years with the pros, I've never talked to a player who could remember having won a single match where he (or she) hit the ball so hard and so well that his placements outnumbered his opponent's errors. Gonzales, Kramer, Laver, Billie Jean King — all they could remember was people losing to them.

So reconcile yourself to the fact that the day is never going to come when you can play an opponent of comparable ability and just yo-yo that person around the court by hitting with wild abandon and unbelievable accuracy. Your goal must be to play the high-percentage shots, get the ball over the net and inside the boundaries, and let your opponent take the crazy chances.

This is what the dinker does so well. He (or she) takes three steps to the right, hits the helium ball and says, "Here's one more chance. Why don't you take it?" And if you get it back he says, "Here's another one. Why don't you take that?" He keeps throwing up "moonballs" while you sit back there with all your fancy moves, cracking off net-skimmers. The dinker has never hit a hard ball in his life: he just keeps tightening the noose until finally you get so frustrated that you try to end the point with a fancy shot, which of course goes into the net.

No one likes to play dinkers because they drive you crazy. You're always saying to them, "Why don't you stand up and play like a man?" But as I'll point out during the book, dinkers win for good reasons. They have mastered several basic physical laws and psychological ploys which make them winners in the Ds, the Cs, the Bs and two rounds of the As in almost every tennis club around the world. You may make jokes about the dinkers, and they may have few friends, but their living room shelves are lined with trophies.

Learn to Buy Time

One of the basic mistakes made by most beginners and intermediates is their failure to buy time on every shot. Instead of beginning their appropriate backswing the instant they determine the direction of their opponent's shot, they delay until the last moment. Suddenly the ball is on top of them or they have to lunge to make the hit, and thus they seldom feel comfortable or in charge of the situation. They can't understand how the pro makes it look so easy.

If this is your problem, you must concentrate on turning your body and your racket back the instant you see the ball leave your opponent's racket, then quickly get into position so that you can step into the ball properly. You want to *work hard getting to the ball early so that you can be absolutely calm as you take your swing.* It's too late to yell "help" when you're hitting the ball. I've found that when you take your racket back early, your concentration is focused upon directing the ball to a target. But when your racket goes back late, the tendency is just to be content with any kind of hit possible.

One bad habit that leads to timing problems is to subconsciously wait for the ball to clear the net, or even to land on the court before you get your racket back. You have to break this hypnosis by telling yourself to *take the racket back before the ball passes your opponent's service line.* That's how quickly you should react. Think about your opponent's baseline as position No. 1, his service line No. 2, the net No. 3, and your service line No. 4. Then strive to get your racket back by the time the ball has reached position No. 2.

PHOTO BY JOHN G. ZIMMERMAN

Another warning: whether you're playing singles or doubles, never let your feet fall asleep. They've got to get you to the ball in time to allow you to look great. Some people develop fantastic strokes but unfortunately they're 15 feet away from the ball when it bounces. Even a player as great as Arthur Ashe admits that he still writes notes and puts them under the umpire's stand to remind himself to keep his feet moving.

I have to warn you, however, that getting to the ball in time and good stroke production are not synonymous. If you know how to swing properly, then extra time is very beneficial. But if you've developed a lousy stroking pattern, arriving early only gives you more time in order to hit a crummy shot. Some people are uncomfortable — even fearful — when they have too much time; they don't know what to do with it. Thus they often fall into an unconscious rhythm trap: as the ball slows down, they slow down proportionately so that they are out of position no matter how fast the ball comes. If they are slightly late when they play against a person who hits the ball hard, they are slightly late against someone who hits softly.

"Keep Your Eyes on the . . . "

Like everybody else since the infant days of tennis, you've been told to "Keep your eyes on the ball." You may even be guilt-ridden because you

22

Some players never complete their shot properly because they subconsciously think their opponent is hitting a shot at the same time — and they must hurry to reach it.

can't read the writing on the ball, or see it hit the strings, and your friends say they can. But don't let them fool you, for the ophthalmologists tell us that nobody can focus their eyes that well. Still, the effort to focus *attention* on the ball is important in two ways. First, this keeps your eyes off distractions such as your opponent. After all, tennis is a game where you hit the ball, not your opponent. Second, this helps insure a hit on the center of the strings by keeping your head down and eyes fixed on the point of contact.

You may be thinking, "If it's so important to keep your eyes on the ball, why do I see pictures of the pros hitting with their eyes focused out ahead of the ball?"

Well, several years ago, after realizing that nobody can actually see a ball in focus at or near impact, I started telling students to keep their eyes on the blur. Then I was told by an ophthalmological researcher that people with accurate vision can't even see that much. The eyes can follow a ball in focus until about five to seven feet before racket impact, and then they lose track, due to a sudden head shift. That's why tournament players subconsciously learn to take their cues for a stroke while the ball is still far from the point at which they intend to hit it.

Trying to get people to still concentrate on following the ball into the racket for as long as possible is doggone tough. For one thing, a tennis ball is a lot smaller than most people think. The golf ball is tiny but the clubhead is small, too, and you know you have to stand there and really concentrate on making contact. In tennis, however, you feel like you have a big war club in your hand and you can't possibly miss, so your attention begins to wander.

Furthermore, people tend to be opponent-oriented rather than ball-oriented. In fact, I have a theory — as yet unproven — that some players think there are two balls in play simultaneously. Just as they start to swing, they subconsciously think their opponent is also hitting a ball, and thus they try to rush their own stroke to begin to chase their opponent's mysterious shot. I try to cure this syndrome by reminding people, "If you're worried about your opponent's next shot, don't bother, because your shot isn't going over in the first place." *Remember, there's only one ball in play and you have it — your opponent can't hurt you until your shot lands on his side of the net.*

Another way to help you take a good look at the ball is to relate to cues on your follow-through. For example, on the forehand don't look up to see where the ball is going until your upper arm or shoulder touches your chin.

On the backhand, wait until the arm is extended upward before you let your eyes go to your opponent. Don't worry; you can "re-track" the ball before it reaches the net and you will have plenty of time to prepare for your next shot.

Take Good Care of Each Shot

Most players have a tendency to think there are a tremendous number of shots on every point. People will talk about how they like to set their opponent up with a variety of shots, or they'll be thinking to themselves as they play, "I know I'm crummy now but on the eighth shot I'll be great." Unfortunately, a point rarely lasts that long. The tendency is to remember the rally in '38 when the ball went over the net 25 times, while forgetting that in club tennis most points end after the serve, or the service return, or one or two shots after that. That's why I tell people, *take good care of the shot you're on — it's probably your last.* If you approach tennis with this in mind, you'll find yourself developing far better concentration and stroke production.

The Basic Law of Tennis: Learn to Hit the Same Old Boring Winner

What tennis actually comes down to — stripped of the trick shots, the weird, sensual body movements, the best in equipment and clothes, the search for the latest theory — is a dedication to those fundamentals supported by physical laws. You may think, "Yeh, but I want to have fun out there, I want a little variety. I want to try lots of different shots, move the ball around, keep my opponent guessing." Well, *losers* have tons of variety; their shots fly all over the court — and often beyond — simply because they fail to swing the same way twice in a row. Champions are those who take great pride in just learning to hit the same old boring winner.

The only problem with playing a "straight down the middle and deep" system is that you need a high frustration-tolerance threshold because you're not trying anything fancy to end a point quickly. Most people don't have the patience to try to outsteady their opponent. They say, "Jeez, the ball's gone over the net three times. I've got to come in and do something *big.*" So they try to hit a drop shot or they go for the lines and that's when they die. It's not easy to hit those big-time shots, so just be happy to keep the ball in play. Stick to the fundamentals and try to master them first, then you can get fancy. But you'll probably find an interesting thing happening along the way: *the better you play the more simplistic you become in your approach.* You find that you don't need to get fancy. It's usually the players who just can't win who feel they have to showboat. This type of player hangs around every club in the country, scoffing at regular forehands and backhands, while saying, "Man, I just want to serve, volley, attack, and hit the overhead smash." He glories in hitting the cover off the ball and has very little respect for the common shot. But that "common shot" is what makes Chris Evert the queen of them all. She doesn't try any fancy stuff. She's patient. She takes care of simple fundamentals — hour after hour of practice, getting the ball deep. She rarely is the first to hit a short ball, so nobody can really hurt her consistently; when they do try to come to the net she can thread the needle with her passing shots. She doesn't have a big serve nor the world's strongest volley, but she has shown that a forehand and a backhand can take you right to the top.

Just as Chrissie will raise the level of the game, so will Jimmy Connors. Whether you like him or not, he'll make his challengers develop good strokes on both the forehand and backhand because he keeps dogging them and dogging them until they miss. And he'll force better serving because he has a murderous service return.

Go for Form, Not Touch

Obviously, to hit the same old boring winner you must develop an efficient and consistent stroking pattern. My goal is to have you master a swing that will hold up when you have Excedrin headache number 38: you may feel crummy but if your strokes are grooved, you're still going to play well. That's a nice feeling to have going into a match. Having the basic weapons and an ability to use them is a great leveler against an opponent who has an advantage in size, strength, and/or age but who is erratic in stroke production.

This is why I want you to learn what at first may seem to be a rather rigid game. I'm a stroke-production fanatic. I teach form, and learning to keep the ball in play, rather than a "touch" system. Thus I want you to try to swing with a fixed wrist and a short, controlled backswing on your groundstrokes, volleys, and approach shots. Loose, free-flowing swings might look nice but they have too many extraneous movements that can break down under pressure. Jimmy Connors has literally less racket-head movement than any player I've ever seen. There's little or no whip or roll in his swing — he just locks that racket in and leaves it fixed, then turns with the body. That's why you find him in the finals or semi-finals of nearly every tournament he plays.

In my opinion, when you play with floppy wrists, you're playing with a dynamite fuse. In fact, *laying the wrist back on the backswing or rolling it over as you come into the ball destroys more good groundstrokes than any other single factor.* This is why I feel that the person who plays with his wrist must be much more coordinated than the average fixed-wrist player. He has to rely on touch, and thus he's only as good as that touch on a particular day; when he loses it, he loses everything. He might beat the top player in the club on Saturday — when his game is finely tuned and he's in the right mood — yet turn around and lose to a dinker on Sunday.

You need a much more dependable game than "touch" if you ever hope to win a tournament by lasting through four, five, or six rounds, whether on the club or international level. So cut down the size of your swing, don't try to add a lot of extra sauce on the ball, don't horse around with your wrist, and be patient. Winning will loosen you up. If you don't win, keep working on basic fundamentals and learn to accept responsibility for your own strokes. Remember, in the end the ball goes exactly where you aim it. Plutonium rackets and color-coordinated sweatbands can't bail you out. But a sense of humor will keep you sane.

Chapter Two

"What the Heck Is Ball Rotation and Who Needs It?" You Do.

WHEN YOU LEARN TO CONTROL ball rotation, you can make the ball do funny things — to your advantage. You can make it jump high for little people who hate to hit the ball at shoulder level, or you can make it skid low for tall people who don't want to bend their knees. You can slice it to the left or right to force your opponent to stretch wide for the return, or you can curve it into his body and give him a new navel. Just as the baseball pitcher uses ball rotation to throw a curve ball and win games, you can use spin to change the pace of the ball and vary the rhythm of a match. But to do all these things you must have a clear understanding of ball rotation, and why the ball behaves the way it does.

This is where some beginning and intermediate players start to get a little hostile at my tennis college. They start off by thinking, "Why study physics? That's for the pros to worry about. I just want to learn how to hit the ball right." I'm the first to admit that you can go a long way in tennis without having a clue about what actually happens to a ball when it's hit, *providing* you can master the stroking styles that produce the spin you want on a particular shot. But when you understand the basic principles of ball rotation, and clear away the myths, you're far more likely to dedicate yourself to learning *how* to hit the ball with spin, particularly topspin. Why limit yourself to a flat, horizontal game when ball rotation can help you defeat opponents?

General Characteristics

Every time the ball is hit, some spin or rotation of the ball is produced. There is no such thing as a perfectly flat groundstroke or serve. A ball that is curving generates air pockets, and that air friction makes the ball do certain things. Good tennis players deliberately control this ball rotation and use it to their advantage. There are four major variations:

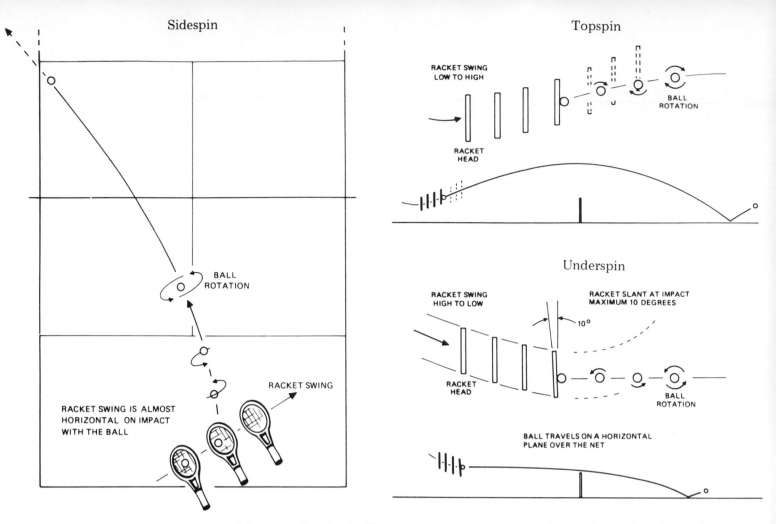

These graphs clearly illustrate the characteristics of topspin, underspin, and sidespin . You need to know how, when, why, and where to use each type of ball rotation.

1. **Topspin** refers to a ball which is spinning from low to high on a vertical axis. (Imagine a dot on top of the ball that moves forward and down towards your opponent.) Topspin generates downward force, so that the ball's path will generally resemble the arc of a rainbow.

2. **Sidespin,** or slice, refers to a ball revolving on a horizontal plane. Sidespin generates a ball which curves to your left or right and carries away from, or into an opponent. It is used mostly on the serve.

3. **Underspin,** or chip, refers to a ball where the imaginary dot on top moves back towards you from high to low; the dot rotates away from your opponent while the ball moves towards him. Underspin generates an upward force until gravity takes over, but that gravitational pull is so great that the ball travels on almost a straight line, rather than in an inverted rainbow arc opposite of topspin.

4. On the typical **spin serve,** the racket brushes the ball about halfway between a full vertical (topspin) and horizontal (slice) spin.

How to Hit Topspin — and Why

I've always been fascinated by the misconceptions that have given topspin a bad image within the general tennis public, particularly the belief that *underspin* is the easier stroke to learn and to control. On the contrary, it's been my experience over the years that underspin is far more difficult to teach to the average player because it demands more talent and timing. I feel that topspin is much easier to impart, more reliable under pressure, and much more valuable to players of every ability level.

Beginners, for instance, should try to hit the majority of their groundstrokes with topspin because it is safer, and it will lead to a stronger all-around game. With topspin from the baseline, you can hit the ball hard while hitting it safely over the net by four to six feet, and the rainbow arc will bring the ball down deep in your opponent's court — thus keeping him away from the net. Sure you can hit the ball hard and keep it deep by hitting flat or with underspin. But you have to play the ball so close to the tape of the net that you have to take all the gamble; you become a Las Vegas player.

More advanced players should heed the words of Jack Kramer, who told me, "The more I see of the great champions, the more I feel they have two common denominators: (1) great speed, which gets them into proper position, and (2) the ability to hit topspin off the forehand and the backhand sides." *Only with topspin can you play an offensive game.* Not only can you drive the ball deep with topspin, or bring it up short, you can pass an opponent who has come to the net, whether down the line or cross-court. Thus you have beautiful flexibility: you can always hit the shot that is called for, depending on where your opponent is positioned.

The Stroke

To impart topspin on the forehand or the backhand, you must contact the backside of the ball with a racket head that is *vertical at impact* and traveling from low to high in the direction of your target. When the racket face brushes against the ball, the ball is lifted up until air pockets begin to generate the downward force that produces a rainbow arc.

On the forehand, for example, take the racket back and then lower your arm and fixed wrist to place the racket at least 12 inches below the intended

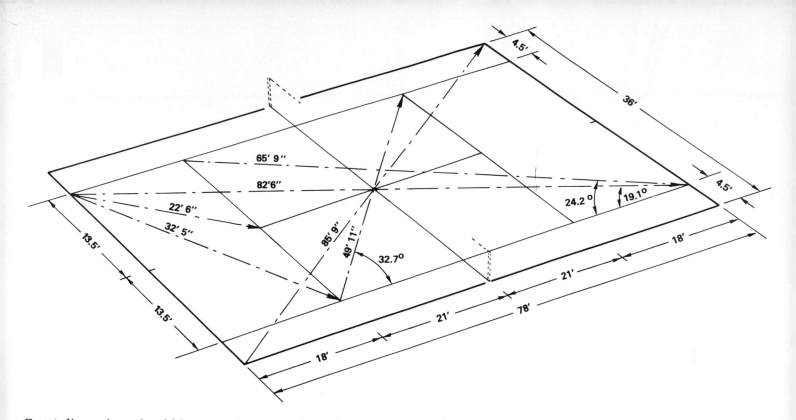

Court dimensions should be carefully studied by all players. Each player should know the precise distance his or her shots normally travel and make appropriate adjustments.

point of impact. Then come up at about a 17-degree angle (using the court as the measuring line) and strike the ball going from low to high, with the racket head vertical to the ground at impact. Follow through with your arm high and pointing in the general direction of your target.

Topspin is responsible for that familiar, if seldom understood line: "Bend your knees." The reason the knees are so important is that if a ball arrives at waist level or below, and you try to maintain a fixed-wrist position (which is crucial), you can't get the racket 12 inches below the ball without bending your knees — unless you simply loosen the wrist and drop the racket head. But when you stand erect and let the racket head fall in this manner, the tendency is to scoop your backhand — and sometimes your forehand — harmlessly over the net. So to insure a vertical racket head at impact, *bend your knees sufficiently to allow your racket head, hitting hand, and fixed wrist to lower together.* By getting low in this manner you can generate power from the lifting action of your thighs and hips as you move into the ball. If you hit stiff-kneed ("Sorry, coach, this is as far as my knees will bend") then your arm is your only source of power.

Another common myth about topspin, which has been perpetuated by some of the greatest players in the game, is that you should use the wrist to roll the racket *over the ball* at impact in order to impart topspin. You'll hear a player complain, "I couldn't get over the ball with my racket face as much as I would have liked," or a tennis commentator will say, "Notice how so-and-so rolls over the top of the ball." Even Laver has talked about hitting his forehand with "quite a lot of wrist" and "coming over the ball with a snap of the wrist."

Pros may have this rolling-over sensation but the question remains: If you

PHOTO BY JOHN G. ZIMMERMAN

All that talk about how the racket face "rolls over" the top of the ball to impart topspin is a myth. In this photo (the first of this nature ever recorded), the hitter tries desperately to roll the racket face over the top of the ball — but to no avail. The racket face is vertical at impact as it moves from low to high. High-speed motion pictures also substantiate that the ball leaves the racket face long before the racket face begins its rollover.

really get the racket over the ball, how the heck is the ball going to go over the net? By rising up through the strings? My research has shown — filming at 12,000 frames a second — that even if the ball is standing still, suspended on a thread, or somebody is hitting the ball to you, it is physically impossible to roll over the ball and maintain racket-ball contact. The ball just goes straight down or into the net. Instead, you must brush the backside of the ball with a racket face that is vertical or nearly vertical at impact and moving from low to high. Remember, we are all controlled by the same physical laws.

Okay, now you want to take a shot at me. You've seen some of those wristy pro players and they're imparting heavy topspin. How do they do it?

It is true that some pros use a lot of wrist in hitting topspin. They will drop the racket head below the intended point of impact with the ball, then bring it up with a big flick of the wrist. However, if the shot is successful, the wrist does not roll over — it is generally fixed at impact and the racket head is vertical, exactly like the player who hits with a firm wrist and lifts his arm up to brush the ball. The key thing to understand is that *relying on wrist action to hit topspin does not mean rolling the palm over and facing it down to the court.* Instead, the racket face and the palm

Ideally, you want to contact the ball with a racket head that is vertical at impact and moving from low to high. The numbers on the chart indicate the degrees of racket angle. If you play well, you'll hardly ever hit a shot with more than a ten-degree racket bevel. That's why it's so important for you to learn what it feels like to have a vertical racket head at impact.

of the hitting hand must remain on the same vertical plane, facing the opponent, with the palm pushing up and finishing across the left shoulder.

For example, people always commented about how Pancho Gonzales got his racket "up and over" the ball on the forehand. This was the reason, they felt, that he could hit the sharp forehand angle shot. But when I studied his stroke on high-speed, stop-action movie film, I discovered that his racket head never rolled over the ball. He *appeared* to roll the racket over after the initial impact, but he actually imparted topspin with a vertical racket head that did not roll over until near the end of his follow-through . . . long after the ball had left his strings.

I'm also challenged occasionally by people who have been told that topspin requires a lot of strength, and that its constant use can wear you out. The first myth is perpetuated by playing pros who have convinced themselves that the wrist and forearm are critical in producing topspin. One pro has even written, "You should work on strengthening your wrist if you intend to use much topspin." Putting aside the fact that you never need to rely on wrist action in the first place, I would agree that a strong wrist is necessary *only when you're late on the hit* and you need a sudden burst of racket speed to impart hard-hit topspin. But I'm not teaching anybody to be late. Skinny eight-year-olds can bomb the ball with topspin simply because they've learned to move into position quickly and then coordinate their body and racket arm as they stroke the ball.

Meanwhile, Bjorn Borg is commonly cited as a player who gets worn out by his reliance on heavy topspin. What critics overlook is that hitting topspin doesn't wear him out, it's the fact that he whacks the ball so hard on every shot, even when he knows he can't put the ball away. If he could learn to "soften up" and conserve his energy, he would be just as effective at one-third the speed. Still, I'd like to do what Borg does and hit all that topspin and be crummy and tired out — and worth $300,000 a year.

The Uses of Topspin

Remember that tennis is a lifting game, and to hit groundstrokes *hard* — with the greatest depth and safety — you must build your game around topspin. If you try to slug the ball with an erect body and a horizontal, across-the-body swing, you have very little margin for error between the tape of the net and the baseline. It's scary how accurate you have to be.

When you try to drive the ball deep, it never seems to come down in time —
if only the court could be three feet longer, you'd be sensational. But then
when you try to hit "net-skimmers," the net seems to stop every other shot;
you "own" the tape of the net and you can't understand why you can be so
unlucky. The reason, of course, is that a ball hit on a horizontal plane begins
to drop sooner, just like a bullet that is shot off in a physics lab vacuum. In
a vacuum you must aim the gun at a 45-degree angle to make the bullet
travel the greatest distance. Aim the gun parallel to the ground and the
fired bullet begins to drop much sooner. A tennis ball is no different, except that outdoors the air is denser and the ball must be aimed at about 50
to 55 degrees.

When I point out these facts to people, they get all stoked up. They think
I've unlocked the secrets of this game. All they have to do is drop their arm
and racket together below the ball, maintain a fixed wrist, swing low-to-
high and aim four to six feet over the net. "Piece of cake," they think. Unfortunately, when they go out to play, they can't get their knees to bend or
their racket and racket arm down below the level of the ball. Instead of
swinging on a low-to-high plane they simply bevel their racket under (meaning the bottom edge of the racket is turned up) and the ball goes over the
back fence.

Remember, the body — as well as the racket — must move from low to
high, and the racket face must be vertical at impact.

Some dinkers get around this problem by going plunk . . . plunk . . . plunk.
They hit the ball high and deep ("moonballs") with very little energy out-
put. By letting gravity do their work, they never get tired while you wear
yourself out trying to slug the ball harder and harder from a deep position.
I'm not suggesting that you should play like a dinker, especially if you enjoy having a lot of friends, but they do apply some sound physical — and
psychological — principles in their approach to the game, which I will detail
in Chapter Eight.

Besides giving you a greater margin for error, a second reason you want to
hit groundstrokes with topspin is that topspin produces a high bounce and
gives your opponent a difficult shot to handle. High bouncing balls up at
chest level drive everybody crazy, pros included, because you can't get your
body into the shot; the only alternative is to try to take the shot on the rise,
shortly after it bounces, and this takes real skill. On the other hand, those
low, hard "net-skimmers" that look so nice will bounce short and come up
waist high, making it easy for people to just throw their rear end into the

shot and crack off a winner. Furthermore, topspin shots which land near your opponent's baseline may drive him to the back fence and leave him vulnerable to short returns up near the net.

Third, if your opponent likes to come to the net when you hit a short ball, your ability to hit topspin passing shots close to the net will help nullify his tactical advantage, and will make him hesitant about even coming to the net. These shots, hit down the line or cross-court, will give your opponent trouble even if he reaches them in time to make a return volley. The reason for this is that balls hit with topspin dip down after clearing the net, making the volley more difficult to execute: your opponent must now hit up over the net instead of down. Hard, flat, horizontal drives can also pose problems for a person at the net, but the pressure is on you to thread the needle: if you elevate the ball too much, your opponent can simply let it go past, and out of bounds. But he has to make a play on topspin because he knows that even a high ball may come down near the baseline.

Sidespin

The sidespin, or sliced shot, is achieved by brushing across the back side of the ball, with the racket continuing on to the right. It is used primarily on the serve to pull an opponent "out of court" or for outright aces, and on "peel the orange" volleys where you want to sharpen the angle on your volley and help slow the ball down. Although I tell students to visualize peeling an orange when they make this type of volley, this is only to give them the right imagery. The face of the racket actually travels on a horizontal plane and makes a direct hit on the back side of the ball, which then makes a very sharp angle and dips.

Underspin

Despite my emphasis on topspin, never accuse me of not teaching underspin. When properly mastered, it can be used effectively on the following shots:

1. Underspin is a basic ingredient of the good approach shot, which you use to take the net when your opponent hits a short ball. Since underspin is

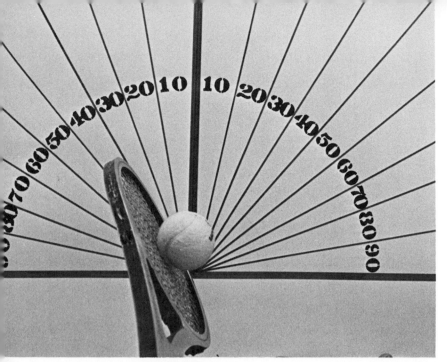

Just as there's a myth that you must come over the ball to hit topspin, some people believe that the racket must come *under* the ball to impart underspin. This, too, is incorrect. Notice in this photograph that even with the racket beveled 30 degrees, the ball is clearly not contacted on the bottom.

Even on this severe "chip" backhand, the racket doesn't come close to the bottom side of the ball. One should think of the racket face meeting the "lower back side" of the ball, just below the equatorial line, to produce underspin.

hit with a lower trajectory than topspin, the ball skids low instead of bounc-ing high, thus forcing your opponent to hit up from a low position. If you are coming to the net, this guarantees a rising ball for your volley.

2. A ball hit softly with underspin (or backspin) tends to "die" when it hits the court, thus making it invaluable for drop shots, stop volleys, and softly hit short-angle shots that are designed to fake out your opponent when he is deep, not when he is at the net.

3. On volleys, you can use underspin to reduce the speed of the ball after it leaves your racket. Pros who have the touch will also use it on service re-turns to take the speed off their opponent's serve. But most people raise the ball up when they try this.

4. On the backhand it gives you a nice *defensive* shot from the baseline, providing you can learn to control it under pressure. You'll often see the pros hitting underspin backhands from baseline to baseline, since without swinging hard they can hit the ball deep while slowing it up. This gives them plenty of time to get in position for their next shot, and by slowing the ball up they can sometimes upset their opponent's rhythm. The ball will also bounce low because of its flat trajectory.

Underspin vs. Topspin

No matter what some coaches and pros may preach, hitting the backhand with underspin is a tough play. Only talented players can hit this shot well with any consistency, and then only through experience, practice, and con-centration. The reason for this, physicists tell me, is that the minute you begin to favor underspin, by bringing your racket from high to low, you not only must make corrections with your wrist, you must manipulate five vari-ables: (1) the speed of your opponent's shot, (2) the ball rotation that your opponent has hit, (3) the angle at which you must come down on your swing, (4) the angle at which you must bevel your racket, and (5) the speed at which you must swing down with that beveled racket.

Little wonder that people have a tendency to lose control on underspin. If they hit the ball up, or hit it hard on a horizontal plane with underspin, the ball has a tendency to sail and keep on going until gravity takes hold. (Research shows that this is especially true when hitting in the wind.) Thus, when you hit with underspin you must calculate — under pressure — how hard you should hit the ball and how much you should bevel your racket so that the ball will come down in time to land in your opponent's court. Most people can't make these decisions with any consistency because they seldom practice. So when they try to hit the ball hard with underspin — trying to win a point — they usually have to walk out the gate, pick up the ball, and come back for the next point.

On the other hand, if you just concentrate on hitting your backhand (and of course the forehand) with topspin — by swinging from low to high with a fixed wrist — you can hit the ball almost as hard as you want and still be safe. No matter what your opponent hits, or what pressure you're under, you can take his shot and return it with topspin. Instead of five variables, you only have to deal with two — the vertical angle at which you are going to elevate the ball and the forward and upward angle of the swing. You fix the racket and leave it alone, then go back, down low, and come up through the ball. Sure it's tough to get that racket and the racket arm down low, as well as the knees, but as I'll discuss (in Chapter Three) this is more of a mental barrier than a physical problem: people can bend their knees to sit in a chair at home, but they just can't seem to do it on the tennis court.

Another problem with relying on an underspin backhand arises when your opponent rushes the net. You can't drive a backhand past him with underspin — unless you're an absolute rarity like Kenny Rosewall — nor can you hit cross-court just over the net with power. Underspin shots hit hard enough to pass a person at the net tend to travel 70 feet or more. The court is 78 feet long, but if you want to pass your opponent with a cross-court shot while he's waiting to volley, you must be able to break the ball off inside of 65 or 66 feet. You just can't do that with hard-hit underspin. You can try, of course, but the ball will either go out or so close to your opponent that he will have an easy volley.

My approach to tennis tries to minimize every possible chance for error. I want you to build a game based on taking the percentage shot, and knowing how to execute that shot under pressure. That's why, in my opinion, when you rely on topspin rather than underspin, you have a much more dependable ally. The crucial question with topspin is: "Can you get it over the net?" If you can, then it works in your behalf. Very few people have ever hit the ball with topspin and watched it go over the fence. There's seldom this confidence with underspin. Oftentimes it goes over the net and just keeps right on heading north.

Topspin is the only stroke in tennis that allows you to slug away and get rid of frustrations without worrying about losing the ball. I've noticed over the years that many people tend to choke because they can't hit the ball hard. They're naturally strong, or frustrated, and they want to hit all-out on the ball, but if they've learned an underspin game, they aren't allowed to do this; they have to baby the ball. *You rarely have to finesse topspin.*

I'm convinced that every young player coming up in tennis — boys and girls alike — had better learn to hit topspin off both the forehand and the backhand if they expect to remain competitive in the coming years. The great young players — Connors, Borg, Vilas, Evert — are topspin artists on both sides, and even the young champion coming up, Tracy Austin, has used topspin since she was five years old. Although Françoise Durr has been ranked in the world's top ten for practically a decade, she admitted the deficiency of her game to *Sports Illustrated* back in 1971: "If I had my life to do over," she said, "I would be a topspin tennis player — instead of playing the flat game I do now."

If you have the feel for underspin, and you can mix it in with topspin, terrific — you'll be using both in the finals. But when you lose that feeling on underspin, you also lose your confidence because the variables are so difficult to control.

This was once pointed out to me by Rod Laver, who attributed a great deal of his success at Wimbledon to his ability to topspin off both sides. He talked about the intense pressure at Wimbledon, and the pageantry that preceded every match: being driven to the stadium in a black limousine; hundreds of people pounding on the windows wanting your autograph; going to the locker room and then to the waiting room — just you, your opponent, and one official — and finally out on the court, where you bowed to royalty and then began to warm up. The grass could be bad and the ball could take bad hops, but you realized that in spite of everything, this was the most important tournament in the world; if you could win here just once, you were home free.

Knowing what that pressure could do to players — he once saw Bob Mark serve a ball up into the grandstands as he warmed up — Laver's strategy in warmups would be to start hitting into his opponents' backhand, since most of them would underspin that shot, instead of using topspin. Rod knew that underspin was only defensive, and required touch, which was hard to come by at Wimbledon because you were so nervous. Plus it's tough learning to control underspin on grass right away when the ball is taking bad hops. As a result, Laver's opponent would be losing his confidence before the match even began. But Laver would immediately start off hitting topspin on both sides as his way to combat the pressure. He would flail away, and at first the ball wouldn't go exactly where he wanted it — but boy, the doggone thing would go in. Pretty soon he would have the nervousness worked out of his system, and *then* he would go to work on his underspin shots. By this time his opponent would be praying, "Dear God, please let this be my day," because he had already lost his touch.

Not that Laver really needed a psychological edge when he was in his prime, but that's how important he felt topspin was to his game.

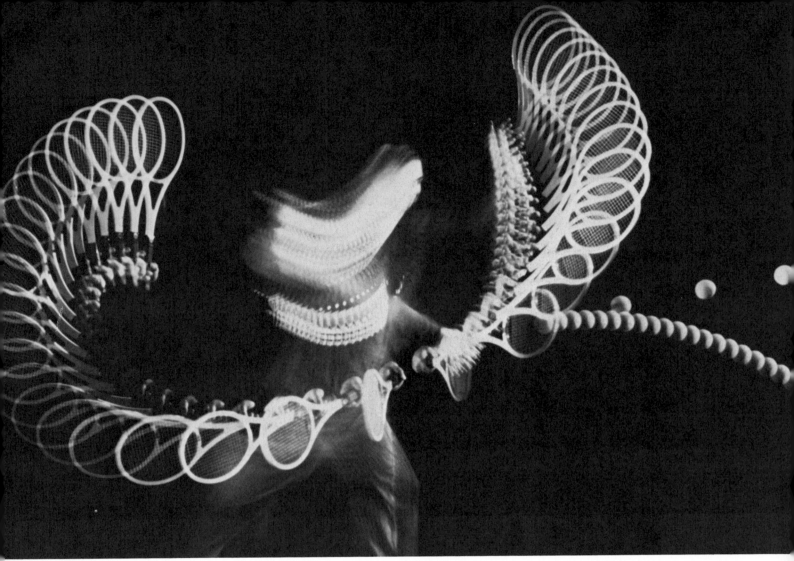

PHOTO BY JOHN G. ZIMMERMAN

This is the loop forehand used by most male and female professional players. In this photograph, the initial backswing has already been effected, so that you can observe the continuous motion of the loop swing once the racket begins its drop. Notice the space between each racket image: the wider the space, the greater the racket's speed. Thus, the greatest racket speed is recorded two to three feet before the racket meets the ball. One physicist has stated that many players pick up six miles per hour in racket speed for every foot of drop on the loop section of the backswing. Also observe how small an arc the hitting hand actually makes. There's very little hand swing to a good stroke.

Chapter Three

The Forehand

ONE OF THE CURIOSITIES of tennis is our love affair with the forehand. Most people regard it as their biggest weapon, the one they can rely on under pressure. On the forehand there seldom is the sense of panic that occurs when the ball is coming to the backhand side. Yet in all my years in tennis, I haven't found one pro player who could quickly name ten great forehands in the history of the game. But there have been dozens of great backhand hitters. And by "great" I mean someone who, while under stress, can place the ball near the intended target.

Psychology aside, the reason for this disparity between the two strokes is that the forehand — physically — is a more difficult shot to hit accurately than the backhand. On the forehand, when you begin to hit a ball which is even with or slightly in front of your body, the hitting arm starts to pinch against the body. Anticipating this pinch, most players relax the hitting elbow and wrist a little too early and then wrap the racket around their body on the follow-through, instead of going out toward their target. Many times the racket arm ends up around the neck, leading me to wonder why I've never read the headline: "Man Hangs Self on Forehand Follow-Through."

If this is the way you swing, and you want to save your neck while developing a winning forehand, then your goal should be to effect a low-to-high stroke pattern that produces topspin and allows you to follow through out toward your target — instead of the adjacent court.

Another warning: if you're thinking, "I don't need to work on my forehand — it's terrific," just be honest with yourself. What are you comparing it *to?* Many people claim to have a strong forehand, but when we get out on the court I discover that they've simply been comparing it to their backhand. Their backhand is crummy, but their forehand is a shade better than crummy, so they have a real "weapon." Don't let this kind of reasoning keep you from developing a good stroke on both sides.

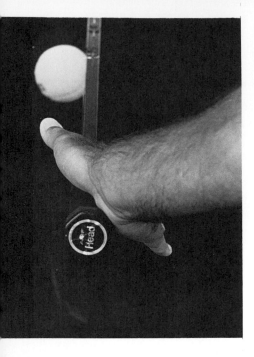 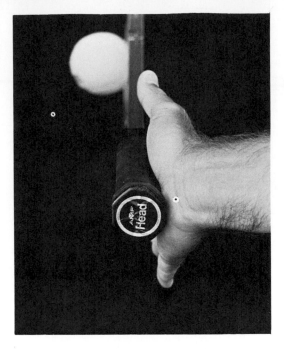 

The Continental forehand. Notice that the center of the palm sits on the top right side of the racket handle.

The Eastern forehand. Notice that the palm sits on the back side of the handle, parallel to the racket face.

The Western forehand. Notice that the palm sits mostly on the bottom side of the handle.

Forehand Grips

An opposite view of the Continental forehand.

The Eastern forehand.

The Western forehand.

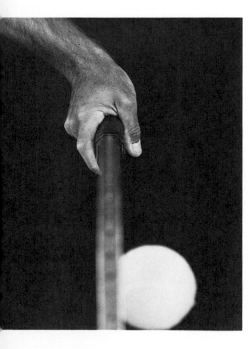  

The Grip

Those of you who scoff at the importance of the grip need to realize one thing: no matter how many adjustments you might make in your swing, *a proper grip will last for the rest of your life.* That's fairly crucial, so don't think you can go out and hold the racket any way that feels comfortable. Furthermore, your grip dictates the position and comfort of your wrist, knees, and body. Except for underspin shots, the racket face should be vertical to the ground when it meets the ball. Thus you want a grip that will necessitate the least amount of wrist motion in order to produce a racket face that is straight up and down at impact. Whatever grip you adopt will place some amount of awkwardness or stress upon the forearm and wrist, but the Eastern grip, in my opinion, demands the least adjustment and produces the most consistency.

Special names have been given to the forehand grips based upon the position of the palm against the racket handle.

When the palm sits primarily upon the top right side, the grip is called the Continental. It requires a strong wrist and is used by many professionals for both forehand and backhand strokes.

When the palm sits mainly on the back side of the handle, it's called an Eastern grip. The palm and the racket face are on the same plane, which gives the sensation of hitting the ball with the palm of your hand. This is the most common grip.

When the palm rests primarily on the bottom of the handle, so that the palm points at the sky, it's called a Western grip. This is the least common grip, although some players use it to great advantage.

The Eastern

If you are righthanded, start by holding the throat of your racket with your left hand so that the racket face is vertical to the ground. Then hold the racket at waist level with the right palm vertical and your fingers pointing slightly downward at approximately a 45-degree angle. The thumb should overlap and lie next to the middle finger, with the index finger spread. Now hold the racket out away from you and look at the top edge of your racket and the top edge of your right palm to see if they are both absolutely vertical. Test yourself by placing the racket on edge on a table

Terminology

The terms used in these two photographs are used throughout this book. Know them well and this book will mean more to you. On the forehand at impact, notice: (1) the shoulder housing the hitting arm, (2) the non-hitting arm, (3) the back shoulder, (4) the front shoulder, (5) head fixed and eyes focused on the point of contact, (6) hitting even with the front side of the body, (7) weight transferred to the front foot, (8) the racket face vertical and the racket head that has not fallen below the level of the wrist, (9) the back hip, (10) the front hip.

to see what it means to have the face straight up and down. Remember, if you play this game right you'll rarely hit a shot that requires the racket to vary more than 10 degrees from this vertical position.

Many people discuss "shaking hands" with the racket in order to achieve the proper grip, while others suggest putting the right palm against the strings, then sliding the hand down the racket to the grip. But I find that many people shake hands differently, while others achieve a unique position with their palm as they slide it down from the face of the racket.

Everybody wants to know, "How can you tell if your grip is right when you are playing a match?" A good pro can detect a quarter-inch flaw in your grip from 50 feet away, but it gets a little expensive having him watch your match from the bench. Short of that, all you can really do is learn through repetition and by "feel" when your grip is right. You can check your grip between points to see if the palm and the racket head are indeed vertical, but "feel" is all you can rely on as you play, especially if you switch grips between the forehand and the backhand, which I advocate. So begin to think kinesthetically. Close your eyes and try to achieve the perfect grip, then open your eyes and see if you are right. Even when you buy a new racket, test the grip with your eyes closed. (Don't feel you're alone with this problem. I'm always amazed by the number of good players who begin to lose their "grip" on occasion.)

The Continental

The Continental brings the palm of the hand an eighth turn higher on the racket handle. But this requires you to change the wrist position as you hit in order to effect a vertical racket head at impact, and I don't like anything that forces you to play around with the wrist. (If you're holding a racket, try the Continental; get that sensation I'm talking about.) In my opinion, by forcing greater wrist play the Continental is destructive to consistent play for 95 percent of the people who use the grip. Jack Kramer is even more adamant. He feels the Continental grip has done more to destroy good groundstrokes than any other single factor.

Yet the battle goes on. One of the arguments for the Continental, for example, is that it is used by many of the top players — especially the Australians. But that is the point: you have to be extremely talented to use the Continental and play a winning game. Or, put another way, you must be more coordinated. Even then you leave yourself vulnerable. If you hold the

On this backhand volley, notice:
(1) the shoulder housing the hitting arm, (2) the non-hitting arm, (3) the back shoulder, (4) the front shoulder, (5) head fixed and eyes focused on the point of contact, (6) the front foot, (7) the back foot, (8) weight transferred to the front foot, (9) the front hip, (10) knuckles of the grip pointed toward the target, (11) index finger on the grip spread, (12) ball being contacted away from the body, (13) racket head pointed at about a 45-degree angle.

Continental you tend to pull across the body in a big way. Thus, every time you reach out in front to hit the ball — especially on the forehand volley — you tend to hit only cross-court because that's where the face of the racket is automatically pointed. You have to make a difficult adjustment in order to hit down the line. That's why when pros like Segura and Kramer played Gonzales, they would run like heck for the cross-court return when he had a forehand volley. They knew that when he volleyed out in front, his racket face pointed to his left naturally. Kramer states that he was able to build 14 courts and 5,000 square feet of clubhouse on the Palos Verdes Peninsula (the Kramer Tennis Club) because Gorgo — as Gonzales is known — had a bad grip on the forehand side when they played their head-to-head tour in 1949, which Kramer won, 97-26.

The Western

Players such as Harold Solomon and Marita Redondo have developed fine forehands with this grip, which places the palm partly under the racket handle. On surfaces where balls tend to bounce high — notably clay — the Western is ideal. Hold the grip yourself, and notice how easy it is to produce a vertical racket head at impact when the ball is chest high. But when the

(1)

(2)

(3)

(6)

(7)

(8)

(4)   (5)

The Loop Forehand

(1) The ready position, just before the player (Richie Ley) moves to the ball to hit a forehand. (2) As soon as the player determines the direction of the shot, he pivots his entire body quickly and takes the racket back to "buy time." Notice the racket face is turned slightly down. Weak players often have the racket face positioned up at this stage. (3) A rear view of the initial forehand backswing using the loop. This is the end of the backswing turn before the player drops his racket and racket arm as he steps into the ball. You should learn to run with the racket in this position. (4) The hitter has completed the downflight of his loop swing, gaining racket speed, and is now ready to transfer his weight out onto the front foot. Pay special attention to the downturned racket face. (5) A rear view of the racket face at the lowest point of the loop swing. This racket-face position is crucial to a good swing, for it allows the hitter to lock his wrist and assures him of a vertical racket when he meets the ball even with the front side of his body. Unfortunately, few people ever get their racket and racket hand down to this low position, and thus they never have a natural lifting motion. (6) When the racket meets the ball, the racket face must be perpendicular to the court to produce the desired topspin. Also notice how the racket is slightly higher than the level of the wrist. (7) The follow-through continues toward the intended target, but the nose of the racket is not pointed in that direction, for this requires a wrist snap of at least 45 degrees. The hitter's head remains fixed with eyes still focused upon the impact area. The head should not be raised until the upper racket arm touches the chin, thus assuring a smooth swing. (8) If the desired follow-through shown in the previous photograph feels too rigid, a simple elbow bend will provide the relaxed feeling you seek. However you finish, don't twist or roll the hitting arm, since this can lead to tennis elbow . . . and hospitals don't stage many major tennis tournaments.

ball bounces low — especially on grass — the Western places such a severe strain on the wrist and forearm that it's difficult for players to hit with any authority. As fine a player as Solomon is, when he gets on grass he's in trouble because the ball skids and stays low longer, making it more difficult to handle with his grip.

The Ideal Stroking Pattern

Before breaking down the forehand into specific elements, I will explain the stroking pattern I seek. I like to have people see the complete stroke and how the pieces fit together. Then I work backwards, filling in the details according to how much students can grasp and assimilate. Grooving the ideal stroking pattern is the name of the game, a matter that requires considerable time and practice — whether you're just beginning or you're trying to replace a stroke that is encrusted with a number of incorrect movements. But try to make the changes that you feel are important and see if your game doesn't improve. (If what I say makes sense, but you refuse to experiment and you continue to lose with your same old strokes, perhaps you're a little masochistic. In that case, look around for a sadist to play each week and you'll always have a grand time.)

From a ready position, your backswing should begin the instant you detect the direction of your opponent's shot. Tell yourself, "It's a forehand!" and rotate both shoulders back simultaneously to begin your backswing pivot. This turns your left side toward the net. Using the loop swing (analyzed later), take your racket back at eye level and away from your body until it points to the back fence. Pause here until the ball approaches, then step out with your front foot — keeping your weight equal over both feet — and bend your knees so that you can drop your racket and racket hand approximately 12 inches below the intended point of impact. Stepping out on the front foot and lowering the racket and racket arm should take place simultaneously. This enables you to transfer your weight forward and up as your racket moves from low to high and strikes the ball with a vertical face. Try to have your eyes follow the ball as far as you can into your racket strings and leave your head down, in a fixed position, so that you will not disturb your stroking pattern. Don't lift your head until your upper hitting arm touches your chin on the follow-through. You should finish with your hitting arm pointed skyward and directed at your target, while the racket itself is facing to your right. Trying to point the racket at your target will force an awkward wrist turn that can produce tennis elbow.

If you can visualize your follow-through "reaching toward the sky," this will give you a greater respect for getting the racket down at the lowest point of your backswing, in order that you can swing from low to high. No matter how low the ball is coming, fight to get your racket and racket hand below the intended point of impact and lift up, so that your body can supply power along with your arm. Don't forget: *tennis is a lifting game*. A person 6'6" tall, standing behind his own baseline and looking over the net, cannot even see his target areas on the other side. (Caution: On fore-hands and backhands, whenever I talk about getting the racket head 12 inches below the intended point of impact in order to hit with topspin, don't get the impression that you simply drop the racket head by loosening the wrist. You must lower the hitting arm, the wrist, and the racket *as a fixed unit*, so that your hitting hand is also 12 inches below the oncoming ball, on the same level as the racket head.)

Now, with an overview of the forehand in mind, strive to make your body accommodate the ideal swing. You can have your body twisted cra-zily, your legs crossed, and a finger in your ear, but if the stroking pattern is perfect, and the racket head is vertical at impact, you can make the play. Conversely, you may have very sensuous and beautiful body movements on the court, but if your racket head is crooked at impact you'll seldom get the ball in. Certainly you want to be relaxed out there, since excess muscular tension inhibits free movement. But never let your entire body go loose. People who try to tell themselves, "Relax, dummy, relax," tend to let their racket arm relax and they generally finish second in a field of two. Instead, learn to keep your racket arm fixed and your racket face in a steady position as you take your swing. You may feel a little stiff at first, but the more you keep the ball in play — and win matches — the more you'll find yourself loosening up.

Finally, when you're out on the court playing, and you want to remember just one key thing on the forehand, tell yourself: "Play with the palm." For as your palm goes (using the Eastern grip), so goes your racket head — they must move in sync with one another. If you can keep the palm turned slight-ly down on the backswing and then have it vertical at impact, your racket head will do the same. Think of them moving together in this pattern and you will be forced to develop a correct stroking pattern.

The Loop Swing

What I'm advocating in this book, on both the forehand and the backhand, is an identical loop swing, as opposed to "straight back." This is a controversial issue among teaching pros, yet I find it interesting that most of those who teach "straight back" use the loop when they go out to play — as does virtually every player in pro tennis.

Advocates of the straight-back swing argue that the average player can understand it more easily, and other pros state, "I teach straight back because the loop takes too long." Yet I've found that the loop can be learned by nearly everybody, and a test at my tennis college showed that both swings reach the same impact point at about the same time. I allow my students to use a straight-back swing if they prefer, but I remind them that the loop will produce better results in the long run.

To visualize the loop swing, try to think of a little hairpin turn taken in two parts. First, bring the racket back at about eye level and wait for the approaching ball. Then, in a continuous motion, drop the racket and your hitting hand 12 inches below the intended point of impact, and come forward and up through the ball, toward your target. On the backswing, remember to keep your hitting shoulder *raised* until the racket is pointed to the back fence. Try to get the feeling of a little lift going back, as if you were taking your racket hand back, down and around a large beach ball. One important movement that will help you to get down is to lower your hitting wrist and the butt of your racket to your right thigh (if you are righthanded) so that you can have a natural lifting motion. Some pros will literally brush the butt of their grip against that right thigh on a low ball, and then follow through like a bowler. This allows them to stay on a natural line to the target.

One reason I advocate the loop over straight back is that the loop is more rhythmical and produces significantly more power and control. Physicist Pat Keating has researched both swings and found that on the loop, the racket head gains approximately *six miles per hour of racket speed* for every foot it drops on the backswing. Thus, on a normal loop swing, where the drop from highest point of the backswing to the lowest is about four feet, a person should gain 12 miles an hour in racket speed with an uninterrupted drop. This increased racket speed has a multiple effect on the speed of the ball, and it helps explain why little kids who use the loop can hit the ball so hard. In contrast to this, the person who goes straight back to the low point

The loop swing is effected in two parts. First, the player should immediately turn his racket back to the two arrows and wait for the ball. The second part of the swing is continuous from the two arrows around, down and up to the completion of the follow-through.

The straight-back swing completely eliminates the loop. The hitter takes his racket back on a straight diagonal downward (as indicated by the arrows), and then moves up along the same line as the loop swing.

of his backswing has gained zero miles an hour as he starts to move into the ball. He must use a lot more muscular effort to gain sufficient racket speed in a short period of time.

A second virtue of the loop is that the stroking pattern you effect is identical for both the forehand and the backhand. By always getting your racket and racket hand 12 inches below the intended point of impact (at the farthest point of your backswing), you groove the same stroke for every height of the ball. Your stroking pattern will always look the same, except for extremely high or low bounces, and you will find it easier to conceal shots from a person at the net, since he or she can't detect whether you are going to drive or lob.

Third, those instructors who teach a straight-back swing will argue, "If you want people to get down lower than the intended point of impact, they're already down with straight back." Unfortunately, I've found that most straight-back players fail to do what they think they do. They swear they lower their racket 12 inches below the intended point of impact, in order to hit with topspin, but their racket actually remains waist high or above. Thus, when they lean into the shot, their hitting arm goes up even farther and raises their racket higher than the oncoming ball. This forces them to make last-second adjustments in their swing just to contact the ball on a horizontal level. These "adjustments," of course, are what cause them to look different from the successful pro.

Those straight-back hitters who learn it right — by taking the racket back at waist level and then dropping it to about knee level — are actually using a modified loop swing. Far more often, however, those people who get the racket low do so by taking the racket straight down on a diagonal line to the lowest point of the backswing, which of course costs them a power-producing loop. (See photographs on page 50.)

If you're a successful straight-back player, don't change. But I encourage the rest of you to go out and watch the pros hit their forehands and backhands. Nearly all of them will have basic loop swings, unless they're intentionally hitting with underspin.

The Forehand in Detail

Now that you have the desired forehand stroke in mind, I'll go through the entire swing in more detail. Only by concentrating on these specific details can you hope to develop a stroke that keeps the ball in play under pressure. You may wonder why I seem to be so obsessive about grooving the proper stroking patterns. My reason is based on a simple physical law, translated here into tennis terms: "Any extraneous movement by the racket which deviates from the ideal stroking pattern demands a corrective measure in the middle of the stroke to bring the racket back to its original position." In other words, an incorrect movement by the racket — such as that caused by a floppy wrist — is really a twofold error, and two errors actually add four extra movements. So when you keep making seemingly minor "adjustments" in your swing on every shot, all you're doing is making corrections. My object is to eliminate as many of those corrections as possible.

Ready Position

Many people become enamored of the ready position because it's one of the few things they can master early. They don't have a forehand or a backhand but they've got the best ready position in the club and you can spot them a mile away.

Nevertheless, I've never been too concerned about a standardized ready position because some people can make fast exits from unique stances. Besides, many top pro players assume a different type of ready position before the ball is struck by their opponent. The idea, therefore, is to find that stance which will produce *the fastest first step towards the ball and the fastest turn of the body* in order to get in position for the shot. To test for this, go out on a court and have a friend time you with a stopwatch. Face an imaginary opponent, racket in hand, while straddling the center stripe. When your friend says "Go!" turn and run to either singles sideline. Do it over and over again to both sidelines until you find the ready position which gets you there the fastest. Remember that when your opponent is about to strike the ball, you don't know if your next shot will be a forehand or a backhand, so be ready to pivot for either stroke with equal ease.

The Backswing Pivot

The more I teach this game, the more I emphasize a proper backswing. I want my students to realize, "As the preparation goes, so goes the stroke," because once you're in the middle of your swing, you're locked into that shot. It's a myth to think you can "guide" the ball or control it with last-second adjustments in your swing. In fact, *unless your opponent's shot is traveling at an unbelievably slow rate of speed, there can be no adaptive behavior in the middle of the swing that can be positive in nature.*

Therefore, keeping in mind that your ultimate accuracy on groundstrokes traces back to your initial backswing, learn these two key points as you try to develop a strong forehand: (1) react quickly to your opponent's shot and (2) rotate both shoulders together as you turn your body to take your racket back.

It's impossible to be too early on your backswing, since your goal is never to be rushed on any stroke. The more time you can buy with quick reactions and a quick but fluid backswing, the more easily and rhythmically you can stroke the ball. Remember, too, that the loop swing is not continuous but is taken in two parts. So the moment you see the ball coming to your forehand, turn your body and start the racket back — but save the racket's fall and the drop of your body until you are ready to step into the ball. Even when you run to get into position, have the racket head back at about eye level and pointed upward. If you wait until you get to the ball to take the racket back, you'll always be rushed and you'll produce an erratic pattern of shots. A late backswing, as we shall see, also leads to wrist layback — one of the most damaging errors you can make.

Just as it's crucial to have an early backswing, *never let your racket arm take a solo.* Turn or coil your shoulders simultaneously with the racket so that you can unleash this energy at the ball, for it's the unwinding of the body that supplies the added power at impact to go with the power generated by the forward movement of the hitting arm. When you pull the racket back alone, you get an isolated arm movement going forward, and this demands a much stronger arm. But by coiling the body in sync with the racket, you can turn into the shot and hit the ball very hard with less energy input.

Preparing early and rolling the non-hitting shoulder inward on the backswing is such an elemental — yet often overlooked — factor in good tennis that Kramer hated to even rally with players who didn't have this grooved into their stroke. He'd say, "Jeez, kid, if you don't turn your shoulder, how in the heck do you ever expect to play this game?" To force his own front (left) shoulder to turn inward, Jack would hold his left hand up by the throat of the racket, which pulled his left shoulder back as he made his turn. On the follow-through he would catch the racket again, so that his racket was never far away from his left hand.

(1)

(2)

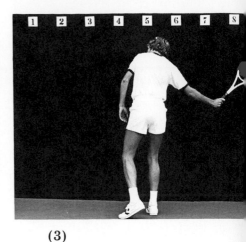

(3)

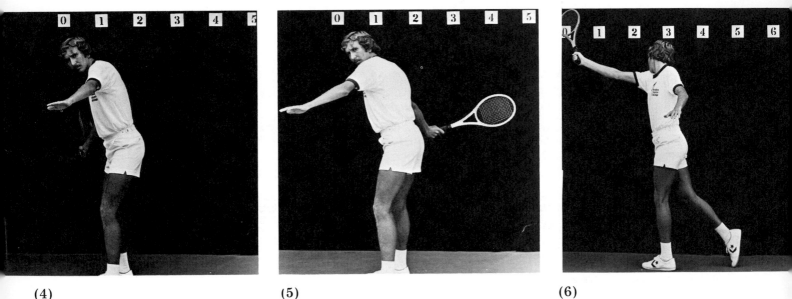

(4)

(5)

(6)

The 24-Foot Swing

(1) In this photograph sequence, each number is spaced 1 foot apart, to help you realize why some faulty forehand swings total 24 feet or more. Here, the center of the racket face is directly under the 2-foot mark before the backswing begins. (2) The backswing has begun and a simple shoulder turn has moved the racket nearly 3 feet. (3) The hitter has completed his proper backswing and now begins the dropping motion of the loop swing. Total distance covered: 7 feet. (4) A front view of the desired backswing shows that the racket is still visible. However, there are few great forehands in the game because most players fail to stop their backswing here. (5) Instead, the typical player adds 4 feet to his backswing by letting the wrist lay back. This 4-foot layback requires a 4-foot correction, increasing the length of the swing by 8 feet. (6) The forward motion into the ball and the follow-through cover 9 feet, meaning that the racket face has now traveled a total distance of 16 feet with the proper backswing; some of the greatest forehands total as little as 15 feet. A wrist layback, shown here, forces the racket to travel 24 feet or more.

Another way to help yourself turn back, on both the forehand and backhand, is to imagine that your initials are on the back of each shoulder blade and you want to turn and show people who you are. Little kids get the idea quickly and some of them will turn that shoulder back and say, "Hi, I'm Jimmy."

The Racket, the Wrist, and the Palm on the Backswing

Throughout my discussion on the forehand and the backhand, I want to emphasize that it's not how hard you swing, or the strength of your arm that will make you famous. It's how well you keep your body and your racket *moving in sync*, by going back together, forward together, and then up together. Thus you don't want to do anything that will destroy the proper relationship between your body and your racket arm. Easy to say, hard to do, but there are ways you can minimize breakdowns under pressure.

To begin with, my observation over the years has been that the *body* seems to have an innate ability to turn into the ball at the proper time. I'll hit balls to absolute beginners and tell them to "swing when you think it's time." If I just watch their bodies move into the shot, I think, "terrific." Yet they rarely hit the ball properly because the racket is out of sync: it's either too high, too low, too early, or too late, or a combination of the four. And the culprit, of course, is the racket arm.

The Racket

Let the pivoting of your shoulders turn the racket back, with the racket head raised substantially higher than wrist level, at approximately a 45-degree angle. If you pivot the upper body, the racket should travel no farther than pointing straight at the back fence, and that should happen automatically if there has been no wrist movement. In fact, some of the better forehands on the pro circuit do not even come back this far. By shortening your backswing in this manner, (1) it's easier to keep the racket arm moving in synchronization with the body, and (2) you get the racket head on the ball consistently because the racket has a shorter distance to travel to meet the ball. (Some pros urge average players to swing "straight back" to avoid a common error on the loop: starting the backswing too high. That's why I teach loop swingers to simply bring the racket back at eye level and maintain a short backswing.)

In contrast to a controlled backswing, think what it means to let the

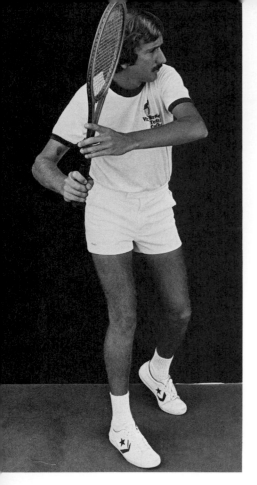

To prevent wrist layback, slightly bend and raise the elbow of your hitting arm (called "leading with the elbow") on your backswing. This makes it almost impossible to lay the racket head back. In fact, if a wrist layback is your problem, you should wait for a shot with the bend already in your elbow, so that all you have to do is turn and hit.

racket come well behind your body by letting the wrist "lay back." To illustrate, if I said to you, "I only want your swing to be 15 feet long from beginning to end," you'd think I was crazy. "Fifteen feet! Heck, that's ten feet too long." Yet most people have swings that total 23 to 25 feet.

For example, players with a correct swing will normally have a minimum backswing of seven feet, and then eight feet forward — or 15 feet. But when most people get the racket pointed to the back fence, they fail to stop there the way they should. They let the wrist lay back and the racket continues around for another four feet — meaning an additional four feet to bring the racket back to the original desired position. If you're wondering why you are always late on the ball, this may be the answer. So go to work on a nice 15-foot swing and you'll gain a lot of valuable time.

The Wrist

If you hope to produce a vertical racket head at impact, *your hitting wrist must be kept firm and must not change its original position on the backswing or forward motion.* No matter how fluidly you swing, if you allow the wrist to "lay back" on the backswing, the racket head will go out of sync with your shoulders. Believe me, you'll save yourself tons of grief as a tennis player if you can prevent this from ever happening. For when you lay the wrist back, you not only have the initial error, you must now make an excess movement to get the wrist — and the racket — back in sync with the body.

The problem, of course, is how to keep your wrist from laying back. First, don't take your racket arm back in isolated fashion. Have your body do the work by rotating with both shoulders while your wrist remains firm.

Second, as you take your forehand backswing, *lead with your hitting elbow slightly raised and bent as you draw the racket back*, instead of maintaining a straight arm. Try this yourself by placing your back foot up against a line and then seeing that your elbow passes the line slightly before the wrist and racket on the backswing. The more you tend to lay the wrist back, the more you will have to raise and bend the elbow. Experiment to see what it takes to keep the wrist in its original fixed position.

Third, remember to regard the loop as a two-part swing and not one continuous motion. Get the racket back quickly, then save the drop for when you step out on your front foot. When you start your swing too late — either with the loop or straight back — you might think that you can recover by suddenly stopping your racket arm on the backswing and moving

To test for unwanted wrist layback and a wrap-around follow-through, the hitter places his back against a fence and practices a backswing and follow-through without ever touching the fence with his racket.

quickly into the ball. But research shows this doesn't happen. When your arm suddenly decelerates, the racket *accelerates* and keeps going back, producing wrist layback. Only by getting the racket back early enough to recover from this deceleration-acceleration, and by leading with the raised elbow, can you keep the racket moving in sync with the body. Once again: *the success of your forward swing is almost completely dependent upon your backswing.*

The Palm

Remember, you want to keep the face of your racket and your palm moving together in their original position, since direction and accuracy are best controlled by your palm. If you keep your palm and the face of your racket lined up in exactly the same manner, then all you have to do is keep your palm moving toward the target and you're home free — if you supply the right elevation.

In order to produce a vertical racket head at impact, *your palm (and racket) must be turned down or faced down slightly at the end of your backswing.* You can test this for yourself right in your living room. First, if your racket face is straight up and down at the lowest point of your backswing, and you keep the wrist fixed as you move into an imaginary ball, you'll find that your racket is facing *upward* at impact.

To correct this, place your racket with a vertical face at the point where you normally contact the ball. Now lock the wrist at that point. Without moving your wrist position, slowly allow your racket arm to creep backwards in a natural motion, retracing your forward movement. At the lowest point of your backswing you will notice that your racket face is not vertical, but is pointing to the ground. You will think, "If I swing like this I'm going to hit myself in the foot." But then move the racket forward, without changing your wrist position, and bring it to the impact point. The racket should now be vertical again. Repeat the drill and take a good look at each stage of the swing. Even close your eyes and try to feel what it means to have that racket and the palm pointed down toward the court. If the racket face is not ending up vertical at impact, experiment with the palm until you discover how much you should face it down on the backswing. Leading slightly with the elbow on the backswing will also help keep the palm down.

When you try this drill, remember to start and end with the racket where you actually contact the ball. For instance, don't make the mistake of lining up the ball straight off your right hip. The racket face may be vertical at this point, but you actually contact the ball 12 inches later, which means that the bottom of your racket will come under.

Pros like Rod Laver and Bjorn Borg really push that palm down on the backswing — without changing their wrist — when they plan to hit with topspin. Try it yourself and see how "clean" and how solid your stroke feels when you contact the ball properly. If the ball keeps hitting the net, or even your own side of the court, don't be discouraged, and *don't bevel the racket face to adjust.* All you have to do is bend your knees so that you can hit properly from low to high.

Bending Your Knees and Getting the Racket Low

We tell everybody going through the tennis college that we can make them famous by Friday if they can get to the ball and learn to do three "simple" things: get the racket head and racket hand 12 inches below the intended point of impact, contact the ball with a vertical racket head, and follow through up under their chin on about a 17-degree angle from the court. Unfortunately, you have to practically beat people over the head to get them to bend their knees and drop their racket hand below the ball — all in the same motion.

One problem is that it's an unnatural feeling to get the racket low and maintain that position on the backswing. When some people get lower than the object to be struck, they feel like they're going to miss it; others are handicapped by their memory of hitting a baseball with a level swing. Another hang-up is that most people haven't bent their knees since 1938. I'll see a gal in the restaurant sitting down to eat lunch, and an hour later she'll tell me out on the court, "Honest, Vic, my knees really don't bend." Furthermore, people often have an image of themselves which is very different from that revealed by our videotape cameras. I once had a man tell me,

The best way to learn the proper wrist position for when the racket contacts the ball is to stand sideways and place the racket face flush against a fence. That's the wrist position you want — for the rest of your life!

Practice Tip: Self-Evaluation on the Wrist Position

On a hard-hit shot, you can vary the ball 30 feet in any direction by moving your wrist just one inch during the swing. That's going to put you in deep trouble. The problem is to correct the error, but first try to discover where the racket is going astray, whether on the backswing or while moving into the ball. Fortunately, there are ways you can analyze yourself on the court or at home to see if you are achieving the correct wrist position to begin with, and to check if you are rolling your wrist or laying it back or otherwise tampering with what should be a fixed position.

1.   Stand sideways to a fence or a wall with your front foot angled against the fence. Achieve the proper forehand grip and place the racket face flush against the fence, where you normally contact the ball. The racket face should be vertical, parallel to the fence, and slightly higher than the wrist. If you want to measure the correct position, the bottom edge of the racket head should be at the same level as your index finger.

Now, whatever wrist bend there is in your hand to keep your palm and the racket face parallel to the fence (and perpendicular to the ground) is the wrist bend you want to maintain for the rest of your life. Never change this bend at any point during the swing unless you become an extremely proficient player. Even then, remember that pros who use a lot of wrist action are playing seven days a week and wristy pros sometimes go sour.

2.   To practice the "feel" of keeping your wrist fixed on your backswing and through contact with the ball, swing very slowly, then stop just before the intended point of impact and analyze the surface of the racket face to see if it has remained parallel to the fence. Also try to swing with your eyes closed to keep yourself honest.

3.   If you are righthanded, place the thumb and middle finger of your left hand on the wrist of your hitting arm and feel exactly what it means to lay the wrist back or roll it over. You'll discover where your problem is starting, and what it takes to maintain a firm wrist.

4.   Stand with the toes of both feet against a line on the court and take a swing. If the racket crosses the line on the backswing, then you're taking it back too far. For a visual check in your living room, you want to see the entire racket at the end of your backswing. If it disappears behind your body, then chances are excellent that you're laying the wrist back.

5.   Attach a yardstick to the surface plane of the racket and try to keep the yardstick from laying back on the backswing. You actually want the yardstick and racket faced slightly down as you go back. The yardstick magnifies any wrist movement and thus helps identify the problem area.

6.   The next time you are rallying, freeze on your follow-through, then allow your shoulder to be the only moving joint as you lower your arm back down to where you normally contact the ball, off your front side. If the racket face is still vertical you know you haven't moved your wrist on the swing. But if the racket face is pointed up, then it was turned under when you hit, and whatever it takes to roll the racket back to a vertical position is the amount you have moved it during your swing.

The hitter (Mary Ley) reaches the farthest point on her backswing. A chair has been appropriately placed to guarantee the proper knee bend for a waist-high, or lower, shot. At this point she will do three things simultaneously: (1) begin the curved downflight of her racket on the loop swing, (2) step forward with her left foot, and (3) sit her rear end in the chair.

Bingo! She makes a perfect three-point landing.

Now the player uses her thighs to push up and out of the chair, which helps lift the ball over the net.

The hitter double-checks her follow-through. Note the direction of the butt of her racket (toward the court), and the height of her follow-through.

Practice Tip: Vic's "Sit-and-Hit" Chair Drill

When hitting groundstrokes with topspin, it's your knees that will allow you to lower your body so that you can hit with a natural lifting motion. Stiff knees, especially on balls bouncing waist high or lower, generally lead to a dropped racket head and ineffective stroke patterns. So if your knees seem chronically stiff on the tennis court, try my "Sit-and-Hit" Chair Drill to give yourself an idea of just how much your knees should bend on most groundstrokes, and what it feels like to coordinate the body and the racket arm on the loop swing.

Stand with your back to an average-sized chair or even a park bench as you wait for a court, and imagine that a ball has just been hit. Pivot your body and take your racket back in a loop swing. As your racket and racket hand drop to brush your thigh, lower your rear end and step forward simultaneously with your front foot. Your rear end should touch the chair or bench as your front foot finishes the forward step. Think of making a brief three-point landing with your racket, rear end, and front foot. You're now ready to come forward and up with a low-to-high motion. (On the backhand, do the same thing.) Also remember to practice keeping your head fixed and eyes down on the point of impact as you come up. If you get in the habit of looking up to see where the ball is going as you lift up, you may disturb your stroke pattern.

Most people refuse to bend their knees as low as I ask because they're afraid they won't have enough strength to come back up. But if you stick with this drill you're going to get your thighs in shape while your stroke improves.

in all seriousness, "You know, I think something's wrong with your TV camera. It doesn't show me bending my knees."

Then you have the corporation president who sits in the classroom the first day and gets all stoked up. He's thinking, "I manipulate planes and trains every day. If all I have to do is control three little variables in tennis, I'll be famous by 2:30." So he rushes out on the court, takes a couple of swings, and asks expectantly, "How am I on this backswing?" Even though he thinks his racket is low, it very often is higher than his own head and we have to say, "You're still a little high." Intelligence tells the guy he has to get lower, so he really bends his knees, but the doggone racket stays up around his head. "I've got it!" he thinks. But we could use his racket for a hat rack.

Remember, it's easy to visualize getting low but quite another matter to actually do it. You have to fight through an invisible barrier to bend the knees and bring the racket down *together*. Try to realize that you probably can never get low enough. Exaggerate, because even when you think you are low, you probably are still too high — until you've grooved the proper swing. I've seen Laver touch the court with one knee to hit a ball just above knee level, yet most people won't even bend down for a ball that "high." They simply say, "No problem, I'll just make this little adjustment in my swing," and instead of almost scraping the court with their racket and racket hand, they simply loosen their wrist, drop the racket head, and bevel the racket face. This usually produces an exceptionally high shot over the net, or the back fence.

Every time you fail to get your racket and your racket hand lower than the approaching ball at the farthest point of your backswing (ideally, 12 inches lower), you must alter your stroke in order to produce a correct, vertical racket face at impact. If your goal is to play a consistent, topspin-oriented game, then failure to get low on every groundstroke will force you to have a different stroke for every height of the ball — and that's a losing formula in good tennis.

Timing the Drop on the Loop Swing

Unless you are late arriving at the ball, I don't want to see you take a continuous loop swing. You'll develop a much more consistent, error-free swing if you turn your shoulders and get the racket back quickly — pointed to the back fence — and then delay the drop of the racket and racket arm until you step into the ball. Even from a dead start, this drop generates significant kinetic energy and thus greater power in your swing than if you simply take the racket straight back down to about knee level before moving into the ball.

The problem is to learn when to bend the knees and to let the racket and racket arm drop as the ball approaches. Try my "sit-and-hit" drill to learn the right coordination of movements, then get out on the court to develop the proper timing when a ball is in play. Try to find a ball machine or a friend who can feed you dozens of balls in the same area so that you can concentrate solely on lowering the racket with a fixed wrist as your thighs start down and your front foot goes out. Remember, your weight is equally distributed over both feet at this point, and now your racket arm and thighs are free to come forward and up together as you transfer your weight into the shot. The result is maximum rhythm and power from your swing.

If you drop the racket too fast, you have to wait on the ball at the bottom of the loop, and thus you may as well eliminate the loop, since you've just lost the potential kinetic energy gains of a continuous motion from the top of the loop through impact. If you're late with the drop, you suddenly have to cut across your body in order to meet the ball in time.

Contacting the Ball

The ball should be contacted when it is even with or slightly *in front* of the side of your body closer to the net, while the hitting elbow is approximately six to ten inches *away from* your body in a slightly bent position. The further away from your body the ball is at contact, the more power you get from the same expenditure of energy, providing you can maintain a firm wrist and still feel comfortable. (Remember: as you stand sideways to the net, "away from" means the direction your belly button is pointed, and "in front of" means the side closer to the net.)

There are two other important considerations about the ball and the racket at impact. First, learn what it means to actually have the racket face vertical at impact (which is a prerequisite of topspin). Most people don't have this feeling. I'll ask players to take a practice swing with their eyes closed and stop their racket where they normally meet the ball. Then I ask, "How does it feel?" They say, "Terrific." But their racket face is generally pointing to the sky and their shot is on its way to the next county. Then I ask them to keep their eyes closed and I adjust the racket to its proper position at impact. Again I ask, "How does this feel?" They say, "Crummy." But I tell them, "Remember this crummy feeling . . . it will make you famous."

Second, it's a myth that any player can "feel" the ball on the strings or "guide" the ball toward the target. Research has shown that the ball is on the strings for only four to six milliseconds before it releases; when you feel the ball touch the strings, it's already gone and on its way. This doesn't mean you can contact the ball and then go anywhere with your follow-through. On the contrary, the racket contacts the ball for such a brief instant that you want to develop a low-to-high swing that enables you to meet the ball within a 6- to 18-inch span. This allows you to mistime the ball and still be good. A swing that is horizontal in nature makes timing much more difficult by allowing you only one point where you can contact the ball and make it be successful.

Play the Ball, Not Your Opponent

Remember, you don't play people in this game. The only thing that's going to make you famous is your relationship to the ball, so take good care of it. Keep your eyes on the ball for as long as you can, and concentrate on the point of impact until your upper arm or shoulder comes up and brushes your chin. Then lift your chin and let your eyes track the ball out over the net. When you leave your eyes down that long, you get a panicky feeling that your opponent's return shot is going to hit you in the ear. But in reality, when hitting from the baseline in this manner, your shot will not even reach the net by the time you raise your eyes to follow the ball. Try it! You'll find that you have plenty of time to stay over the ball and still get ready for your opponent's return.

Since our eyes can't track the ball all the way into the racket, I've lately been telling my students, "Keep your head down and try to see the racket pass in front of your eyes." Try this drill: rally with a friend, and whenever one of you doesn't watch the racket pass by your eyes at or near impact, that person yells, "Stop." At first your rallies will end after one or two shots, but they will lengthen out as you learn to concentrate on watching the ball as it approaches you, and then the racket.

Keeping your eyes down on the point of impact is also a guarantee that you will not lift your chin early, and thus disturb the relationship between

your head and the racket. If the center of the strings of your racket is about to strike the ball, and you suddenly lift your chin, this is going to lift your racket and cause you to hit off-center. That's one important reason why you occasionally — frequently? — hit "wood" shots off the edge of your racket.

Some coaches argue that when you leave your eyes down until your arm touches your chin on the follow-through, your shoulders "freeze" and you cannot move them properly as you contact the ball. But I can't buy that concept. Leaving your head and eyes down is also one key to a good golf swing, and it certainly doesn't stop your shoulders or hips from moving efficiently through the ball in that sport.

Remembering the proper follow-through will also help keep your head down as you stroke the ball. It's like shooting a camera: some people have a tendency to think they've taken the picture before they actually release the shutter, and thus they pull away at the wrong moment. In tennis, if you fail to realize how important it is to go all the way up and out on the follow-through, you have a tendency to pull off the ball at or before impact. I watch people all the time who lift their eyes and pull their head up before the ball even reaches the racket, yet they swear they actually see the ball hitting the strings. Therefore, don't be in such a hurry at impact; "hang on" to the shot for as long as possible, even though the ball is here and gone in an instant.

If your head lifts before you contact the ball, the racket may lift off its intended stroking pattern. In this photo, the hitter practices holding his head down while completing the stroke. Try it. You'll find that you can use thigh-power to lift your body without jerking your head upward. (See other forehand drills, page 78.)

Go After the Ball

Not only on the forehand but all your strokes, always strive to play the game *out in front* (towards the net) and *away from your body* (towards the sidelines) — never up close. Be aggressive and go after the ball. Don't let it come to you. Step out, and then move into the ball as you hit so that your weight and forward inertia can produce maximum power. Don't hit with your weight on your back foot and don't back up unless you are absolutely forced to by a deep shot. The weaker your arm, in fact, the more you must step forward to play good tennis. When you're late getting to the ball, and you must hit off your back foot, your only salvation is the strength of your arm. People who swing "all arm" also have a natural tendency to roll their arm and smother the shot.

The farther out in front you can step, and still maintain good balance, the

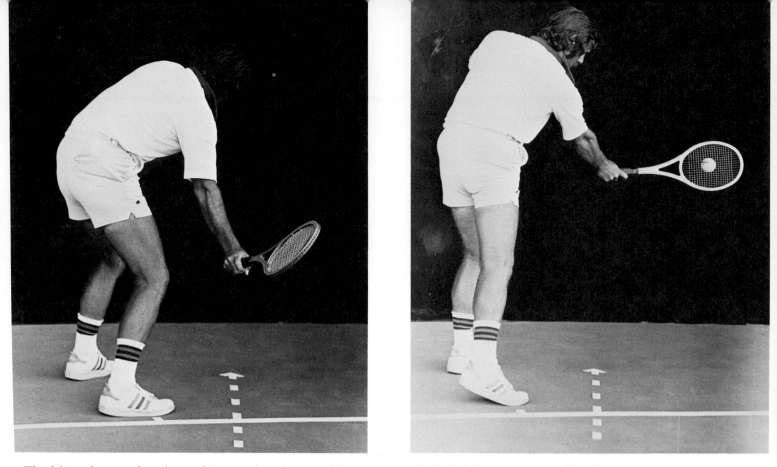

The hitter has used a piece of tape pointed toward the net post to help him practice an "inside-out" forehand swing. The forward motion of the palm, wrist, and forearm should move out and away from the body; this produces more power. At impact, notice how the racket face is parallel to the baseline and the net, while the palm faces the target.

longer you can keep your palm and racket going to the target. A long step forward gives you a greater range in which to meet the ball and still produce a successful shot. The shorter your step, the shorter your follow-through will be, and thus the more you will tend to pull across your body. A horizontal swing is similar to a spinning top, which must keep its balance over the center point. That's why people who swing on a horizontal plane take shorter steps: when they try to take a long step into the ball they have a hard time judging their swing.

After the hit, you can let your back foot come up to meet your front foot but don't let it come off the ground in a forward step, for this spins the body on a horizontal plane and usually effects a somewhat horizontal swing.

Swing Inside-Out, Like a Golfer

If you are turning from golf to tennis, and you have a good golf swing, you should be the happiest person alive. All that money you spent on lessons is now going to pay off in dividends because the efficient golf swing and the proper forehand share many important similarities, such as: (1) the head must be kept down and eyes fixed on the point of impact, (2) the shoulders must rotate in sync, slightly before the ball is met, (3) the real power is derived from the movement of the hips and the thighs as you contact the ball, and (4) there is an "inside-out" movement of the body and arms before impact so that the club or racket makes solid contact with the ball.

Most tennis players, especially those who swing on a horizontal plane, have difficulty in grasping the inside-out concept. They are accustomed to starting their swing out away from their body, and moving into their body with the forward motion of their hitting arm. This swing pulls the ball cross-court and with less power. Hitting inside-out, however, means the hitting arm is fairly close or "in" to the body on the backswing and the forward striking motion is away from the body. At first you get the feeling that you're going to hit the ball off to the right of your target. That, in fact, is the *feeling* you want. But if you can get your racket and racket hand lower than the ball on the backswing and swing inside-out, your palm and racket face will point to your intended target at impact, and will often be parallel to the net.

The inside-out motion contributes to a successful forehand in many ways. First, it leads to greater control and consistency by allowing the racket face to remain on target with the ball much longer than does a horizontal swing. If you can develop a stroke that keeps your palm going toward your target even before you strike the ball, you increase the distance in which you can make contact and still make a good hit. Second, inside-out keeps you from pulling across your body. Third, it forces you to contact the ball out away from your body, which lengthens the radius of your stroke and thus gives you more power with the same energy input. And fourth, since your energy flow is out toward your target, you can pull off one of the game's toughest plays: the passing shot down the line when your opponent is coming to the net. Yet swinging inside-out does not restrict you from hitting cross-court.

Assuming you get down properly with your thighs and your racket, *the movement of your hips is the key to the inside-out movement.* As you shift your weight forward into the ball, rotate your hips slightly ahead of your upper body (as in golf) so that your right hip turns in toward the target. Think about rolling your hips into the ball and directing your body inertia out toward your opponent's backhand (assuming you are both righthanded). Knowing when to turn the hips is a tricky little maneuver, and some people find it easier to visualize their palm swinging out toward the right net post, instead of trying to relate to their hips. But remember, use your arm more to perfect the stroke pattern, and let your body generate the power. Relying on your arm to supply the power will only lead to a greater number of errors.

One reason most tennis players have trouble swinging inside-out is that they simultaneously try to swing on a horizontal plane. You may think, "I'm so accurate that I can swing horizontally, hit the ball out toward my target, and then follow through across my body." But if you can do that, I'd like to get it on film, because I've never seen it happen before. *You can't fight physical laws.* When you swing horizontally, your hips want to bring you around like a spinning top, and it's virtually impossible to snap them forward and out toward your target. You are swinging from outside-in, across your body, and your racket face can only stay pointed toward the target for an instant. This doesn't allow you much margin for timing errors.

The Real Power Is in Your Lift

People often tell me that they've read, or have been told, to "stay down with the ball" on groundstrokes. This always baffles me, since I've only seen one pro player stay down after contacting the ball, and that's Françoise Durr on the backhand. But I have seen great players get down to the ball and then lift their bodies in synchronization with their forward and upward stroke. They know that getting low is futile unless you also come back up, and that the real power in your swing is generated by *lifting* with your thighs and rear end as you swing into the ball, coupled with a turn of your hips. You should remain *over* the ball as you lift, with your eyes down on the ball — but never stay down, unless you want your grandmother to beat you in straight sets.

When you go out to meet the ball, step out flat on your front foot, then suck your stomach in and lift hard with your thighs and rear end. Remember to keep your eyes down as you lift — don't be so eager to see where your shot is going — and keep your head fixed. It's a mistake to think that lifting your body means that you should also throw your head back. Nor do you ever want to lean back, by throwing your front hip or your shoulder back. *Always keep your body, hitting arm, and racket traveling toward your intended target as you move into the ball.*

A good way to develop your stroke and to get your legs in shape as you rally is to intentionally hit balls on the rise by getting down in a low position. This forces you to use your thighs to lift the ball over the net. You'll find that you can get low and still make the play by tapping the power in your thighs, instead of relying on the strength of your arm and the bevel of your racket.

The Importance of Your Palm

You can have the greatest footwork in the world and beautiful, sensual moves, but if you're holding an Eastern grip and your palm is not vertical at impact and pointing straight toward your target, you're going to die young. For example, if you can make the palm go straight down the line, the ball will follow, providing you have the proper stroke and the right elevation. But if the ball hits the net post, you'll know that your palm was pointing there at impact.

Watch the top players. When they are having trouble, or they feel their swing is out of kilter, they often will take their palm and start swinging it toward an imaginary target, trying to regain the proper sensation. Even at Wimbledon you could see Kramer and Laver shadow-swinging with their palms. So "think palm" and you'll be on the road to a trusted forehand.

Two warnings: (1) It's almost impossible to keep the palm going toward the target unless it is lower than the ball on the backswing. If you are higher than or on the same level as the ball, centrifugal force will drive you around to the left as you contact the ball. But if your palm and the racket are lower than the ball on the backswing, you'll find that the palm stays naturally on line with the target. To visualize hitting out toward the target with your palm perpendicular at impact, think about the bowler's motion. The only way he can release a ball straight down the alley at his target is to have his arm swing from low to high, on a vertical axis, as he delivers the ball. If he uses any other motion, centrifugal force will drive his ball off-target.

(2) To allow for timing errors, try to keep your racket going parallel to the net as long as possible, but don't push or force your palm out to achieve this; if you have to use a fancy wrist movement, then you're changing your wrist and racket face position.

The Crucial Role of a Fixed Wrist

One of the major goals of this book is to convince you how important it is to get your hitting wrist in perfect position, and then leave it fixed throughout your swing. If you can hold the proper grip and form the proper wrist position — and hold them firm — you can mistime the hit yet still effect a shot toward your target. But if you lay the wrist back on the backswing or roll it over as you come into the ball, then you throw everything out in favor of the touch system. Even if, at times, you have the coordination and the talent to play with your wrist and hit a target area under stress, you'll probably be an erratic player forever. You'll be famous one day, a toad the next. For when you lose your "touch," you lose everything. Instead of adjusting and coming close to a good hit, you don't have a clue where your next shot is going. That's why I'll guarantee you: if a person can snap his wrist well — on groundstrokes and volleys — and still be successful, he's on the pro tour.

Hitting with a lot of wrist action not only demands concentration and super timing every day, it leaves you nowhere to turn for advice on technique. A coach can't teach "touch" — he can only ask you how you feel. Wristy players are always coming through my tennis college and saying, "Jeez, I'm trying to work on your strokes but I just don't have the feel today." Well, they probably haven't had the feel since they started playing tennis, because the wrist play requires just too much from the average player. The person who rolls his wrist before impact, for example, reduces the range in which he can hit the ball on the money with a vertical racket face. He must time the inertia from the roll of his wrist and then he must curb that inertia so that the wrist doesn't roll over once it is parallel to the net. This takes perfect timing and control. Conversely, when you can fix the wrist and leave it alone, and swing on a low-to-high plane out toward your target, you have a much longer range in which to hit a good shot.

The Follow-Through

Most players think their stroke is over the instant they feel the ball touch the strings, that they can now go anywhere with their follow-through. Thus they suddenly pull their racket off to the left and look up quickly to see where their shot is going. Remember, however, that even though the ball is on your racket strings for only four to six milliseconds, *try to see how long you can hang on to your follow-through rather than how quickly you can let it go.* It isn't that you can actually feel yourself guiding the ball (that's a myth) but that this kind of concentration keeps you from pulling off the ball before impact is actually made.

Also, *strive to have your follow-through finish at the same point,* whether you are hitting a ball at chest level or down around your knees. Except for extremely high bounces, begin your backswing around eye level, go back, and then drop your racket hand and fixed wrist 12 inches below the ball and hit up. If your wrist is fixed, and your arm comes up as I've suggested and touches your chin on the follow-through, then you'll automatically produce the same follow-through finish on every stroke. If you fail to follow this sequence, you will add different strokes for different heights, and thereby develop a nice inconsistent forehand.

One way to check your follow-through and to find the desired finishing point is to take a proper swing while standing near a fence. When your upper arm or shoulder touches your chin and is fully extended out towards the sky, see where the racket is pointed on the fence. Put a ball or a piece of cloth in that spot on the fence and then practice finishing there for an imaginary high ball and for one that is only six inches off the ground. This will get you into a uniform follow-through position. You will learn what the length of each swing has to be and the sensation which accompanies each swing when the ball is at different levels.

I stressed earlier in this chapter that if you know that your follow-through must reach a particular place, then you have a greater respect for getting the racket down on the backswing. Similarly, if you think you can hit the ball and go anywhere, then you figure you can start anywhere. Going to a specific spot on the follow-through doesn't necessarily guide the ball. It simply helps to keep you from pulling off or pulling up before the ball has left the racket. There is so much energy flow coming into the ball that any last-second adjustments can only lead to trouble.

Remember: *a good follow-through is really the product of a good backswing.* Their success is intertwined. If you can comfortably reach the follow-through position that I seek, then it means you were prepared properly on the backswing, and you had an inside-out forward motion. Although it is true, "As the follow-through goes, so goes the direction of the ball," it's more important to realize: "As the backswing goes, so goes the follow-through" — for most people.

(I mentioned earlier that I prefer a simple follow-through that keeps the wrist firm and the racket arm in line with the intended target. However, if this feels rigid and uncomfortable, simply bend the elbow at the end of the swing.)

The hitter (Richie Ley) freezes his body on the follow-through to check out his stroke quality. If his weight has transferred properly from back to front foot, he can lift his back foot off the ground and still be well balanced. Theoretically, this is how you should finish for nearly every stroke you hit, no matter how low or high the ball bounces. This in turn will help you develop the consistent stroking pattern you need on all groundstrokes.

Self-Evaluation on the Follow-Through

A teaching pro is certainly not the only person who can detect flaws in your swing and suggest remedies that can lead to good tennis. If you know the basic elements of a good stroke, and some of the common errors, you can evaluate yourself while rallying before a match or while practicing. One excellent method is to simply freeze on your follow-through and look for the following tip-offs:

1. Is your weight forward on your front foot?

2. Can you lift the back foot off the ground and maintain your balance on the front foot? If not, you haven't shifted your weight and you are failing to utilize the power in your legs; the chances are excellent that your body hasn't lifted two inches.

3. Is your upper hitting arm under your chin and pointed out toward the target?

4. Are your eyes still fixed on the point of impact?

5. Has your head remained in precisely the same position as when the ball was contacted?

6. Your belly button should be facing your opponent and should not have gone beyond that point.

7. If you have hit with an inside-out motion, your right knee will have come up close to your left. Ideally, the back foot should not have moved forward, but if it has, then no farther than the front foot.

8. Bring your hitting arm back to the point of impact and see if the racket face is still vertical. Or has your wrist rolled — over or under — or shifted dramatically?

Some players will even freeze and take a look at their follow-through while actually playing a match. They know they have a full second with which to take a quick look at their body before they need to prepare for their opponent's shot. Yet when we ask people to try this at the tennis college, they just can't bring themselves to do it. They're so worried about not having enough time to handle their next shot that they don't want to see if they are actually taking a good swing. Their only criterion is whether the ball lands in or out, irrespective of how crummy they might swing. All I can urge you to do is: *don't delay solving your problems.* Don't balk. Eventually you have to check out your swing and see what you are doing wrong if you want to start making improvements. So don't keep waiting until "the next shot."

72

Common Forehand Problems

Following are many of the common forehand problems and the prescribed treatment as already described in this chapter:

Your Shots Keep Going to the Left

The most common cause is that you are pulling across your body, which is usually caused by a horizontal swing and improper movement by the wrist. A second reason, though rare, is that you may be impacting the ball too far in front of your body. Your hips will have completed their turn at impact and you will be out of sync and hitting with less power. Andres Gimeno, in fact, is the only successful player I've ever seen who could contact the ball more than 12 inches out in front of his body.

When you swing on a horizontal level, centrifugal force drives you around and causes your follow-through to cross your body instead of going on a line to your target. To play tennis as dictated by physical laws you must get your body down and your racket below the ball so that you can swing naturally from low to high while maintaining forward movement toward the target. Rather than have your racket start and finish on the same plane, visualize it moving from low to high.

Other reminders:

a. When playing inside the singles sidelines, you have only 19.1 to 19.6 degrees variation on your follow-through from the baseline if you try to shift from your opponent's backhand corner to his forehand corner.

b. Develop an inside-out stroke so that your palm and racket can travel out as far as possible toward the target.

c. Don't let the ball get too close. Stride into the ball with your hips leading slightly, and transfer your weight to the front foot. This keeps you from pulling back or hitting from your heels or the back foot as you swing.

d. Keep your head fixed and eyes down on the point of impact until the ball leaves the racket strings. If your head turns or lifts during the hit, your body will tend to move in the same direction and pull the racket with it.

e. When you reach the front side of your body on the forehand, you have a tendency to break the elbow and pull the ball to the left, unless you develop a low-to-high stroke and maintain a fixed wrist. Check to see that your ini-

The wild and unnecessary follow-through.

Ball too close to body.

Ball too far away from body.

The player who watches his opponent instead of the ball.

The player who refuses to bend his knees and must therefore drop his racket head.

The player who lets the ball get behind him and must hit down on the ball. He can't figure out why the ball hits the net.

The player who never goes out to meet the ball, although the ball often comes back to meet him. His front foot should be planted on the ground before he starts moving forward into his shot.

The player who heard he should get his racket under the ball for underspin.

The wrong-foot-forward syndrome.

tial wrist position is proper and that you're not laying the wrist back or rolling it over before or during impact.

Missing the Ball Completely

When you are swinging in a northerly direction and the ball keeps heading south, you are in deep trouble. One reason is that you very likely are watching your opponent instead of the ball. Even though your eyes cannot track the ball as it approaches impact with your racket, *try* to look at the seams of the ball, or read the writing, or watch the wool come through the back side of the strings — anything to get you to concentrate on making good contact. This also helps keep your head down so that your racket isn't pulled away at the last moment in your eagerness to see where the shot is going. A good drill is the "stop-rally drill" explained on page 64.

Finally, your only goal should be to hit the ball. Most beginners are thinking of two things simultaneously: hit the ball and get it in the court. So just take one goal at a time.

Your Shots Keep Going to the Right

The cause of this problem is that your racket head is late coming through as you swing into the ball, and this difficulty can stem from a number of factors: you're late getting to the ball, you're starting your swing too late, your wrist is laid back, or your backswing is too long.

Learn to get that fast first step the instant you see the ball leave your opponent's racket. Turn your body and racket back simultaneously, instead of using an isolated arm motion — then delay the drop of the racket and racket arm until you're ready to step into the ball. Test yourself to see if your wrist is laying back on the backswing. One way to check this, as well as the length of your backswing, is to stand with your back against a wall or a fence. Take a practice swing and if your racket bangs against the barrier on your backswing or follow-through, you are taking the racket back too far, or swinging too far across on the follow-through.

The Ball Is Landing Too Short

a. One reason may be that you are hitting on a horizontal plane, which causes the ball to begin its drop sooner, unless hit harder. Instead, swing low to high, elevate your shots, and let the higher arc and topspin bring the ball down deep in your opponent's court. Remember the "sit-and-hit" drill (page 60) to remind yourself how low you must get, even on a waist-high shot.

b. You may be "arming" the ball, which means an isolated arm motion and little input by the body. This is caused by hitting from an open stance, which decreases hip rotation potential, and failing to turn your front shoulder as you take the racket back. Instead, try to show the back side of that front shoulder to your opponent, and then step in to the ball.

c. Your wrist may be rolling over. Work to keep the wrist fixed while increasing your body movements (i.e., turning the shoulders) to supply the power.

d. You may have a fixed wrist, but the top edge of your racket is leaning forward or backward. Work against a vertical wall or fence to find the wrist position that produces a vertical racket head at impact.

e. You may simply be hitting too weakly, in which case you need to increase your hip movement, and the lifting motion of your thighs, to gain more power. Remember the inside-out golf swing.

f. You may even be hitting with excess topspin, which is a nice problem to have, especially when your opponent is at the net. All you have to do to hit deeper is to *decrease* the upward angle of your forward swing.

The Ball Consistently Goes Too Long

Either your shots have insufficient topspin — in which case you must increase the angle of your low-to-high forward swing — or the bottom of your racket is leading (which means the racket face is tilted up.) For the latter problem, check your wrist position to see that it produces a vertical racket head at impact. If the racket is turning under, the reasons could be that you are hitting off the back foot, leaning back, lifting your head too early, or your palm may not be pointed downward at the lowest point of your backswing. So work to maintain a steady racket head, and then get your body moving in sync with your swing. Concentrate on stepping into the ball and

The Two-Racket Forehand Drill

The two-racket drill is used to check body and racket synchronization. The hitter holds a second racket at her shoulder, parallel to her hitting racket. Ideally, this second racket held against the body should make nearly the same stroking pattern as the hitting racket if body and hitting racket are "in sync" (the front shoulder and hip turn slightly ahead of the swing). When trying this drill, stop at several points during the swing and see if the two rackets are maintaining their original visual relationship to each other. In the fourth picture, as the ball is struck, the left shoulder has moved slightly ahead of the hitting racket.

(1)

trying to take it more on the rise, instead of hesitating and letting the ball play you.

Overhitting

It just may be that it's more important to your ego to hit the ball as hard as possible than to worry about keeping it in play and winning a lot more often. If that's the case, I can't help you. But if you don't have the competitive temperament to slow down your swing, and you also want to win, then you must learn to increase the angle of your low-to-high lift so that you impart severe topspin. Then you can get rid of all your frustrations and still keep the ball in the county.

Other Forehand Drills

1. You want to keep all movements out in front of your body, on the backswing and the follow-through. To test for this, stand with your back flat against a fence or wall and practice taking a swing. To keep from touching the fence you must have a nicely controlled swing that goes inside-out. You can test yourself on the court as well. Stand with your front side to the net

(2)

(3)

(4)

(5)

This is the backhand loop swing, which forms the same stroking pattern as the forehand loop on page 40. Notice the similarities: the drop of the racket on the backswing, a ball which is contacted at the peak of its bounce, and the high follow-through. Observe, however, that the ball is contacted much farther out in front of the body on the backhand, and that the player's head drops low and then comes up as a result of the lift by the thighs. Notice, too, how the left hand makes its own little loop in sync with the hitting hand.

and draw an imaginary line from that front side to your target area. Now try to keep your swing from taking the racket across that line.

2. Jack Kramer has always insisted that nobody can really develop solid groundstrokes unless he or she turns the non-hitting shoulder inward to start the backswing. I mentioned earlier how he would put his left hand on the handle of his racket in order to pull that shoulder back. Another drill you can use to help develop a kinesthetic "feel" for the proper loop swing is to stand sideways to the net and place the butt of your racket against your front shoulder, then take a swing. Turn the front shoulder, take the racket back at eye level, go down, forward, and then up. Taking your front shoulder through the same stroking pattern, in miniature, as your hitting arm will give you exactly the sensation I'm seeking.

3. Try the same drill using two rackets, one held in perfect hitting position, the other held against the front shoulder. Ideally, both rackets should stay the same distance apart throughout the swing, since your body — on the loop swing — must make the same movement as the hitting arm. If not, they will begin to spread apart and you (or a coach) can discover exactly where your trouble starts. Another benefit of this drill is that your knees are forced to bend properly if you hope to keep your rackets in sync.

4. To help steady your head and keep it from lifting too early during impact, use the "neck brace drill," in which you place your non-racket hand behind your head and then hold your head down as you swing.

Chapter Four

The Backhand

I KNOW I'VE TOLD YOU that the backhand is actually physically easier to hit than the forehand. But we all know that's not the way it is *psychologically*, right? If you're like the average player, you're pretty relaxed on the forehand, but when you see a ball coming to your backhand you cringe, "Dear God, it's a backhand!" and your racket goes up in defense. When rallying before an important match you try desperately to look good by hitting everything off your forehand, while hoping your opponent doesn't discover the fact that your backhand is non-existent. You may even be thinking, "I know I don't have a backhand, but I've got a terrific forehand and a great serve, so I can win anyway." And you probably will, too — as long as your opponent agrees to have a forehand contest. But good players will never give you a chance to hide a severe weakness. Instead of simply attacking your backhand at every opportunity, they will first drive the ball wide to your forehand, which opens up the entire court. If you manage to get the ball back, they will just hit to your backhand and you have no choice but to try to hit it.

So why continue to be defensive — and vulnerable — with a stroke that can be an offensive weapon? When you develop a good forehand *and* a good backhand, you make your strong side even stronger because you don't have to give ground. Instead of overplaying your strength, by running around a weak backhand to hit a forehand, you can stand where you should and thus conserve energy while forcing your opponent to hit better shots.

If your backhand is an obvious handicap, let's break down your swing and start over. And if you feel that you already have a good stroke, many of the checkpoints and drills in this chapter should help sharpen it up — and put it to the test.

What we all want to *strive* for, in my opinion, is a Don Budge backhand. Nearly everybody agrees that Donald, the Grand Slam winner in 1938, had the greatest backhand in the history of the game. He was the only player I've ever seen who could take Gonzales' serve — in its prime — and pound it back off the backhand. Gonzales would serve and attack against everybody;

Backhand Grips

The vertical ruler simulates the palm placement on the Eastern forehand grip, before you shift to the Eastern backhand. The horizontal ruler simulates the palm placement on the Eastern backhand. In other words, I'm advocating a full 90-degree turn.

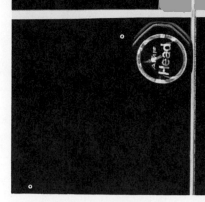

he took the net easily against Laver, and he defeated Rosewall consistently by moving in on his backhand. Yet when Budge and Gonzales played in the early 1950s, and Budge had been out of the game for nearly five years, he still had such a lethal backhand that Gonzales literally could not come to the net when he served to that backhand, for fear of being passed.

Thus I've never been too shy about admitting that Budge has been my model on the backhand ever since I was a senior in high school. Having heard about his backhand, I hitchhiked into Detroit to see him play Bobby Riggs during their barnstorming tour in 1947. I took along a 3-by-5 card that was punched with different-sized holes, and all during the match I just followed Budge through one of those little holes, trying to focus on different aspects of his strokes and his body movements, particularly on the backhand. That's when it really struck home how important it is to swing from low to high with a *lifting* thigh motion, for I realized that Budge played with his knees, thighs, and hips, as well as with his arm. He would get his body and his racket low and then lift out toward his target, brushing the ball with heavy topspin that enabled him to get great depth *and* blistering speed. Years later, Jack Kramer would tell me, "The thing I always remember about Budge's backhand is his butt stretched up on the follow-through, his hitting arm extended high in the air, and the ball going by me at 120 miles per hour."

When I began giving lessons I added a few of my own interpretations to help my students *try* to swing like Budge. For example, I needed a gimmick to help them to keep the racket face going through the ball — out toward the intended target — and to finish high, instead of pulling it across their body in the Humble Harv fashion. Finally I came up with three initials which have always worked pretty well: A.T.A., for "Air the Armpits." You laugh, but today I have students all over the world telling their opponents, "A.T.A., dummy!"

Another concept I emphasize today is that *the knuckles on your hitting hand dictate the success of your backhand*, just as the palm is your guidance control on the forehand. Try to see how long you can keep the knuckles pointed to the net, going out to the target, and skyward, for they are identical in purpose with the face of your racket.

Keeping "A.T.A." and the knuckles in mind should help you understand why a strong, accurate backhand is dependent upon swinging from low to high with a vertical racket head at impact, and why a horizontal swing is going to prevent you from making any real gains in this game.

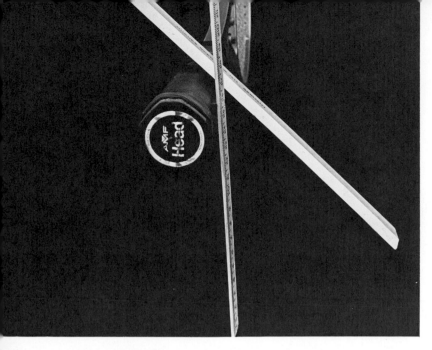

Many teachers and players, however, recommend only a 45-degree turn, which takes you to a Continental.

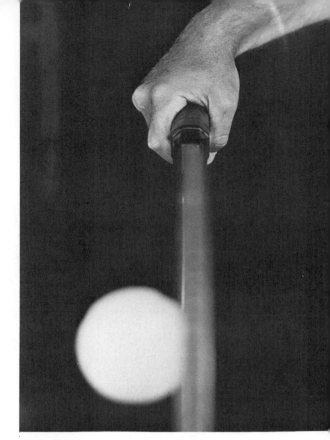

The Eastern backhand grip places the surface of your palm across the top bevel of the racket, and requires less wrist adjustment.

The drawback with the Continental, in my opinion, is that you must place the wrist in an awkward position in order to get the racket face vertical at impact. This is why so many players who hold the Continental elect to hit the backhand with underspin rather than topspin.

The thumb should be placed at a diagonal across the back side of the racket handle. It should never be placed straight across. Nor should it be placed underneath, since this requires greater strength at impact. Think of the thumb as an aid to control the direction of the ball. With this grip, as long as the front of the thumb is facing your target, so is the racket face.

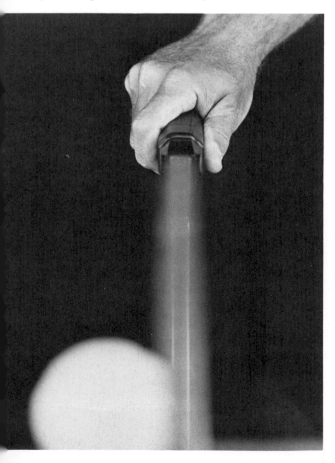

The Grip

If you can perform two separate tasks simultaneously (and most people can with practice) you should switch grips when you turn from the forehand to hit a backhand. I advocate the Eastern backhand, with the palm moved to the top of the racket, the knuckle of the index finger riding the top right ridge, and the thumb placed *behind* the racket handle to provide a brace-like stability when the ball is contacted. Many people hold their thumb under the handle because they feel as though the racket is going to fall out of their hand, but this tends to take more strength to hold the racket steady at impact.

When I get people to hold the Eastern backhand for the first time they think, "This stupid shot is going to hit me in the foot," because the racket head feels like it is pointed down. *But this grip position provides the most stability and requires the least amount of wrist adjustment in order to produce a vertical racket head at impact.* You thus minimize your errors in hitting the ball.

The Continental — halfway between the Eastern forehand and the Eastern backhand — is the most common alternative grip, especially among the pros. Many top players hold a Continental for both grips, not because they think it is better on the backhand but because they feel there is insufficient time to change grips in a game where the ball is coming back at them at 90 or 100 miles per hour. *Don't fall for this myth.* Research at my tennis college has shown that if you can perform two separate tasks simultaneously you can change grips faster than you can take a single step. See for yourself. Practice switching grips for five minutes every day as you step towards an imaginary shot, and in a week or two your hands should beat your feet every time.

The Continental is made for the backhand volley and is fine for the backhand chip or underspin. But for basic topspin drives from the baseline it requires a strong wrist and a roll of that wrist to bring the racket straight up and down at impact. Mastering this wrist play is asking too much of just about everyone. Far better, it seems to me, to take the time now to learn to switch grips, and then build a winning game on something far more dependable than "touch."

The Swing: An Overview

One reason the backhand produces so many unhappy, contorted faces in contrast to the forehand is that people tend to regard it as some weird stroke, unique in itself, when the truth of the matter is that the forehand and the backhand should have identical stroking patterns and the same basic body movements. (The only real difference — and an important one — is that you must step into the ball and swing sooner on the backhand side because your hitting arm is much closer to the net.) Thus, as I describe the backhand, I will remind you of the similarities with the forehand while detailing those aspects of the swing that differ slightly from the forehand.

The instant you see the ball coming to your backhand, turn the shoulder of your hitting arm and your racket back simultaneously so that your arm doesn't make an isolated movement. This places your side to the net and enables your body and racket to move in sync.

Just as on the forehand, I prefer to have you take a short loop swing. Start by bringing your racket back at eye level or slightly higher, and out away from your body. (Holding the throat of the racket with your non-hitting hand will help keep the racket head up on the backswing.) Maintain a rigid hitting arm and a fixed wrist, keeping in mind that your hips and thighs will supply most of the power you need.

When the racket is pointing to the back fence or slightly beyond, step out with your front foot and drop your racket, fixed wrist, and hitting hand approximately 12 inches below the intended point of impact. This will enable you to make a low-to-high forward motion as you shift your weight into the ball. When you lower your body, the throat of your racket should almost brush the back thigh going down to help insure a natural lifting motion. The racket face should also be slightly turned down, facing the court, at the lowest point of your backswing.

Remembering that the loop swing must be continuous from the moment you begin the drop, come out of your low position by lifting up hard with your thighs and stomach muscles. Contact the ball 12 to 18 inches *out in front of your body*, with your hitting arm fully extended and the racket face vertical. Then stretch your body out toward the target and up, while getting the feeling of your hips snapping into the ball and carrying out; don't let them pull you around.

Your eyes should follow the ball as long as possible and remain fixed near the point of contact until your racket arm is pointed toward the target and

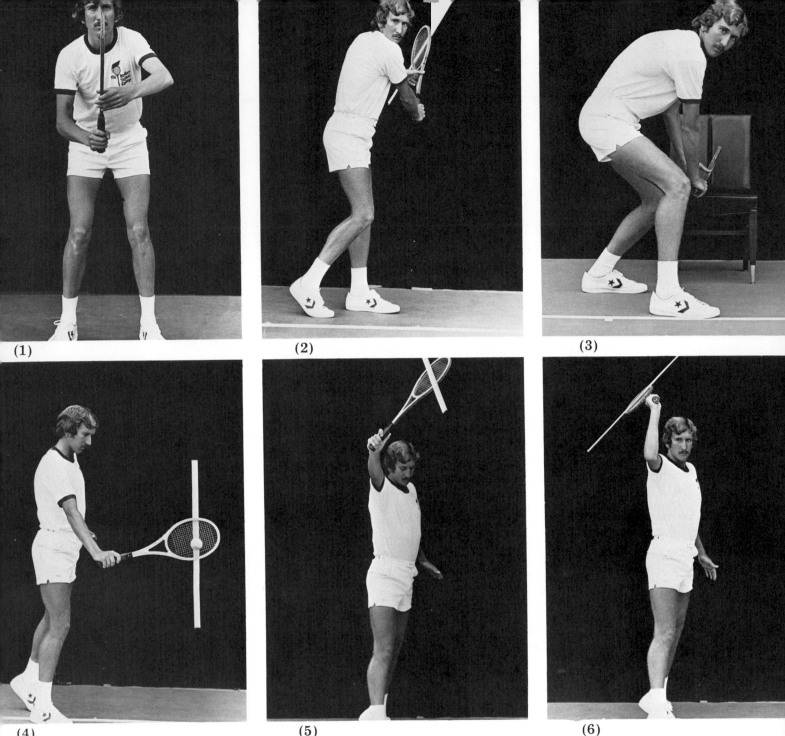

(1)   (2)   (3)

(4)   (5)   (6)

The Loop Backhand

(1) You should assume the same ready position on the backhand as you do on the forehand. Hold a forehand grip to begin with, then switch when you see the ball coming to your backhand. Notice that the hitter carries his left elbow high, which helps insure a short backswing. (2) As you turn back, simultaneously switch to a backhand grip. The backswing is short and a fixed wrist will keep the racket face pointed slightly down. The racket should not lay back behind the hitter's body. This position ends the first part of the backhand loop swing. At this point, the hitter will bend his knees and step into the ball, while dropping his racket and fixed wrist 12 inches below the on-coming ball. (3) At the bottom of the loop swing on a low shot, the racket throat should reach the left knee before beginning its forward and upward movement. Place a chair behind you and try to hit it with your racket as you go down to give yourself an idea of how low you must get even for a waist-high shot. Also notice in this photograph how the right hand is close to the right thigh at the lowest point of the backswing. Nearly everybody makes the mistake of taking the right hand back to the left thigh, which causes the racket to stick up in the air rather than being faced slightly downward. (4) The hitter contacts the ball out in front of his body with a vertical racket head that is slightly above the level of the wrist. He gains power from his leg-lift. (5) The hitter has straightened his knees and extended his body so that he finishes up on the toes of both feet. Rod Laver and Don Budge are two players who often lifted completely off the court. Notice the similarity of the backhand and forehand follow-throughs, and also A.T.A. (Air the Armpits). (6) The hitter has relaxed his elbow for a more comfortable follow-through.

skyward at about a 45-degree angle. You want to get down to the ball, and then stay *over* the ball as you come up — *but don't stay down,* or all the power for your shot will have to come from your arm. Lift up with your thighs and keep the racket going parallel to the net as long as you can. Think of hanging onto the ball — pretend that you're not going to let it off the strings — and this will help keep your racket face pointed toward the target. *Don't let anything pull you off on the horizontal.*

Key Elements of the Swing

The Backswing

Remembering the forehand, react quickly and get your racket back immediately but *don't let your hitting arm take a solo.* Righthanders, cradle the throat of the racket lightly with the left hand as you turn back and this will keep both shoulders rotating as a unit. Leading with the left elbow going back — as long as you don't let the elbow drop — will also help keep the racket face on the ball.

If you turn your body properly, and maintain the appropriate fixed-wrist position, you don't have to make a big play on the backswing in order to hit with power. All you need is a short, efficient backswing with the racket pointing no farther than perpendicular to the back fence. You can bring your racket back farther, in order to conceal your shot or to apply excessive brush topspin, *but only if you have a good turn in your upper body, not because your wrist is laid back.* Thinking you can take a big backswing by simply playing with your wrist is one of the most common mistakes made on the backhand.

In fact, people worry so much about their backhand that they tend to increase the length of their swing instead of shortening it. When you take the hitting hand back too far, this pinches the racket against your body and you have to flick your wrist out to compensate. Your shoulder is a radial point and as you take the hitting arm back, the racket has a tendency to lift up, and even get higher than the approaching ball. Take a racket right now and test this for yourself.

Another persistent error on the backswing concerns the elbow of the hitting arm. When you bend this elbow at any point — instead of maintaining an extended arm — the wrist has a tendency to go loose and your racket face will suddenly point to the sky. This forces you to straighten the elbow and use a lot of wrist action in order to get the racket into a correct position at impact. Most people, unfortunately, can't make this "adjustment," and thus their racket face is tilted back at impact, ready to produce a "sky ball."

Remember, too, how a quick, controlled backswing that allows you to wait for the ball will help prevent the problem of "deceleration-acceleration." Just as on the forehand, when the arm decelerates at the end of your back-swing, the racket continues to accelerate. This produces wrist layback if you are not careful, and particularly if you are rushing to complete your swing. But when you "buy time" and fix the racket on the loop swing before letting it drop, then deceleration-acceleration has already been absorbed.

Fighting to Get Low

Although I don't have the physiological research data to support this state-ment, I've found that the tennis racket does a funny thing to your legs: it locks your joints. How else to explain the fact that people can't bend their knees when they get a racket in their hand? They can sit down and eat lunch, and they can climb into the bathtub, but put them on a tennis court and their legs are like yardsticks. Even the racket seems to be held up by some invisible force. One voice inside keeps saying, "Get your body and racket down, dummy," while the other voice is arguing, "If I get lower than the ball, I'll miss it."

Nevertheless, you have to remember that making successful groundstrokes depends on your ability to *bend your knees and drop the throat of the rack-et to your back thigh* so that the racket head is below the intended point of impact. The lower you get, the easier it is to stay on line with your target, for you now have a natural pendulum movement, like the motion in throw-ing a bowling ball. Think, for instance, about getting low and bowling with the back side of your hitting hand.

Always try to get too low. Imagine that your hitting knuckles are falling and that they are going to touch the court. To realize just how much you must bend down, even for a ball at waist level, try my "sit-and-hit" drill, where you sit in a chair as your racket drops and your foot steps out to meet the ball (see page 60). Several other drills will help you learn what it means to get the throat of your racket down properly without simply loosening the wrist and dropping the racket head, as the average player seems to do.

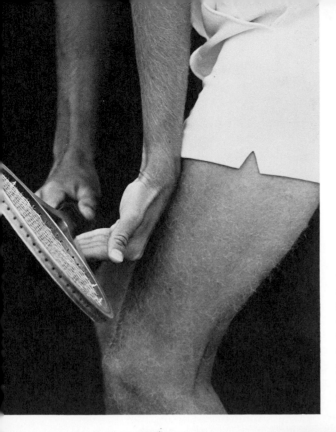

Very few backhand hitters get their racket low enough on the backswing to effect a natural upward and forward swing. This photograph shows a close-up of the hitter's extra effort to actually touch his left thigh with the throat of his racket. Try it yourself. Take your left hand off the racket and place the back of that hand against your thigh and extend the fingers. Then bring your racket back and down, and see if the throat can brush these fingers. That's the cue that your racket is getting low enough.

Here's a front view showing how you want to get that racket down. People always say, "Jeez, who wants to get it down that far?" And my answer is, "Winners."

a. Have a friend hold a stick at waist level or lower; then try to bring your racket under the stick as you make your move into the ball.

b. Righthanders, hold the back of your left hand against your left thigh and stick out your fingers, then try to have the throat of your racket brush these fingers on the way down.

c. Righthanders, learn to make a perfect lefthander's forehand by cradling the throat of the racket with your left hand on the backswing. Then come down and have the left hand — still holding the racket — touch the back thigh. At this point release the left hand and the right arm will complete the swing.

Unfortunately, when people try to touch their back thigh going down, they cheat so much it's scary. They'll drop their racket two inches and ask expectantly, "Am I getting down?" That's why I've always wanted to invent a little sensor device that could be strapped to your thigh, so that when the hand cradling the racket on the backswing came down and touched the sensor, it would cry out, "You're the greatest!" and you would know that you were free to go forward and up. Plus, your ego would get a nice boost.

Timing the Racket's Fall

The idea of "working hard to swing easy" is even more important on the backhand than the forehand, since on the backhand you must contact the ball farther out in front of your body in order to hit with maximum power and accuracy. Therefore, the instant your opponent hits the ball, run to get in position with your racket already back. Even if the ball comes straight at you, get in the habit of turning back as fast as possible. Then it's only a matter of learning how to coordinate the lowering of your racket, your fixed wrist, and your knees.

When you bring the racket back you can delay the drop without any loss of power. But once you let it fall, keep the swing continuous, for the fall is what produces significant kinetic energy gains. If you drop the racket too soon, you'll lose the rhythm and power of the racket and body moving together into the ball; your only option will be to "arm" the ball over the net. If you let the racket fall too late, you'll be forced to swing horizontally just to get a piece of the ball.

Try to learn to time your drop by experimenting against a ball machine, or with a friend who will hit you 30 or 40 balls in a row. Only through repetition and experimentation will you learn to sense where the ball must be before you can start your drop. One little experiment you can try is to hold your left hand behind your back as you swing at the ball. This not only lets you know if your racket falls too early or too late, it also shows you that a nice easy fall by the hitting arm can provide plenty of power.

Contacting the Ball

Remember what I stressed earlier on the forehand, that to play this game with power and accuracy, you must go out to meet the ball. Be aggressive. Don't let the ball play you; don't back up out of hesitation or fear, because you will always be crowded and cramped trying to take your swing — and closeness of the ball to your body will force a bent elbow, especially on the backhand. You can have the racket fairly close to your body and still make a hit. But when the *ball* comes closer than about four feet from your body (for adults), you're in deep trouble, my friend.

If you are always late contacting the ball, the most likely reason is an incorrect belief that you should hit the backhand the same distance from your body as the forehand. But as the photos on page 92 show, the forehand can be contacted even with the front side because the shoulder housing the hitting arm is on the back, whereas the backhand must contact the ball farther out in front, when your hitting elbow is about six inches away from your body, because the hitting shoulder is closer to the net. This enables your hips to pull through on an inside-out axis while gaining the greatest amount of power from your thighs and rear end.

As your body moves into the ball, keep your head fixed and eyes down; *try* to see the ball at impact, even when this is visually impossible. When you feel the racket contact the ball, stay with your stroke — don't suddenly pull off the ball, or stop your follow-through, or jerk your head up to see where the ball is going. *Remember, a fixed head helps insure a consistent hit on the center of your strings.* Some critics of the lifting motion argue that people tend to throw their head up or back when they lift, but you can keep it down and over the ball if you concentrate.

Footwork

Try to envision a baseball hitter striding forward into the ball, or a boxer stepping in to deliver his punch. You want to step out on your front foot as

Here's the same view for a left-handed forehand and a right-handed backhand.

This photograph shows a hitter stroking a backhand and forehand simultaneously. Notice that the ball is contacted 12 to 18 inches farther in front of the hitter's body on the backhand than on the forehand. Remember, the shoulder housing the hitting arm on your backhand is closer to the net. Thus, you must start the forward motion on your backhand sooner because you must meet the ball sooner.

the racket drops, and then transfer your weight forward as you push your body up. If your front foot lands parallel to the net you'll risk twisting an ankle, and if you finish flat-footed you'll lose power. Nor do you want to let the back foot come past the front foot, for your hip will spin you around on the horizontal. Stepping across with your front foot also leads to a horizontal swing and a shot that is pulled off to the side. If you are righthanded, think of stepping toward the left net post with the toes of your front foot.

Generating Your Power with the Lift

You don't need a strong arm to hit a hard backhand. Your arm's job is to hold the racket steady in the proper position. *If you can bend your knees and get your racket low, then the rising motion of your body will supply all the power you need.* In fact, when I worked with the Argentine Tennis Federation in 1967, I learned that you don't even need to hold the doggone racket to play this game. I had a blacksmith build me a belt holster that could hold my racket straight out from my thigh with a vertical racket face. Then I stood at the baseline with my arms folded and had somebody throw a ball to my backhand. I would go down, come up, and hit the ball over the net every time, just by using the power in my legs.

This was the key to Budge's backhand. He played with his thighs, hips, and stomach while his hitting arm was synced with his body lift along the desired stroke pattern. After watching him play in Detroit years ago, I spent the next three or four weeks trying to emulate his stroke. I would go out on the court, stand in front of a fence, toss the ball up, and let it bounce. Then, keeping my racket arm stiff while bending my knees, I would just lift with my thighs and rear end and hit the ball into the fence. Gradually I would move back and strive for a little more rhythm, always using my body and doing little with my racket arm. In less than a month I had my basic backhand.

You can learn to time your lift in much the same way. Hit against a fence, use a ball machine, or have a friend stand off to the side about 15 feet away and bounce the ball to your backhand. At first, just try to relax and get the feeling of the proper stroke in slow motion. Use your body to supply the power and see how slowly you can go and still lift the ball over the net. You'll find that you can swing very slowly and still hit the ball pretty darn hard — *if* you learn to utilize the power in the lower half of your body.

Let your swing flow and just get the rhythm. Don't worry about where the ball goes, or even that you keep missing it. Try to exaggerate. Come right off the ground when you lift — but don't lunge — so that you understand what it really means to lift. On your forward motion, turn your rear end into the ball, then lift out towards the net and up. Stretch those stomach muscles and come up on your toes as you hit through the ball; make the calves and thighs really work for you — *feel* them pull you up.

I can't emphasize enough how important it is to let your body come up as you hit. Yet people going through the tennis college are always trying to fake us out. They shout "Lift! LIFT!" thinking they've really stretched out, when all they've actually done is step out and land flat-footed. Good coaches, however, won't be fooled by grunts and groans. They simply watch your rear end to see whether or not you lift. So don't get lazy down there. Get way down and then go way up. I once saw a film of Budge where he took a ball

The hitter demonstrates the inside-out movement on the backhand side. This time he uses tape pointing to the left net post, and he attempts to make the knuckles of his hitting hand continue on the tape line until he meets the ball.

just inches off the ground, yet still finished up on his toes on the follow-through.

The more you insist on staying down, the stronger your arm must be. Françoise Durr is virtually the only top player I've ever seen who stays down on the ball on the backhand, and she had an unorthodox grip to begin with. Plus, she's one of the strongest players off-balance I've ever seen. But nearly all the top players realize that you bail yourself out of a hole with your rear end, not your arm. They know that by learning to use the power in your thighs you can take a low-bouncing ball and still hit it over the net with power.

A final point to remember about timing your lift is that you must have your body and racket moving forward and up *together*. If they move in sync — and the racket head is vertical at impact — you can take a ball right against your body and still bang it over the net. Don't try to make last-minute adjustments in your swing; just pull the elbow back a little bit, shorten the radius of your swing, and thrust yourself up. But if your racket is up and the body is down, or vice versa, then you don't have a prayer.

The Inside-Out Concept

Getting low with your body and racket and lifting up with your thighs will be useless if you don't learn to hit through the ball with an inside-out motion that keeps the racket on line with your target. This is no less important on the backhand than it is on the forehand (see page 66).

To visualize what the inside-out motion means on the backhand, stand with your back against a fence or wall and practice swinging out away from your body. This forces you to swing inside-out in order not to touch the fence on your follow-through.

Also try to get the feeling of turning your back hip into the ball, and then carrying that hip out toward your target and up. With your body coiled at the end of your backswing, think about turning the hip "in and then out" — not in and around on a horizontal plane. Focus on your lower body and make your hips and knees do all the work. When the pros get caught on their back foot, for example, they snap their hips through and still hit with power. But this requires getting low and then pushing the hips forward while carrying them out toward the target. If you swing on a level plane, inertia is going to drive your hips around horizontally and it will be difficult if not impossible to keep the racket from following.

94

On the backhand, the desired racket-face position is vertical at impact, and the hitting arm is well in front of the body. The hitter should go out to meet the ball. Conversely, notice what happens to your racket face when you lean back (second photo.) The hitter has not changed his good, firm, initial wrist position, yet his leaning body has produced a 20-degree movement in the racket face at impact.

Another problem occurs if you pull your rear shoulder back, or lean back, as you are making your lift. This pulls the racket off-target. Instead, the rear shoulder must go out towards your target in sync with your hips and the knuckles of your hitting hand. Turning this shoulder inside-out enables you to lengthen follow-through.

The Crucial Fixed Wrist

Just as with the forehand, if you ever want your backhand to be a pal under pressure, don't horse around with your wrist. Leave it fixed and your arm extended throughout the swing, while your body supplies all the rhythm and power you need. Remember, *you don't want to make any adjustments with the wrist in order to produce a vertical racket head at impact — unless you think that you can win by relying on "touch."* But as I warned you wrist players earlier, most of you will never know from day to day what kind of player you are because the fluctuations in your game will be too great. You have to meet the ball so far out in front of your body on the backhand that if you have a loose wrist, you'll never be able to control the ball consistently.

If you buy my rationale for a fixed-wrist position, you first must know when you have the appropriate wrist position at the beginning of your swing. Using the same drill as on the forehand, stand with your right side against a fence. Place the racket flush against the fence, about waist high, with the racket head slightly higher than the level of your wrist. Then move away from the fence until your elbow is a finger's length from your body, and your arm is extended. Now leave the wrist alone because you're perfectly placed for a backhand. Get the sensation of how the wrist feels in this position because that's where you want to leave it on the backswing and through impact for the rest of your life.

When you take the racket back from this beginning position, the racket face should be pointed *down* at the end of your backswing and you will probably think, "This crummy shot is going *under* the net." But if you keep the wrist locked as you complete your swing, you'll see that the racket becomes absolutely vertical at impact.

Thus you want to concentrate on keeping the racket head slightly hooded (facing down) as you take it back, with your hitting knuckles pointed to the court as you reach the bottom of your backswing. The natural tendency is for these knuckles to be facing up on the backswing because the el-

The same fence drill used to determine the correct wrist position on the forehand can be used on the backhand (as shown here for a left-hander). Remember, the backhand must be contacted farther in front of your body, so stand away from the fence, making certain that the elbow of your hitting arm is at least a finger-span in front of your body.

The hitter shown here (a righthander) has learned to carry the elbow of his left arm high to avoid a wrist layback.

bow bends, which is why most players end up adjusting their swing to hit with underspin. But your goal is to hit with topspin, which means you must *push those knuckles down* as you draw the racket back. Have the left hand help out by pushing down on the throat of the racket. You can lift with confidence and hit the ball as hard as you want with topspin *if* you know your racket is going to be straight up and down at impact, and your forward and upward swing is nearly vertical, as Bjorn Borg's is. Playing with a fixed wrist and an extended hitting arm will give you this assurance. If the ball starts going past the baseline, just push the knuckles down more and lift on a more vertical angle.

Even though what feels wrong on the backswing is actually right, most people go for comfort. Their wrist is often perfect or just slightly off when they start their backswing. But then their wrist has a natural tendency to lay back when the elbow breaks, which causes the racket to turn under. These people must now snap their wrist forward in order to produce a vertical racket face at impact — a "touch" play that helps distinguish them from the champions. This inability to judge the amount of wrist roll is one reason why they also produce such an interesting variety of backhands — into the net, over the back fence, or bloopers to their opponent.

As you concentrate on maintaining a fixed-wrist position, don't forget to *let your body turn the racket back.* Most people are lazy with their bodies and thus they bring their racket back by simply bending the hitting elbow or laying the wrist back, which leads to a "slapping" motion as the elbow leads the way into ball contact. This is one of the most common problems on the backhand and can be corrected by maintaining an extended hitting arm while pivoting with the body.

Unfortunately, most losers will change their stroke to accommodate an improper racket head, rather than changing their body movements to accommodate a properly placed racket head. These players think they can stand stiff-kneed and swing with a low-to-high motion by simply loosening their wrist to drop the racket head, and then beveling the racket face — instead of getting their body low and lifting up with a vertical racket face that is slightly higher than the level of their wrist. As a result, they must scoop the ball over the net rather than lifting it up and over with the power and accuracy of topspin.

Another example is the player who tries to lift with his body from low to high, but his shots keep going out because he has an improper wrist position. Yet instead of finding the correct wrist position to accommodate his proper stroke pattern, he immediately changes the nature of his backswing and swings from high to low to accommodate his incorrect wrist bend.

I want you to swing at a normal speed — with a low-to-high motion — and if your wrist position is proper the ball should land inside your opponent's court or very near the outside boundaries. You should be able to see the topspin arc effect take place and this should give you the confidence to make a slight wrist adjustment or grip change to give you the consistency you want. But if you don't have this confidence, and a willingness to experiment in making corrections, then you'll simply leave the racket alone — in its incorrect position — and try to change your swing. When you start to "choke," for instance, you will start leveling off your swing instead of lifting up from low to high.

So get the racket set perfectly, keep your arm and wrist fixed, and work on achieving the proper body movements. Your body can be absolutely perfect but if the racket is slightly off at impact, you take gas. If your racket is perfect, on the other hand, you can do a lot of crazy things with your body and still make the hit.

The Follow-Through

If you can remember "A.T.A." (Air the Armpits) and "knuckles" as you swing, this should help give you a greater respect and the proper imagery for developing the correct follow-through.

"Air The Armpits" reminds you to extend your hitting arm upwards after you contact the ball until it's pointed toward the sky, not a side court. Don't hold the arm back — let inertia carry it up. Keep telling yourself, "The stroke is never over," and when you think you've gone far enough, go a little farther. You have all this energy input going forward and up, so don't suddenly let it end. Think about forming a little archway with your arm and the racket and literally walking underneath.

Moreover, "as your knuckles go, so goes your racket head." Thus you want to try and carry your knuckles out toward the target and upward. Don't jab or cut across or swat at the ball, and don't fall back. Hit through the ball and go all the way up. If you can do this, and the racket head is vertical at impact, then you're going to come pretty close to an accurate placement.

Put me to the test on an empty court. Stand near the baseline, gently throw the ball up in the air, and let it bounce. Take your backswing and then keep your knuckles on an absolute straight line to the target and see how close the ball comes. Even after making contact, keep your knuckles going toward the sky. There are two basic variables on every shot: width and length; and if you can make your knuckles go inside-out and face your target all the way from impact on, you will control 50 percent of your backhand. All you have to worry about then is length. Yet most people yank their knuckles off target by pulling across their bodies, and with only 19.1 degrees margin, they "die young."

A third little guidance checkpoint can be the thumb of your hitting hand, if you hold the Eastern grip with the thumb placed behind the racket handle. Try to visualize the thumb following out towards the target, the same as with the knuckles. You may even want to make a dot on your thumb and then try not to let that dot come off the target line as you play.

A Follow-Through Checklist

Spend time testing your own backhand: when rallying or during a match, freeze on the follow-through and take a look at your body, not where the ball ends up. Here are some points to look for:

a. Can you lift your back foot off the ground without falling? If not, you haven't transferred your weight forward to the front foot.

b. If your front foot is perfectly flat or your knees aren't straightened out, you didn't lift up with your thighs and rear end.

c. You should be able to drop a plumb line from your front shoulder to your front foot.

d. Righthanders, your racket should be pointed slightly to the left of your target if you have swung properly with an inside-out motion.

e. Did you A.T.A.? On the forehand, a checkpoint is your arm coming up under your chin. But your arm is going away from your body on the backhand, so to see if you've really stretched your arm up properly, it should be pointed to about 1 or 2 o'clock. Some top players, in fact, will be literally vertical, with their arm pointed skyward.

f. Your upper body should finish slightly facing the net, as your eyes remain fixed on the point of impact.

g. Moving only your shoulder joint, let your hitting arm fall back to where you think you contacted the ball, then see if the racket face is vertical. If not, you haven't maintained a fixed-wrist position, or you must correct your grip.

Some people will run a mile to avoid hitting a backhand.

h. If you consistently pull across your body on the follow-through, the problem can usually be traced to either a high backswing or getting too close to the ball. By remaining too high on the backswing, you allow centrifugal force to drive you around on the horizontal, which makes it impossible to swing out towards your target. Letting the ball get too close generally forces the hitting elbow to bend, with the racket following the elbow around. When you swing on the horizontal or let the ball get too close, you must throw your front hip back in order to make contact, which results in a pulled shot.

i. If your racket head is vertical at impact, and you are hitting with topspin, but the ball keeps going in the net, then you must get your racket lower on the backswing in order to produce more of a lifting motion. If the ball is going *too long*, you need to increase the angle of your low-to-high motion so that greater topspin will bring the ball down quicker. The crucial point is: *don't change your racket head to make these corrections — only the angle at which you swing.*

Backhand Tactics

If your backhand is an embarrassment to you, even among loved ones, your first goal must be to focus on the problem and not try to hide it by always running around to play forehands. *The longer you attempt to cover up a lousy backhand, the more you ingrain your fear of the shot — and fear inhibits learning.*

You're probably thinking, "Yeh, but I see the pros run around backhands to hit a forehand all the time." This is true, except they do it for entirely different reasons.

First of all, when your opponent is rushing the net, you want to hit the ball with topspin so it will go over the net and down at his feet. This forces him to bend low and lift the ball, which produces a defensive shot and thus an easier volley to handle. If you can topspin your backhand when an opponent is attacking the net, great. But most backhands tend to produce high balls because most people tend to hit them flat or with underspin. Forehands, however, have a more natural tendency to brush the ball and it's easier to keep the racket face on a vertical plane, which facilitates topspin. Thus, when top players have a choice they usually opt for their forehand.

Second, you can be late on a forehand and still hit with topspin. If you are late on the backhand — where the ball must be contacted farther out in front of your body — you can only underspin. That's why, on service returns especially, you will see the top players try desperately to run around backhands because they can be late and still whip off a topspin forehand that makes the ball dip down at the feet of the onrushing server.

Topspin vs. Underspin

Contrary to what some instructors preach, hitting the backhand with underspin (or "slice," as it is incorrectly labeled) is not only a tough play but a defensive weapon at best. Whereas topspin enables you to play aggressively on any surface, underspin is a delicate "touch" shot that only talented players can hit well with any consistency, and only then through experience, practice, and concentration.

If you concentrate on learning to hit with topspin, you can slug the ball almost as hard as you want and still be safe; when you start hitting long you simply increase the vertical angle of your swing to produce greater topspin. But the minute you begin to favor underspin, by bringing your racket from high to low, you not only must deal with the five variables I discussed earlier (page 36), but also you lose some tactical advantages.

Still, people talk about underspin being a reliable shot. Even Kramer used to get on me a little bit. He would say, "Work on that chip backhand, kid,

The length of the dotted line is 65'9'' — a tough shot even for great players to make on their backhand (or their forehand). That's why the attacking player has positioned himself over the X. He is now midway between the best shots his opponent can hit, whether down the line or cross-court. In intermediate tennis, this range is usually less than shown here because most players are unable to hit excessive topspin on either the backhand or the forehand.

because it's pretty safe to hit." But it's only easy if you have the touch. When people try to hit that shot hard under pressure, it often goes into the net or over the fence.

Another virtue of topspin is that you can hit short or long — on any court surface — and hit it hard. Underspin doesn't give you this flexibility. Very few people can drive underspin on the backhand, nor can they hit short-angled shots with enough speed to get them past a person at the net. Remember, balls hit hard with underspin have a tendency to travel 70 feet or more, and the distance from the baseline singles corner to your opponent's service-line corner on the diagonal is only 65'9'' (see page 30). To "own" that shot you must be able to hit the ball with topspin and bring it down inside of 66 feet. Hard-hit underspin will simply not come down in time. You can try, but the ball will either sail out or come so close to your opponent that he has an easy put-away volley at the net. Everyone uses Kenny Rosewall as an example of someone with a very successful underspin backhand passing shot. But he's the only player I've ever seen who can hit a hard cross-court diagonal with underspin. Even then he has to practically hit the sideline every time.

Now, these figures may seem unimportant to you if your opponent simply plays from the baseline and never tries to rush the net. In fact, underspin enables you to hit the ball deep without swinging hard, and by slowing the ball up it provides you with more time to regain position while possibly upsetting your opponent's rhythm. However, if you try to improve and you begin stepping up in competition, you are going to play people who rush the net on every short ball and who try to hit an approach shot or volley to your backhand. In that case you have only three sound options: (1) lob over their heads, (2) pass them down the line, or (3) hit a cross-court diagonal. If you can only hit a backhand on the horizontal or with underspin, the last option is virtually impossible. Thus you give away one-third of your opportunities.

I remember watching Stan Smith lose to Pancho Gonzales in Las Vegas about 1970. Stan's biggest problem that day was that he was chipping his backhand — hitting with underspin — and the wind was blowing his cross-court shots out. I thought, "Why doesn't someone teach Stan to topspin off the backhand? Then he could control the shot much easier and he could pass people like Gonzales instead of having to play the ball defensively."

Well, about three days later I was at the Los Angeles Tennis Club and Stan was out on the court like a beginner, throwing the ball up and working on a topspin backhand. He would let the ball bounce, take his racket back at eye level, then drop down with his thighs and lift up as he hit the ball. Once he had that shot under control, he had the final weapon he needed in order to become the world's No. 1 ranked player by 1973. In fact, after Stan won the World Championship Tennis title in 1973, Arthur Ashe pointed out that he now hated to play him because Stan had learned to topspin his backhand cross-court, which made him lethal all over the court.

Developing a Passing Shot

Another technique that will make you famous on the backhand is your ability to hit the ball on a straight line when you want to. If you can drive the ball down the line as your opponent rushes the net or when he (or she) has already gained control, you can take away his tactical advantage. You either win the point outright, or you pull him so wide that unless he volleys strongly you have a wide-open court for your next shot. Moreover, when your opponent knows that you can pass down the line, he must play you honestly: he can't "cheat" to the middle of the court to cut off the cross-court backhand that is virtually automatic if you can only swing on a horizontal plane.

Developing the vertical, low-to-high swing that enables you to pass down the line has been the main goal of this chapter. You have only a 24-inch margin of safety in order to hit a good passing shot between your opponent and the singles sideline, and you'll rarely ram it down this narrow alley by swinging horizontally. You may *think* you're talented enough to pull off this shot by just making a little "adjustment" in your swing, but first put yourself to the test.

This is my favorite drill to help you develop the proper inside-out swing, and to have you appreciate how difficult it is to hit backhand passing shots unless you swing from low to high with an inside-out motion. Mark off a 24-inch "alley" down the singles sideline (with tennis ball cans, for example) and try to place every shot inside the lane. Be happy if you can manage to beat yourself in a little game where you bounce the ball and hit it down the line, giving yourself a point when your shot lands in the "alley" and a point against yourself when it doesn't. Drills like this will help you realize the importance of owning an inside-out motion where your hips, shoulders, knuckles, and hitting arm all follow through toward the target.

Hitting with Underspin

If after all my arguing you still want to pursue an offensive underspin backhand, let me clear up three common myths. First, nobody has a "slice" backhand. Second, you don't hit "under the ball." And third, the wrist is in a *fixed* position at impact if you take the proper stroke.

Photographs give the impression that underspin is achieved by slicing under the ball. I have even heard pros claim that they lay their racket back as much as 45 degrees for a severe "chip" backhand. Yet high-speed photography reveals that top players such as Bob Lutz contact the *lower back side* of the ball, barely below the halfway mark, with a racket face that is *nearly vertical at impact*. Our research shows that the racket can be beveled back no more than 10 degrees at impact if you expect to hit the ball reasonably hard and keep it in play, even from baseline to baseline. The only time you actually want to try to hit "under" the ball is on trick shots, where you want to impart such severe underspin that the ball will bounce backwards when it hits your opponent's court. But first win the Nationals, then you can worry about this shot.

Another problem in visualizing and executing the proper underspin stroke is that pros such as Rosewall unintentionally mislead people by laying the racket head flat on the backswing. You see this all the time in pictures of players preparing to hit with underspin. What still photographs don't show, however, is that when Rosewall comes around and makes his hit, the wrist is locked in tight, his hitting arm is stiff, and the racket face is nearly straight up and down *just before impact and through contact*. He doesn't let his wrist go loose, nor does he allow the racket head to move freely through the air. To achieve this he must use a lot of early wrist action, which is just too difficult for the average player.

A final point to remember when hitting with underspin is that although you strike down on the ball with a high-to-low stroke, you must take the racket right back up after impact if you hope to get the ball over the net. Generally, you want a stroke pattern that resembles the high-low-high curve of an archer's bow.

The Two-Handed Backhand

The two-handed backhand has gained considerable status in recent years, thanks to Jimmy Connors, Chris Evert, Bjorn Borg, and other expert practitioners. Indeed, this stroke may give you the aggressive, reliable backhand you dream about — providing you understand your own physical capabilities.

First of all, everybody tends to forget about the two-handers who can't beat Mickey Mouse; these players hit unnaturally and they fail to get any racket speed or control going through the ball. On the pro tour, you see only the successes, not the youngsters who couldn't make it because of a weak two-handed backhand.

Secondly, you need to have more than a little natural ability and coordination not only to play well with two hands, but to convert from one hand in the first place. The most important requirement is *a supple upper body*. Most people in this game are arm swingers rather than upper-body swingers, and the habits they have ingrained make it difficult to adjust to a good two-handed movement.

Familiar with these factors, if you still want to try to hit with two hands, give it a try. Most players can't control the ball with one hand, so if you can learn control with two hands, I say great. When starting out, try to realize that what we're actually talking about is a two-handed *lefthanded* forehand on the backhand side (for you righthanders). The left hand and the left side are dominant as you strike the ball. Thus you should practice the drill where you learn to hit a lefthanded forehand (page 106), for this is exactly what you need to achieve with a two-handed backhand.

You should hold an Eastern forehand grip with the left hand, but you have

Try the two-racket drill on the backhand to see how well you are synchronizing the movements of your body and your racket.

two options with your regular hitting hand. If you're fairly talented and comfortable on both sides, and you're pretty sure you'll stick with the two-handed stroke, continue to hold a regular Eastern forehand grip. Then you don't have to switch grips between strokes. But if you don't feel natural hitting from the left side, and you're undecided about two hands, you should hold an Eastern backhand, because the chances are good that you will eventually revert to a one-handed backhand, and you will thus already have the proper grip.

One argument against using two hands is that it reduces the reach you have. It is true that you reduce your reach by half the width of your body. But reach isn't the problem for most people. If you have reasonable reactions, and you can move your feet, you can retrieve most of your opponent's shots anyway. But once you get to the ball the problem remains, with one hand or two, how to hit it over the net properly. This reduced reach is more than compensated for by the fact that you actually have two forehands. This gives you a better opportunity to topspin off both sides, since you have a split second longer to contact the ball on the backhand side.

Other Backhand Drills

1. You need to keep your body and racket arm synchronized for better rhythm, power, and a shorter swing. To see if you're doing this, and to prac-

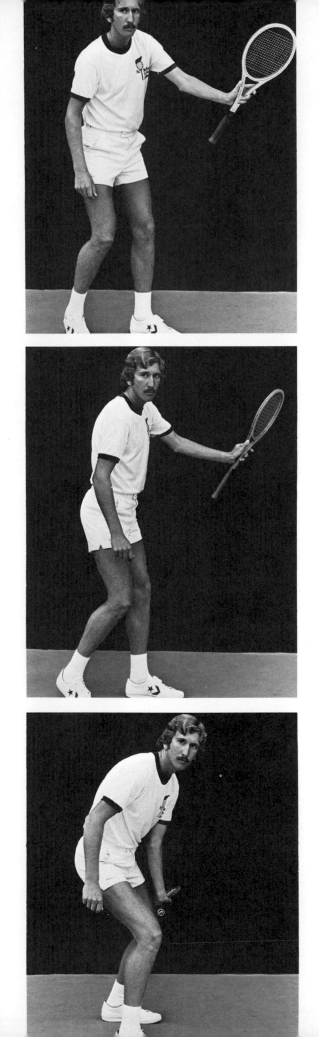

The "Lefthanded" Forehand Drill

The hand that cradles the racket throat can make you famous on the backhand. So practice the precise stroking pattern you seek on the backhand using only your left hand. Work hard to get that feeling of having your left hand touch your left thigh when you make your drop on the loop swing. Once this drill feels comfortable, place your right hand on the racket but allow your left hand to dominate until it touches the thigh. Then have your right hand take over for the upward and forward motion.

A racket cover has enough weight and wind resistance to help you build the muscles you need for high backhands. At home or while waiting for a court, keep the cover on your racket and practice taking the backhand shots you normally use in a match. Start adding one ball at a time inside the racket cover as your strength improves. *Go slowly.* Add only as much weight as it takes to place a moderate strain on your muscular system.

tice the proper movements on the loop swing, try the racket-against-the-body drill discussed on pages 78–79. Place the butt end of your racket on the shoulder of your hitting arm and then go through the swing: turn back, drop down, go forward and up. Try the same thing with the racket on your front hip. Then use two rackets at once, one held in perfect hitting position and the other held against the front shoulder. As you take your swing, the two rackets will remain nearly the same distance apart and will make identical stroke patterns — if your body and hitting arm are properly synchronized.

2. The left hand is basically submissive for most players. They tend to forget it's even there or what to do with it. But you can give it a split personality by telling yourself, "I'm going to learn a forehand with my left hand." First, have your left hand practice a forehand stroke by itself: take it back, down, forward, and up, remembering the rule on the forehand that "as the palm goes, so goes the racket." Then cradle the throat of the racket with your left hand as you begin your backswing and practice making that same motion. Let go with the left hand when it reaches the back thigh at the lowest point of your backswing. Making a perfect forehand stroke pattern with your left hand will help your right hand make a perfect backhand. This also forces you to pivot properly with your upper body.

3. If you can learn to swing with your body, you can have a weak arm and still hold your own on the backhand. But to hit the ball consistently on the center of your strings, and to hit out with power, you need strong extensor muscles. These muscles lie along the top of your forearm and are crucial in maintaining a fixed wrist and a firm, extended racket arm throughout the swing.

Fortunately, you can develop these muscles without investing in a set of barbells. Just put a cover on your racket and practice taking your backhand swing. The wind resistance against the racket cover will give you good tension on the extensor muscles, and meanwhile you are practicing your stroke. Combine this with the "sit-and-hit" chair drill (see page 60) and you will strengthen all the muscles you need on the backhand. As your arm gets stronger, place one ball inside the racket cover, then two, then three, until you get up to six. Pretty soon you'll be able to hold that racket fixed the way it should be, without any flopping about by the wrist.

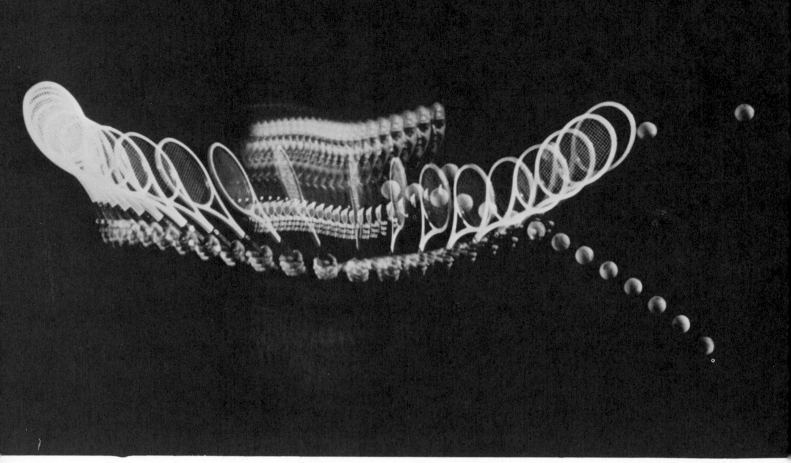

PHOTO BY JOHN G. ZIMMERMAN

The approach shot is the third most important stroke in good tennis, behind the serve and service return. A deep and well-placed approach shot normally renders an opponent helpless. The ideal stroking pattern resembles an archer's bow, with the hitter swinging high to low to high with a slightly beveled racket to impart underspin. The racket does not continue down after impact but is carried back up high on the follow-through, so that the ball is hit deep and not into the net. Notice the path of the hitting hand — it's another visual reminder on this stroke.

Chapter Five

Approach Shots, Volleys, Overheads, and Lobs

I F YOU WANT TO HIT GROUNDSTROKES from the baseline all day, that's fine. You'll get a tan, and you may even be fantastic — as long as your opponent agrees to play the same type of game. But you don't always have this choice in tournament play. You can't say, "Sorry, I don't play against anyone who attacks the net." Therefore, if you're serious about challenging good players, you must learn how to work your way up to the net and how to close off the point once you get there. You must learn how to anticipate the short ball, how to rush in and hit an approach shot, how to volley, how to lob, and how to hit an overhead.

Developing these strokes and an aggressive mental approach will enable you to thrive between the baseline and the net, instead of treating that area as a no-man's-land. Plus, you'll realize how much more fun and challenging tennis can be when you venture out from the security of your baseline.

The Approach Shot

An approach shot is any shot utilized to gain or approach the net, either after the ball has bounced (an approach groundstroke) or while it's still in the air (an approach volley). Normally you will hit this shot near the service line, which is sort of your halfway house between the baseline and the net. Most approach shots are set up by an opponent's weak groundstrokes, but in beginning and intermediate tennis, many first serves and nearly all second serves present perfect approach-shot opportunities.

For some reason, the approach shot is commonly overlooked or downplayed, but I feel it's the third biggest shot in tennis. First comes the serve, which puts the ball in play, and then the service return, which determines where the point goes from there. But then comes the approach shot, the

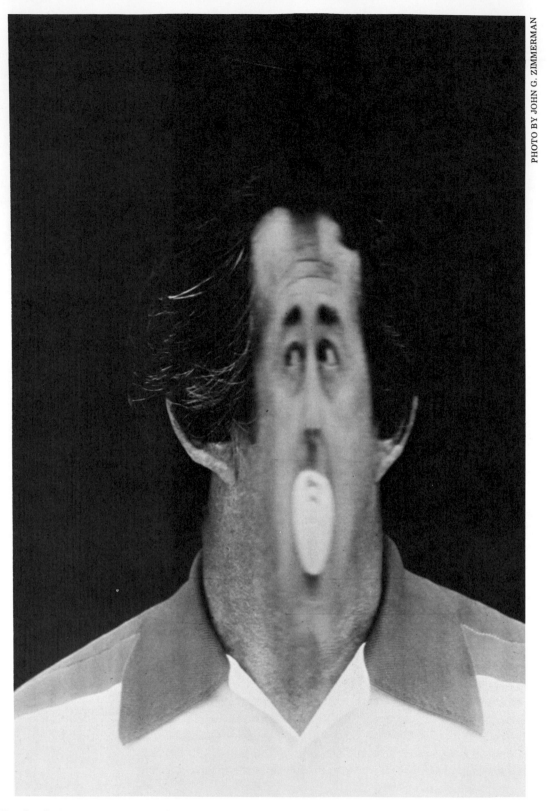

Vic Braden's famous "fuzz sandwich." This is why you need to learn how to volley at the net.

"bread-and-butter" play in tournament tennis and a psychological influence on nearly every point.

In good tennis, the reason you want to work so hard on forehands and backhands — and keeping the ball deep — is that you never want to be the first person to hit a short ball. A short ball enables your opponent to come in, hit an approach shot, and take the net, while you are left with three difficult options: lob over his head, hit passing shots down the line or cross-court, or try to give him a new navel. Whatever you choose to do, the pressure is now on you to execute. In fact, whoever owns the net will control the point nearly every time in pro tennis. Only a handful of players in history have been able to push their opponents around from the baseline, where you can only run a person three steps either way, but up near the net you can angle the ball sharply away from the fastest opponent around.

Unfortunately, many players don't realize the strategic benefits of gaining the net. If they do, and they want to be aggressive, they generally don't have the weapons to get them to the net — meaning strong legs and an approach shot. And if they somehow reach the net, they usually lack the weapon they need to win the point or defend themselves — a volley. Thus I find that most people tend to react defensively rather than offensively when the ball is hit; the closer they get to the net, the greater their anxiety levels. The ball is coming faster and they have less time to react. As a result, if they run in to hit a short ball, they then either try to retreat to their baseline stronghold or they plunge ahead, saying, "Here goes nothing," which is generally true since they don't know how to volley.

Instead of getting caught in this mental trap, *make yourself realize that when you get the first short ball you have been given a gigantic opportunity,* and that the closer you get to the net, the happier you should be. Most points are so short that you can't afford to let your opponent get off the hook by hitting short balls while you camp out at the baseline. Unless you're convinced that you can outlast your opponent from the baseline, you have to learn to attack the net at every opportunity. If he hits patty-cake second serves, never stay back — intimidate him by always moving in, hitting your approach shot, and then taking the net.

Finding Your "Short Ball Range"

Before you can start charging the net, you must learn your "short ball range" — that area on the court where you can hit an approach shot to your

(1)

(2)

(1)

(2)

(3)   (4)

The Forehand Approach Shot

(1) The hitter begins his approach to the short ball hit by his opponent. Notice the short backswing and stiff wrist, which keeps the racket face always on line with the ball. (2) A *slight* downward hit, using the shoulders and a beveled racket, has been effected on the back side of the ball to produce backspin. At impact, the racket face is tilted back from five to ten degrees, and the ball is contacted at chest height. Notice the hitter's eyes focused on the point of contact. (3) Having already produced a backspin on the ball, the racket is brought back up almost immediately to effect the "bow." (4) The hitter never stops his forward motion toward the net. He continues right on through the ball so that his body energy can supply most of the power on the shot and he can move forward into a much more intimidating volleying position. Though many teachers promulgate the "stop and hit" approach shot, you'll notice that most pros hit on the run.

(3)   (4)

The Backhand Approach Shot

(1) The short backswing helps keep the face of the racket pointing toward the ball as the hitter begins his backhand approach shot. (2) The hitter has dropped his front shoulder and has hit slightly down on the ball to produce backspin. (3) He raises his racket on the second half of the approach-shot swing to complete the bow-shaped stroking pattern. (4) The high follow-through is typical of all good backhands. Also notice the footwork here and on the forehand. The back foot should always come in front of the front foot if at all possible.

113

opponent and reach a position halfway between the service line and the net as, or before, the ball is on your opponent's racket. You can find this radius by having a friend yell "now" as he contacts your practice approach shot, at which point you should be in the desired position just described.

Once you know your short ball range, walk around it, get a feel for it. During a match, don't rush in to hit your approach shot unless you see that the ball is going to land in this radius. Otherwise you'll end up attacking balls that are actually too deep, and you will still be running to your position near the net as your opponent hits his return. You'll spend the day trying to hit shots off your toes or saluting those that go whistling by as you run forward.

The Stroke

When you see a short ball coming, work to get a quick jump forward and to have good body balance while on the run. As you approach the ball, turn sideways to the net, but don't "break stride" or stop in order to hit it. Your feet are never in the same position on the approach shot, so don't worry about a standard hitting position — it's the rhythm that you seek.

Keep the racket head high — at about eye level — with your arm and wrist fixed. Take only a short backswing and hit through the ball with a slight high-to-low-to-high motion and a slight racket bevel in order to produce *underspin*. The low trajectory makes the ball skid low when it hits and forces your opponent to bend down for his return. Keep the racket strings on target throughout your stroke and just make a little shoulder turn with a down-and-up loop. Your body moving forward will supply all the power you need. Even though you hit with underspin by pulling the racket down to brush the back side of the ball, *your follow-through must finish high to keep the ball from landing short or going into the net.* Never think that you chip down, or hit down, on the ball. Concentrate instead on carrying your racket back up and out toward your target to hit the ball deep. If you visualize trying to get around the outside of the ball, it will help you to keep your racket head high.

Just as on all your other strokes (except the serve and the overhead) *don't horse around with your wrist.* Leave it fixed throughout your swing and let your body and racket arm do the work. You can't let the wrist go soft, or roll over, or lay back if you hope to have the racket meet the ball squarely. Try to have the arm form a little bow as you approach the ball so that it can make the play as a fixed unit. By fixing the racket head, you can make some fairly large movements with your body without affecting the flight of the ball. But a slight wrist turn makes a giant exaggeration. One reason Jimmy Connors has such great consistency on his approach shots and volleys is that he locks his wrist and his racket head and then makes the play with his body. The racket doesn't turn in his hands, which insures consistency as the racket head comes through the ball. But the average player fixes his body and then turns the wrist under to supply underspin.

Footwork

Although most people are taught to stop as they hit their approach shot, I feel this destroys the rhythm that you seek and your ability to volley effectively at the net. In fact, I've never seen a pro stop and hit this shot unless he is late and the ball is slightly behind him. But if you contact that ball out in front — where you are supposed to — then you can run right through as you hit and move into position for your volley. (Another reason I don't want you to stop as you hit is the matter of deceleration-acceleration. When you suddenly stop running, your upper body continues to move forward and down, while your racket arm goes up to keep your balance. The result is generally an approach shot that is pulled down into the net.)

After hitting your approach shot, keep moving forward to the side of the center stripe to which you hit the ball, halfway between the service line and the net, and three feet from the stripe. You want to be in the *center of your opponent's possibilities*, so the only time you should stand on the center stripe is when you've hit the ball straight down the middle.

When you reach your desired position, stop momentarily with a little check-step — hopefully when the ball is on your opponent's racket strings. Then you can move quickly in any direction without stumbling over your feet. This is where anticipation is critical. Try telling yourself, "Drive or lob, drive or lob," as you study your opponent's swing and the direction of the ball as it leaves his racket. If it's a drive — a passing shot — you want to get two steps forward on the *diagonal* toward the ball. *Don't run parallel to the net.* If it's a lob, turn and try to get three quick steps back. If you can learn to make these movements instinctively, without standing there flat-footed trying to confirm your decision, you may play at Wimbledon yet.

Keep It Deep

Your first goal is always depth. Try to land the ball within four feet of your opponent's baseline, whether you hit the ball horizontally or with underspin. Hitting deep forces your opponent back and gives you more time to crowd the net and to react to your opponent's shot. Conversely, if you hit your approach shot short, with a high bounce, you decrease your reaction time on the next shot and place yourself on defense, even though you are closer to the net.

Jack Kramer wasn't that fast, but his approach shot was so deep and he was such an absolute fiend for hitting target areas that he would get position on you and there wasn't much you could do about it. After hitting his approach shot he would get those extra two or three steps toward the net and shorten the angle so much that it was virtually impossible to pass him, especially from your position about five feet behind the baseline. Former playing great Lew Hoad remembers how Kramer "always hit his approach shot so deep — always in a little two- or three-foot area, either in the backhand corner, in the middle, or in the other corner."

I visited with Hoad at the World Championship Tennis finals in 1975, and we got to talking about how many of today's players don't seem to have a respect for keeping the ball deep, such as on their groundstrokes, approach shots, and second serves. "The emphasis seems to be on just getting to the net, rather than on getting to the net behind the really good approach shot," I said, and Lew agreed. "I can't for the life of me see how they can consistently hit the ball short and get away with it," he said. "When I was playing, you had to really work on your approach shot, because any time you could go to the net, you had to go." We also noted that even though Rod Laver's game was going down, he was the only player in the eight-man finals who had any consistent depth on his approach shots. And Hoad felt it came basically from playing the guys in the older era.

Placement and Target Areas

As you become more proficient, strive to hit nearly every approach shot with underspin to your opponent's backhand corner — a target area four feet inside the baseline and four feet inside the sideline. This is your target for the rest of your life, unless you come up against an opponent who has a stronger backhand than forehand.

Now you're probably thinking, "Wait a minute, Vic. I'm just happy if I keep the ball in the *court* and you're talking about target areas. The only way I can hit that backhand corner is by accident." This may be true, I know, but everybody should at least practice hitting to target areas because this brings about faster improvement and a realization of just how much you need to work on a particular stroke.

There are two reasons why you want to underspin your approach shot and aim it for your opponent's backhand:

a. Whenever you go to the net you want to force your opponent to return the ball high, where you can volley much better. An underspin approach shot bounces low to your opponent, and very few club players will make the effort to get down low for the ball and to lift up with a vertical racket head. Instead, they remain stiff-kneed and simply drop the racket head, scoop down for the shot, and raise it high — which is exactly what you want.

b. Since most players hit backhands with underspin, and balls hit with underspin tend to sail, these players cannot hurt you nearly as much as those who can hit with topspin. When you come to the net against an opponent's topspin shot, the ball often comes over the net and down at your feet, which forces you to bend for the tough shot. That's why you want to keep the ball low even against a player who pulls across on his backhand, because he can take a high ball and drive it on a flat line, just over the net — a difficult shot to volley.

Positioning

A common mistake is to believe that no matter where you hit your approach shot, you should stay right in the middle of the court, close to the security of the center stripe. ("That line is the middle — I will stand on the line.") Yet in reality you are not in the middle but to one side, unless you have hit the ball straight down the middle. As page 118 shows, if you stand on the center stripe for a shot to your opponent's forehand and backhand side, then you leave yourself vulnerable to passing shots down both sides. Instead, you must determine the angle that your opponent has in which to hit and then stand halfway between.

For example, if you can hit to your opponent's backhand, and take your position three feet to the right of the center stripe, there's hardly a player in the world who can pass you on the left if you have good reactions and a decent volley. He must be able to topspin his backhand in order to hit the ball

In taking his ready position near the net, the volleyer straddles the center line only when his opponent is hitting from near the center of his court. The volleyer also moves forward or backward as he determines whether his opponent is hitting a drive or a lob. The circle on the volleyer's side of the court indicates his short-ball range.

The volleyer moves three to four feet to his right when his opponent is hitting from his backhand corner. Few players can hit a backhand winner past what appears to be the volleyer's "vulnerable" left side.

The volleyer moves three to four feet to his left when his opponent is hitting a forehand near the singles sideline. Again, the volleyer is halfway between where his opponent can hit, whether down the line or cross-court.

hard enough, on a cross-court diagonal, to keep it away from your volley at the net. Very few players even on the pro tour can do that. Thus, realistically your opponent can now only go to your right or over your head. *You have just cut off 33 percent of his opportunities.*

When people first try to position themselves correctly, they feel naked leaving all that space on one side, such as when they hit the ball to their opponent's backhand. They don't believe me when I tell them they *want* to tempt their opponent with that "wide-open" area on their own backhand side because it's virtually an impossible shot for the average player to pull off. They say, "Yeh, but what about the guy who hits it in here?" and they point to that little area on the court, inside the 65'9" diagonal (see page 101 photo), that very few people in the history of the game have been able to hit under pressure. I always tell them, "He isn't living, so you're in pretty good shape. Nobody ever 'owns' that shot."

Stop worrying about the extraordinary shot, and be much more concerned about what realistically is possible, given the physical laws and the court dimensions which govern this game.

Put me to the test if you still feel that it's nothing to hit those cross-court shots that dip over the net and away from your opponent. Divide the opposite service box roughly in half with some rope so that you can visualize the 65'9" diagonal as shown on the diagram, then stand on the baseline at your backhand corner, bounce the ball, and just try to bring it down *inside* the diagonal. Keep score as in a game and see if you can beat my concept. Then put an opponent halfway between the net and the service line, three feet to your side of the center stripe, and try to hit the ball past him, while bringing it down inside the court. Unless you can hit with topspin, you will either have to aim the ball too close to your opponent, or you will have to soften your hit, in which case your opponent can easily step across for his volley.

Anticipation

Okay, let's say your only strategy for ten years has been to "hit and stay back," but it hasn't made you too famous. So you're going to start working on your approach shot, and rushing the net a little more often than every other April. Great, except for one warning: you will need more than a good stroke. In order to hit a consistently deep approach shot, you need anticipation and a fast first step forward so that you can reach the ball before it starts to drop after bouncing. This requires that you learn to think and react *offensively*, not defensively.

If you and your opponent are typical intermediates, and you have a baseline rally going, you're waiting for the first short ball, right? Then you can rush in and show off your new approach shot. But when will you get this short ball? *Statistically, on the very next shot.* If your opponent could keep it deep, he wouldn't be playing you — he would be out on the tournament circuit. He might hit an occasional deep shot by accident, but very few people can hit two deep balls in a row by design. So every time your opponent prepares to hit, keep telling yourself, "The next ball is going to be short." Stay on your toes, ready to move forward. *Be surprised if the ball lands deep — never be surprised that it falls short —* and this will change your whole game.

Yet nearly everyone stands flat-footed at the baseline, waiting to see where the ball goes, then they cry, "Oh no, it's short!" and they go running in and reach the ball on the third bounce. They get disgusted that they didn't react fast enough, yet on the very next shot they remain glued to the baseline, and once again they're shocked by the short ball. All day long they hit and back up, unable to realize they're not playing Jimmy Connors. To get your feet moving, make yourself break toward the ball before it reaches your opponent's service line and you'll be on your way to good tennis.

If you can *concentrate, think about always moving forward, and get your feet moving quickly,* you won't need roller skates in order to reach a good hitting position for your approach shot. Then, if you can hit the ball deep to your opponent, and run to your appropriate waiting position, you will be in the same position as the pros: your opponent will be on the defensive and you will be poised near the net. You'll have achieved your first goal — to gain control of the net. But to "own" or hold the fortress, you next need to know how to volley and to defend against the lob.

The Volley

The volley is any ball you hit in the air before it touches the ground. Although you can volley from near the baseline, you generally will volley in the vicinity of the net, a fact which stirs a basic emotion in many players: fear. Beginners and women who play in competitive mixed doubles are always telling me, "I don't want to play the net. I get up there and I'm scared

Practice Tip: Approach Shot Drills

The approach shot is not an easy stroke to master. There's a definite "touch" involved that requires long hours of intensive practice. But if you can learn to hit that baby deep — preferably to your opponent's backhand — you are going to be deadly at the net. The following are some drills that will sharpen your approach shot and help you evaluate your stroke:

1. If you think you already "own" this shot, quit talking big and see how you fare against targets. Set up cans in those four-foot-by-four-foot corners inside your opponent's baseline and sidelines. Then stand at your baseline and have a friend or a ball machine land balls around the service line, so that you can run in and try to stroke the ball into a corner. It's a humiliating feeling to see how far your shots land from the cans, and to realize you can't guide the ball the way you think. But it's a great drill to make you conscious of keeping the ball deep. You can also set up cans in all four corners and then rally with a friend. On every short ball, attack and hit an approach shot and see who's the first to knock over a can.

2. Using that four-foot radius will help you know if you are playing with your wrist. People who use the wrist on this shot will hit an occasional good shot, but when they miss, the variations are great. People who play with a fixed wrist are not as wild.

3. If you want to practice your approach shot under match-like conditions, challenge the person at the club who tries to overpower his first serve (although it rarely goes in) and then hits a meek second serve. This is where you always want to attack and hit your approach shot. But don't give your intentions away. You can't go up to the person and say, "Let's play a match — I want to practice attacking you." Be nice and the person will think, "Gee, they're finally recognizing my talent around here."

4. Most players feel that if they can't look at their target, they can't hit it, and thus they fail to concentrate on simply watching the ball come into their racket. So try this little drill to prove that if you have average peripheral vision, you don't need to look directly at your opponent's baseline corners as you swing. Righthanders, hold a ball in your hand at the point where you normally contact your approach shot, and with your eyes focused on the ball, point your left finger to either corner. Then look up and see if your finger is pointed accurately. If it is, you know you can relax and keep your eye on the ball, not your target.

PHOTO BY JOHN G. ZIMMERMAN

Vic executes a volley. His eyes are glued to the point of impact, and the face of the racket is slightly beveled and pointed at about a 45-degree angle upward. The butt of the racket is pointed down toward the court; try to imagine the butt sliding across an imaginary tabletop, and then rising again.

to death." This is understandable, since anxiety seems to increase proportionately the closer you get to your opponent — because he can easily provide you with a "fuzz sandwich." When you're up at the net, especially in doubles, everything is happening fast and you can sometimes be frightened into inaction. We once had a lady at the tennis college who froze in her ready position, watching the ball come right at her. "This ball is going to hit me," she grimaced, moments before it bounced off her forehead. A friend asked her, "Why don't you move back?" And she said, "When I do, I just get hit one step farther back."

Learning how to volley will help you overcome fears about playing the net in doubles and following your approach shot to the net in singles — not to mention making you a vastly improved player. But then another problem arises. People very often will hit an approach shot and make a great flurry to reach their preferred position halfway between the service line and the net. But when they land on this spot, they say "Made it!" and they aren't about to budge for anything. They think they now control the point, when they actually are in danger of losing because they're not ready for their opponent's return shot. You frequently hear these people say, "Terrific shot, Bertha," as the ball goes zipping by.

Instead of becoming hypnotized in your ready position after hitting an

122

The hitter holds a Continental grip to show why most players have difficulty hitting high forehand volleys with this grip: the racket is automatically angled toward the left side of the court and the racket face is beveled slightly upward. Down-the-line forehand volleys are also a little more difficult to hit with a Continental grip than with the Eastern forehand.

The hitter demonstrates the weakness of the Western grip on low forehand volleys. This grip makes it darn tough to bevel the racket face upward to help the ball clear the high net.

approach shot, *you must go to the net with the understanding that you are going to win or lose the point on the very next shot.* You're not in the middle but at the end of a sequence. In most cases your opponent will either make an error on your approach shot, hit an outright winner, or return the ball weakly, thus giving you a relatively easy volley or overhead with which to end the point.

The Grip

I prefer to have pros and beginners alike use their regular Eastern forehand or Eastern backhand grip when they volley. Despite what you may have been told, our experiments show there is sufficient time to switch grips if you will simply practice switching grips as you take your first step. Also, the rate of speed of the ball hit by many professionals is a rate you're not apt to confront for several years.

I know that many pro players and teachers argue in favor of the Continental (halfway between the Eastern forehand and backhand grips) so that you can use a one-grip game. But remember, *the Continental forces you to be much more coordinated and talented, especially on the forehand volley.* Even top pros like Roy Emerson have admitted it is more difficult to handle the high forehand volley with the Continental because the bottom of the racket is beveled forward and they can't control it. When they try to get their racket out in front to volley into their opponent's backhand corner, the racket points on a diagonal *away* from that corner and they can't make the play unless they compensate by swinging late or they are double-jointed. You try it, holding a Continental grip.

In the first photograph, the volleyer keeps his palm vertical while holding an Eastern forehand grip. The second photograph shows how much the palm must move to switch from an Eastern forehand to an Eastern backhand, on groundstrokes and volleys alike. Some experts say this switch is impossible to make, especially when volleying at the net. There is time, according to research conducted at my tennis college.

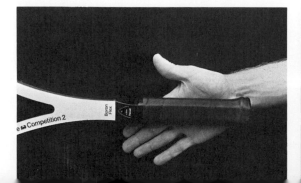

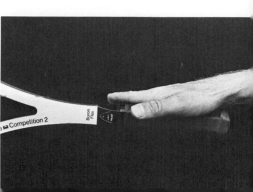

(1)

(2)

(3)

(5)

(6)

(4)

The Forehand Volley

(1) The volleyer has to be ready to move quickly in any direction. The body and foot position which facilitates fast action is the same as for a groundstroke. The placement of the left elbow in this high position forces a shorter backswing on the backhand volley. (2) The volleyer raises his heels and leans slightly forward just before his opponent strikes the ball in order to facilitate faster footwork. (3) This is as far as you should take the racket back as you move into the shot. Leading with the right elbow also prevents wrist layback and keeps the racket face on line with the approaching ball. (4) The volleyer contacts the ball when it is even with his front shoulder. His side is facing the net. (5) If possible, the racket head, ball, and hitter's eyes should be on the same level at impact — which often requires a substantial knee bend on low volleys. (6) Many weak volleyers finish below the tape of the net on their follow-through. I strongly advocate at least an eye-level finish for all volleys.

The Forehand Volley

Make sure you get into a ready position following your approach shot, or anytime you find yourself at the net. This helps insure that you will volley properly. Then keep telling yourself, "Drive or lob, drive or lob," as you watch your opponent take his (or her) swing. Just before he contacts the ball, bring your heels off the ground so that you can push off your toes as you move forward to volley, or as you turn and retreat for a lob.

If your opponent hits a drive, break *diagonally* forward — toward the net post — to meet the ball. Remember, the closer you get to the net, the easier you can close off the point. If you run parallel to the net, balls which are sharply angled will simply get farther away from you.

On all your volleys, *try to visualize a short, punching motion rather than an actual stroke*, because the greater the length of your swing, the greater must be your talent. Your concern is with accuracy and placement rather than speed on the ball, so don't take your racket any farther back than the shoulder housing the hitting arm. Instead of a backswing, think of your hitting palm reaching out to intercept the ball, as if you were catching a baseball.

Your goal is to contact the ball when it is even with your front shoulder and at eye level, so bend your knees to get down on a low ball. Volleying off your front shoulder gives you a clean view of the ball and the racket. If you try to contact the ball too far out in front, you have to contort your fore-

If the average player bends this low, he's afraid he'll never be able to get back up. But low volleys require this amount of knee bend to effectively guide the ball back deep to your opponent. Many of the great volleyers in the 1930s used to end up with their long white trousers completely grass-stained at the knees during Forest Hills and Wimbledon.

arm and wrist to make the hit and you can't judge the ball coming into the racket. Also, the farther out in front you try to hit the ball, the more you must face the net with your body — and the more you face the net, the more your racket tends to pull down rather than carrying out.

At contact, your front shoulder should be towards the net and your racket head pointed upward at a 45-degree angle. Some players prefer to visualize the butt of their racket pointed at the court, as was suggested by Ron Heathrow, a past attendee at my academy for teaching professionals.

Although there is little follow-through on the volley, never let the racket suddenly stop, pull across, or drop; stroke through the ball and carry the racket out toward your target so that you keep the ball deep. *Try to imagine that you are swinging across a high table top, with the racket head always up and the face vertical as you hit through the ball.*

Some pros actually teach their students to lay the racket head back on the volley, in order to snap the wrist into the ball at contact and produce more power. But once again, I argue that *laying the racket back at any point on the volley is the kiss of death.* Instead of fixing your racket with a locked-wrist position and letting your arm and body supply the power, playing with the wrist requires you to judge — under pressure — how and when to snap the wrist so that you can contact the ball properly. As I emphasized earlier in the book, the body has a natural tendency to turn into the ball properly, but the doggone racket fails to stay in sync with the body because the wrist has come into play or the arm is taking a solo.

Just as on the forehand stroke, you can prevent wrist layback by leading slightly with your hitting elbow on the backswing while leaving your wrist fixed. Visualize your arm extending parallel along a line; when you draw the racket back, your elbow should pass the line before your wrist or racket. Then, as you go out to volley, keep your hitting palm and the face of your racket directly in line with the oncoming ball so that your opponent sees only your racket strings, and never the butt of the handle. *Always keep your hitting elbow out away from your body.* Drills where you have a ball or your elbow pinned against your body as a way to prevent wrist layback will only

The kiss of death on the volley is to drop the hitting elbow and push the arm forward, as the hitter is doing here. This causes the racket face to tilt back and thus come off the path of the oncoming ball. Strive instead to carry a high, slightly bent hitting elbow (as in the third picture in the forehand volley sequence on page 124) and this will automatically let the elbow lead the racket on the backswing and prevent wrist layback.

increase this problem — for when your elbow comes in, physiology forces the wrist to lay back.

The Backhand Volley

The stroking principles are basically the same here as on the forehand volley. One difference is that when you step forward to meet the ball, think of your *knuckles* reaching out to intercept the ball, and not your palm. Also, the non-hitting arm can work in your behalf by cradling the throat of the racket on the backswing. But keep this hand and the elbow high and out away from your body so that the racket face is always on line with the oncoming ball, and not laid back.

The instant the ball leaves your opponent's racket, simultaneously turn the shoulder of your hitting arm toward the net and switch your grip from the Eastern forehand to the Eastern backhand. Then move diagonally forward, contacting the ball six to ten inches in front of your body and at eye level. Your body weight transfers from the back to the front foot as you make contact, and the racket head remains up and finishes high on the follow-through. You generate your power on this stroke by the forward movement of your body and by keeping your hitting arm extended, *not* by bending your elbow and throwing the racket head at the ball.

Anticipation

The main reason that most people don't have a good volley is that they don't move their bodies. Self-hypnosis at the net and the fear of making the wrong decision are as destructive as a lack of form. You can have lousy form but if you can get on top of the net you can volley with your earlobe and still make the play. Conversely, even with great form, if you wait for the ball to come to you instead of attacking, you will always be on the defensive, with more difficult volleys to execute.

The reason pros can volley so well is that they start moving as or before the ball is hit, whereas the average player waits until the ball reaches the net. When the pro comes to the net and is about to be passed on either side, he runs one way or the other; he's not afraid to guess wrong. He knows he has to react instantly and that at least he has a 50–50 chance of outguessing his opponent. But the intermediate wants to confirm every decision. You can

(1)

(2)

(3)

(4)

(5)

(6)

The Backhand Volley

(1) Never underestimate the value of getting into a consistent ready position on all of your strokes, whenever possible. You have the time in most cases, and this puts you in position to break quickly in any direction. Notice here how the hitter holds his racket close to eye level, with his left elbow riding high. (2) The volleyer sees the ball heading for his backhand and effects his body pivot, with the left hand helping to guide the racket back. The left elbow remains high and the racket face is ready to meet the ball. (3) The ball is contacted well out in front of the body, and the racket head stays at eye level. (4) A side view of the volley at impact. (5) The hitter finishes with a high follow-through — as on the forehand — and he never lets the racket drop. Most people continue down on the follow-through, which is why so many of their volleys wind up in the net. Even on the lowest ball, try to complete your stroke with a high finish, and see how quickly your volley improves. (6) If your knees and thighs aren't in shape, you're going to be in deep trouble on low volleys. Also remember to keep your eyes on the point of contact.

All four volleyers stand on the center stripe and then stretch for an imaginary cross-court shot to show how crucial it is to get that extra one or two steps closer to the net in order to cut the ball off. When most club players go to the net, they begin inching back as their opponent gets ready to hit the ball. The guy who inches all the way back to the service line will have to call a cab to reach the ball. But the man at the net can literally reach the shot even when his feet are planted.

see him freeze on the center stripe thinking, "Is he going to pass me on the left or on the right? Son-of-a-gun. It was to my backhand," and he makes no move at all. He's got a 100 out of 100 chance of losing — but he's not going to look dumb by running the wrong way.

That's why I like the advice Sandy Mayer said he received from his father: "I don't care if you guess wrong at the net, but you have to go, one way or the other. I never want to catch you standing on the middle line." If more people would learn to do this early in their tennis "careers" — reward themselves for making a move, even if it's wrong — then they would be on their way to a sound game. Yet kids, especially, are so fearful of reprimands from themselves or authority figures for going the wrong way that they begin to build in a subconscious braking system.

Footwork

When you reach a ready position near the net, understand that this is only where you want to *land* — not where you're going to volley — so don't let your heels touch the ground as you wait to see the direction of your opponent's return. Think instead about how fast you're going to have to exit to make your next play. You will be a good volleyer if you can gain *one step forward* by reacting quickly. In fact, you will render your opponent practically ineffective on the cross-court passing shot. The great volleyers get two steps toward the ball and their racket practically crosses the net when they follow through.

Another reason you don't want to get caught back is that the closer you can get to the net, the higher you will be able to volley. But if you hesitate, the ball will drop lower than the tape of the net and you won't be able to make an offensive play. You will have to hit the ball defensively, concentrating on just getting it back into play and deep.

Closing Out the Point

Very often, when you hear the pros say that a particular player can't close out the point, they mean that he doesn't crowd the net by getting those two steps forward; thus, instead of being an immediate winner, he very often loses the point or is forced on the defensive.

For example, the charge against Cliff Richey — at one time the No. 1 ranked player in the country — was that he didn't have enough shots. But Cliff had every shot in the book, plus he could hit the ball deep and keep it in play. What it really boiled down to was that although Cliff actually volleyed well, he couldn't get close enough to the net to really gain the advantage. When I was accompanying the Davis Cup team in 1967, Pancho Gonzales kept telling Cliff, "Learn to close off the point." Gorgo just couldn't understand how a guy could fight so hard out there but then, when he finally got a chance to win the point, he would only produce more opportunities to fight harder by just keeping the ball in play on his volley.

Similarly, I have heard many theories about what caused Stan Smith's decline a few years back. One of my own observations is that Stan somehow lost his confidence about getting that extra step at the net, and thus he could not close off volleys or get good volleying position, a trait which had made him deadly during his years at the top.

Placement

When you are volleying at the net, where should you aim if you have the time? Top players try to hit the ball on a short diagonal, rather than deep and down the middle, because it forces their opponent to run farther. Plus, if their opponent does return it, his body weight carries him well off the court and out of position for another shot.

However, *if you are not positive that you are going to end the point with a short-angle volley, then just strive for depth.* Trying to force short-angle shots will very often cause you to miss. So be aggressive, but don't be impatient when you go to the net. Hitting your first volley deep will still keep your opponent in trouble. Your ability to hit with depth will also give you the confidence to relax and not to panic on your first volley. But if you volley poorly, you tend to regard your first volley as an all-or-nothing shot.

On volleys where you are away from the net, such as near the service line, your only goal should be to keep the ball deep and in play. Don't gamble on hitting the angles. The farther you can push your opponent back, the longer his return shot is in the air and the more time you have to close in on the net for your next shot.

General Tips on the Volley

a. Treat easy shots with the same respect as difficult ones. Very often you will get an easy ball off your opponent's drive but you relax and fail to get your two steps forward. Suddenly the ball loses speed and drops below the level of the net and now you are on defense, having to raise the ball back up again. Furthermore, the softer the ball is coming, the harder it is to volley from a low position. You have a tendency to let the wrist and the racket go limp with the shot, which causes you to dump the ball into the net.

b. When you run for the ball, keep your hitting arm and racket face up. When you stretch to make a hit, no matter how late you might be, keep the face of your racket high — never let it drop. Even on a desperate lunge, if you keep your racket head high you still have a chance to catch the ball on the strings and return it over the net. Try always to finish high.

c. Always be thinking, "Drive or lob, drive or lob," as you wait for your opponent's return. Don't be afraid to guess wrong. Your guesses will become educated guesses as you learn to anticipate.

d. Try to keep your eyes on the ball right into the racket, even on short-

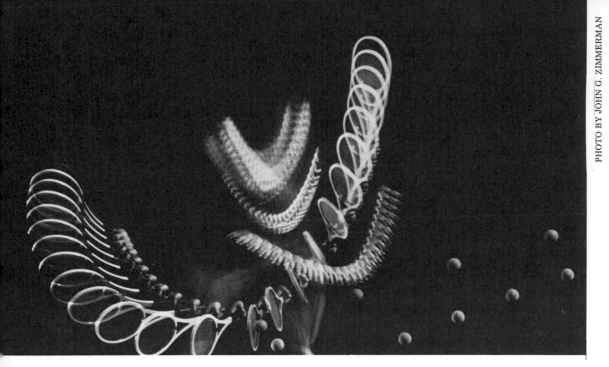

PHOTO BY JOHN G. ZIMMERMAN

The hitter executes a doubles half-volley, with the racket coming up quickly on the follow-through to brush the ball lightly and help it come down faster once it goes over the net. For a deep half-volley in singles you should extend your follow-through toward the net so that the end of your stroke doesn't have such a steep vertical climb. Still, your basic approach to the ball is exactly the same on both shots.

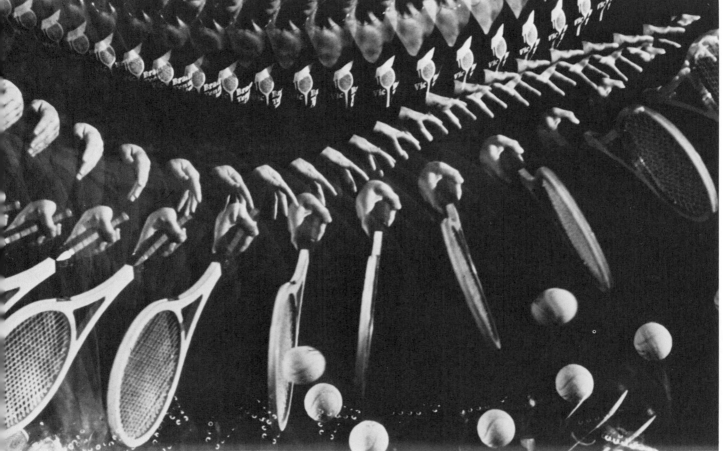

PHOTO BY JOHN G. ZIMMERMAN

The hitter (Mary Ley) shows how low you should get your hitting hand and the racket head to hit a proper half-volley. Notice how the racket head is several inches off the court, and straight up and down on the hit. The body lifts up to lift the ball over the net.

range volley exchanges, because this increases your chances to make the good play and end the point right there. I have a pro doubles film where there are four shots in less than two seconds, and Rosewall has his eyes fixed on the spot where the ball meets the strings for both of his shots.

e. Learn to volley from a deep position, not just up at the net, because very often that's where you are caught if you don't move quickly between the baseline and the net. But remember, the farther back from the net you volley, the more talented you must be. You have to learn to hit out — to almost *lift* that ball from the service line. If you volley down even slightly, the ball will go into the net.

f. A good reminder on volleys at head level or above: people rarely hit them deep enough. Players are so afraid of hitting this shot over the baseline that they snap down severely with their racket, and the ball very often ends up in the net. A corollary to this precaution: the closer you get to the net, the more you have a tendency to relax and swing down. So always keep the racket head up and going out.

g. One reason you may not volley well is that you never practice coming to the net and volleying. But you can't practice effectively or work on your weaknesses if you don't have a realistic idea about what you can actually do with the shot. After a match you may talk about how you were going to the net and volleying like a champ, but most people tend to remember the one or two volleys that they hit well and to forget the ten that they missed. This is why you must have a friend record where your volley is landing during a match, and how effective it really is. You need to learn how well you volley from the service line, from halfway between the service line and the net, and when up at the net. Then you can go out and work on a specific weakness.

h. An excellent drill to help make you react and move quickly at the net is to play without a racket while a friend throws or hits the ball from the baseline. You just try to catch it. This forces you to concentrate on the ball, to hustle into position, and to stretch out for the ball because you don't have that extra racket length to play with. But when you've put a racket back in your hand, don't forget to do what you've practiced.

The Half-Volley

The half-volley is a difficult yet unglamorous shot that must be hit down around your sneakers, just as it bounces off the court. It's almost impossible

The Forehand Half-Volley

(1) The hitter, while moving continuously forward, begins to lower his body for the tricky half-volley. This is virtually his entire backswing. His eyes never leave the ball. (2) A severe knee bend is necessary to keep the racket nearly parallel to the court. (3) Contact is made slightly ahead of the front foot with a vertical racket face that is on the same level as the wrist. Since the racket face is not tilted upward, the thighs must effect the desired lift. (4) The hitter has a high follow-through and continues moving forward to gain a favorable position at the net.

to attack with a half-volley, nor do you arouse much envy by telling friends you have the best half-volley in your club. The tendency is to want to kick at a ball that low or to say, "Play two — I don't hit anything below my knees."

Some coaches, in fact, won't even teach the half-volley. They feel that their students shouldn't let themselves get caught in that area around the service line, that they should either be back far enough to take the ball on a normal bounce or else reach the ball when it's still in the air. But this approach ignores two important realities: (1) Intermediates are caught all the time in that midcourt area, either by "hanging around" waiting to see what their opponent is going to do or by failing to know their "short ball range" on the approach shot; (2) the better you play, the more you need a half-volley to remain competitive. If your opponent has really worked on his service return, he will land the ball at your feet all day long when you rush the net. You'll need to get that shot back over the net and deep if you want to win your serve.

The Stroke

Forehand and backhand half-volleys require a short backswing, good knee bend, and a low-to-high lifting motion with a racket head that is vertical at impact. This produces a slight topspin which enables you to lift the ball up over the net with speed and still bring it back down safely into your opponent's court.

You can't expect to hit a decent half-volley by staying high with your body and simply lowering your racket head with the face beveled back to "scoop" the ball up over the net, as most people try to do. Instead, you must freeze your wrist position, lower your hitting arm, and then use your thighs and the lift of your body to supply the power. The slightest bevel in your racket can drastically affect the ball's flight pattern. But if you know the racket head is fixed, and not beveled, then you only have to decide how much to lift your thighs.

Don't get lazy with your knees. They must lower your body almost to the court so that you can bring the racket face right down to the level of the ball, and then lift the entire body up as the ball is hit. That's why the great old-timers had grass-stained knees on their white pants. Jimmy Connors and Bjorn Borg are the best players I've seen in many years who will get this low on the half-volley, so that their racket is held very close to the surface of the court, face straight up and down and already fixed for the hit.

(1)

(2)

(3)

(4)

The Backhand Half-Volley

The same movements used on the forehand half-volley are required for the backhand half-volley. Notice the high left elbow, even for low balls. Remember, just as on the backhand groundstroke, you can't be late and make a good play. On the backhand half-volley, in fact, I've found that if you get trapped at your feet and you can't meet the ball out in front, you almost always lose the point. So concentrate on reacting and moving quickly to the ball.

Contact should be made immediately after the ball has bounced. Think of hitting the ball and lifting it up over the net, while keeping your eyes down on the point of impact. Don't try to take an early peek at how you did. Keep your head fixed so that it maintains its relationship with the racket, and have them lift together. If you let your head lift up early you will tend to scoop the ball.

If possible, the half-volley should be executed with little or no pause in forward motion so that you won't lose time moving to that side of the center stripe to which you hit the ball, and as close to the net as possible. Don't get trapped on the half-volley by letting the ball land closer to your back foot than to the foot closest to the net; this will force you to stop and make the hit. Remember, too, that the backhand half-volley must be contacted further out in front of the body than the forehand. If you're late on the backhand here, you rarely can make a successful return.

Placement

In singles, just strive to keep the half-volley deep — by contacting the ball with less of a vertical lift — and this will give you time to get good position near the net. Your opponent is generally backcourt on this shot, but if the ball only goes to the service line, he can trot in and give you a new look.

In doubles, you must keep your half-volley as close to the net as possible, so that one of your opponents can't deck a high volley. The pros will try to hit a "soft" shot that goes over the net and dies, forcing their opponents to volley up. But be careful not to also soften the wrist as you make this play or you will dump the ball into the net. Keep a firm wrist, bend the knees, and then rise quickly out of this low crouch with a vertical lift. This enables you to brush the ball lightly, so that once it crosses the net it will begin to descend sooner than the singles half-volley.

The Lob

The lob is the only stroke in tennis that can pull you out of a hole and give you a giant win, even though you have nothing else. People make fun of those players who like to throw up a lob every two or three shots, but they

The only difference in stroke production between a baseline drive and the lob is the bevel of the racket face at impact, whether on the forehand or backhand. Thus, when hitting from the base-line, make every volleyer believe you are about to drive the ball. This draws the volleyer closer to the net and makes him more vulnerable to your lob.

seem to forget that good lobbers have more trophies than any other person in the club.

Try to realize how devastating the well-timed, well-executed lob can be: (1) It can be used like the baseball pitcher's change-up to break up your opponent's rhythm and the pace of a rally; (2) It can be used to buy time to allow you to get back in position after scrambling off-court to make a play; (3) As a tactical weapon it drives your opponent away from the net and allows you to move in and take the offensive; (4) It will tire your opponent by forcing him to retreat from the net and to stretch up to hit overheads.

So learn to lob effectively and see how dramatically it improves your game. As the late Raphael Osuna used to tell Raul Ramirez, currently Mexico's Davis Cup hero: "Remember the lob. The lob, the lob, the lob."

The Stroke

Both forehand and backhand lobs require the same Eastern grips as used on your groundstrokes.

The elevation of your lob depends upon three factors: (1) the degree to which your racket face is beveled or turned upward to the sky, (2) the angle of the forward low-to-high striking motion, and (3) the speed of the stroke. Beginners should first learn to hit lobs high into the air with the racket face turned upwards to the sky, while lifting with a low-to-high forward motion. As proficiency is gained, develop about a 55-degree stroking angle and add a slight bevel of the racket to get under the ball. This will produce the greatest depth from baseline to baseline with the least amount of energy. On the follow-through, make sure you complete your stroke and finish with the racket head high.

The best way to learn to lob is to get out and practice, without the pressure of a match but under realistic conditions. Have a friend hit balls so that you can run laterally along the baseline and even off the court to make the play. If you only practice against balls that come right down the middle you can get into a pretty good groove and begin to think, "Gee, I'm lobbing pretty well." But then you get into a match and you start running laterally, with your energy going away from your shot, and your lobs come up short. (You can also practice on your own by just bouncing the ball before you lob, but remember to run to the ball to simulate actual playing conditions.)

If you can only practice while rallying before a match, try to hit at least 20 lobs and work on having the ball land within five feet of your opponent's baseline. If the ball goes beyond the baseline, practice adjusting the upward angle of your swing and the bevel of your racket so that you can always swing with the same speed no matter what the pressure.

Placement

The most common mistake you can make is to lob shallow and thus give your opponent an easy overhead while you run for cover. One reason you might tend to lob short is that you look at your opponent out of the corner of your eye and unconsciously slow up on your swing. So learn to block out your opponent. Second, if you hit your first lob of the match too long, you generally overcompensate on the next one and hit it weakly to your opponent, who stands there at the net grinning. Thus you lose two straight points on the lob and you're afraid to lob again the rest of the match, which retires one of your greatest potential weapons.

To break these habits, *always attempt to lob five to ten feet too long.* Try to hit your first lob of the match over the baseline. If you are long, try to hit your next one with exactly the same speed but with slightly more bevel in your racket so that your extra length will go into height and still give you the depth you want. Take a hint from the good players. When they lob long they think, "Good, good," because they know exactly how to gauge their correction. That's why you always want to try to lob early in the match so that you can learn from your errors and have your "touch" adjusted by the time you start playing under more pressure later in the match.

Two refinements on lob placement: (1) try to have your opponent look up into the sun, if there's sun, and (2) if you're near one of your baseline corners, try to lob on the diagonal to gain extra distance.

Concealing Your Lob

Most people don't even think about concealing their lob — they're just happy to get it up in the air. But with experience you should try to have your lob stroke resemble your forehand and backhand groundstrokes as much as possible in order to reduce your opponent's effectiveness at the net. When you conceal your intention to lob until the very last instant, your opponent can't anticipate what you're going to hit, and must hold ground until the last possible moment.

Pancho Segura still has the best concealed lob in the game. He looks like he's going to drive the ball, only to send up a lob. This forces you to freeze at the net. You can't anticipate a forehand and step forward to volley, nor can you spot the lob coming and turn to chase it down.

Interestingly, Segura's student, Jimmy Connors, is probably more effective with the lob, and concealing the lob, than any other modern-day player I've seen. Jimmy's not just a big blaster. He's not bashful about throwing up that lob. The same was true with Pancho Gonzales. When I kept informal records on the pro tour, I found that he lobbed better than all the other players. He was really something.

To conceal your lob, remember to turn your front shoulder and have a loop swing identical with your forehand and backhand. This also means running to the ball with your racket head up and already back. Then work on racket bevel. The lob is one shot on which you want to use the bevel of your racket, but obviously this takes a lot of practice and experience. One warning: don't sit back on your back heel as you go to lob because this is a dead giveaway to a smart opponent. Just step into the ball like you are going to drive the ball, only you lob.

The Offensive Lob

The pros can anticipate so well, and retreat so quickly to chase down practically every good defensive lob, that they have brought a new shot into the game: the offensive lob hit with severe topspin. They ride the ball hard and it goes up like a lob, just high enough to be out of reach of their opponent at the net, but when it lands it kicks toward the back fence and is hit hard enough so that the opponent can't get back in time to make the play. Unfortunately, this is a low percentage shot. Even the pros find that it only works about one out of five or even one out of ten times, and that when they hit it too low they just get killed. Big money tournaments will force the top players to refine this shot into a more dependable weapon, but the average player should have it well down on his list of priorities.

Regaining the Offensive with Your Lob

If you lob successfully over your opponent's head and force him back to the baseline, then you should match him step for step and regain the net as he retreats for the ball. However, if you lob over your opponent's head but the ball comes down on a vertical plane and he doesn't really lose ground, then of course you have to stay back and wait for his overhead.

Jack Kramer tells the story of how Dennis Ralston's failure to take the net following his lob helped cost him a Davis Cup match against Australia in 1964. Ralston was leading Fred Stolle two sets to one and was one point away from breaking Stolle's serve in the fourth set. The match seemed virtually wrapped up. Stolle served and took the net, and Ralston hit a perfect lob that drove Stolle back to the baseline. But when Stolle turned around to hit, Ralston was still back. Jack Kramer was doing the commentary for CBS and I remember him saying, "Oh, there's a serious tactical error by Ralston. He should have followed into the net." Given a reprieve, Stolle went on to win the point and was now serving at deuce. On that very next point Ralston made the same mistake and Stolle again won the point. He went on to hold serve and eventually he won the match.

Combatting the Lob

When I talk about how important it is to gain control of the net, people sometimes wonder, "Heck, if that's the case, why can't you just run up to the net and stand there every time?" Well, for one thing, you're not in good enough shape to do all that running. And secondly, you can't always play dummies. People can lob and drive you straight back to the baseline.

Remember, the thing that will make you famous at the net is your ability to get two steps forward or three steps back by anticipating the nature of your opponent's shot — ideally by reading his racket head. Just as getting close to the net will make you a more effective volleyer, your ability to retreat quickly will neutralize your opponent's lob. If you can turn and reach your service line before his lob reaches his own service line, you'll be sensational; even a good club player will never beat you with this shot because people simply do not lob that well, or that deep, consistently.

In reacting to a lob, however, many players make that same old mistake of becoming paralyzed at the net. They say, "Is it going to be a drive or a lob? Son-of-a-gun, it's a lob." Then they run back like crazy but it's too late. People often tell me, "Hey, we have this lady at our club who never misses her lob — she can lay that ball in a bucket." But the chances are excellent that she's not that great a lobber. It's just that her opponents never react fast enough when she lobs. They stand at the net, watching the ball and saying, "Nuts, she did it again." So if somebody is lobbing you all the time, start retreating the instant you smell a lob, and see how well that person lobs once you apply a little pressure.

If you can't follow the face of your opponent's racket to sense if he's going to drive or lob, try your luck at a lob-drive anticipation test. Pick out a person you've always wanted to beat and go out and watch him play. Take along a notebook and a pencil and try to guess whether he's going to drive or lob on each shot. Make your decision just before impact with the ball. If you guess right, give yourself a plus. If you're wrong, then a minus. At first you'll go about 50–50, with one right, one wrong, one right, etc. But before the match is over you should be guessing right almost every time. The reason for this is simple: people simply do not have the ability to hit the perfectly concealed shot. Some players practically call out, "I'm going to lob," and yet their opponents still don't move because they haven't learned to anticipate. Also, people have a tendency to play people — not the ball — and thus are distracted by body motions and fakes. So, first try to learn to follow the face of the racket because that's what dictates whether your opponent is going to drive or lob. If you can't follow the racket face, look for giveaway body signs such as a lower backswing on the lob or a falling back on the rear foot.

Anticipating the lob will be wasted if you don't also get back from the net and set up as quickly as possible for your return shot. I like people to turn and run like a baseball outfielder, looking over their shoulder at the ball. You can backpedal if you know you can move just as quickly while maintaining a good rhythm. When you chase down a lob and you're forced to hit on the run, always try to make the ball go deep so that you keep your opponent from taking the net.

A great tip I got from Kramer, who got it from his coach as a kid, was this: when you're running back for a lob and making an over-the-shoulder return, always try to knock the ball *over* your opponent's baseline. You think you've compensated for how much energy you have going in the opposite direction, but you never have.

On a high lob, you should never let the ball bounce unless it has been hit almost straight up and your opponent has had time to scramble back in position. Then you should let it bounce and give yourself a clean shot, rather than a difficult overhead. But if the ball has any arc to it and is driving you back, contact it in the air as soon as you can. The farther back you get, the more you lose good court position while your opponent regains it. Plus, you are unable to exploit your opponent's power if you let the ball bounce; when it lands, it slows down and loses force.

Another common question I receive is, "How can I keep my opponent from lobbing all the time?" This is actually a specialized problem because most players simply can't lob well enough ever to pose this threat, at least not consistently. However, for those players who do run across this problem, the best antidote is to try to make your shots skid low (by hitting with underspin) and keep your opponent running, especially for short-angle balls. People who lob regularly love it when you hit a nice deep ball that bounces high. They simply stand about five feet behind their baseline and lob the ball easily. But if you can undershot and volleys, the ball will stay low and your opponent will have a tougher play on his part. It's also much harder to lob while on the run.

The Overhead

The overhead smash is a treat for some players. They love the feeling of power and the chance to slam the ball as hard as they want while their opponent cowers on the other side of the net. Yet a missed overhead triggers more response than any other shot in tennis, even more than a double fault or a missed volley. On the overhead there's the sheer humiliation of knocking such an innocent-looking shot into the net or out of play, and the shot preys on your mind for several points afterwards. That's why whenever I was down match point — which happened often when I was learning the game — I always tried to lob. Most players are weak, or certainly inconsistent on their overheads, and they tend to choke more on match point. They're thinking, "Jeez, this is it! If I hit this overhead I'll win the match." Then they proceed to dump the shot because they fail to hit out naturally. When you lob to your opponent under pressure you have double duty going for you: his tendency to choke on the shot, and his subsequent anger if the shot is missed. Your opponent kicks himself for blowing an easy one — "Nuts, I had him where I wanted and I missed it" — while you get a reprieve. In high school I once played a hot-headed kid from Michigan and I was losing 6-0, 5-0, and 40-30 when I threw up a lob. He missed it and he got so mad that I went on to win the match, 0-6, 7-5, 6-0.

Thus it can be a great feeling when your overhead changes from a handicap to a weapon. But this will only come through practice and experience — and learning to treat the shot much as you would a serve.

The Stroke

Hold the same grip that you use on the serve — either the regular forehand grip for some beginners or the Continental for experienced players and extremely talented beginners.

Take long steps to get to the striking area, then short quick steps to position yourself for the hit. If you are retreating for a lob, either try to turn and run back naturally or backpedal very fast.

Use virtually the same stroking motion as you do on the serve, with one exception: shorten the backswing, and thus conserve energy, by simply taking the racket head back at eye level, without letting the racket drop. Then turn forward and let the racket loop down behind your back before you swing up at the ball. You want a controlled backswing on the overhead because the ball is falling from a greater height and at a faster speed than your service toss. *Don't wait for the ball to come to you.* Position yourself quickly and swing upward and forward to meet the ball *in line with your right shoulder*. When you let the ball get straight out in front, you prevent yourself from turning your front shoulder into the shot. Just as on the serve, you want to hit with nearly a 240-degree shoulder rotation so that you maintain rhythm and generate maximum power and accuracy — without trying to slug the ball. Just keep your chin up as you swing and try to maintain a continuous motion.

144

When preparing to hit an overhead, many players normally point their finger toward the dropping ball for tracking purposes. I happen to prefer that people point their elbow first, then point their finger, since this provides greater shoulder rotation and more rhythm.

A minor controversy here is whether you should track the lobbed ball with your left finger, or with the bent left elbow. I prefer to have people point initially with their left elbow — which facilitates a greater shoulder turn and promotes a smooth, baseball pitcher's motion — and then follow out with the finger. This provides a kinetic energy chain moving in sync with the hitting arm.

Players who immediately point their finger at the ball limit their front shoulder turn and diminish the amount of rhythm on their swing substantially. They have a tendency to get too stiff. However, I know I'm badly outnumbered by other coaches on this little point of technique, so if it's too uncomfortable to point with your elbow and you can't even find the ball, then stick with the finger point. But don't be rigid — point it comfortably so you maintain a relaxed upper body pivot.

Normally, you should hit overheads before the ball has bounced, in order to shorten the time your opponent has to get back in position and to increase your angle for hitting put-away shots. But lobs landing near the baseline or those hit extremely high and dropping on a vertical plane may be allowed to bounce.

145

Placement

When hitting overheads from a deep position, speed is not nearly as important as accuracy and depth, since you already have your opponent on the defensive. Just strive for depth and nobody will be able to hurt you. Neither do you want to attempt short angles, unless you are right on top of the net. Frankie Parker was the only person I've ever seen who could hit exceptionally short-angled balls on the overhead from a deep position. That's how rare it is.

However, downplaying the speed of your overhead does not mean you should ease off. Learn to hit all out — while maintaining your rhythm — instead of turning conservative. When you get into a choking, pressure situation it's much better to just be able to hit hard with your normal swing than to suddenly ease off. Early in the match don't be afraid to hit three or four balls out, trying to find your range, because once you find it you will be lethal. But if you turn conservative on this shot, a smart opponent will lob you to death because he knows you can't hurt him.

Although you want to adopt a service motion as you hit your overhead, stop thinking "serve distance" when you visualize your actual target areas. For example, when you serve you have 60 feet from the baseline to your opponent's service line. But when you hit an overhead from the baseline you gain another 18 feet to your opponent's baseline. Furthermore, when you hit overheads from between the baseline and the service line, you still have more distance to play with than when you serve. Unfortunately, many players feel they have decreased the distance available to them, and that they must hit down on the ball — with the result that they always walk up to the net to retrieve their shot. *So when you hit overheads between the baseline and the service line, remember to swing up and out at the ball in order to keep it deep.*

Never be discouraged if your overhead is going long. Depth is the name of this game, once you get it under control. The main reason you may be hitting long is that you are letting the ball get too far behind you as it comes down. To adjust, keep hitting up through the ball, but strive to contact the ball farther out in front of your hitting shoulder. If length is your only problem, you have good form and you're on the way to playing good tennis.

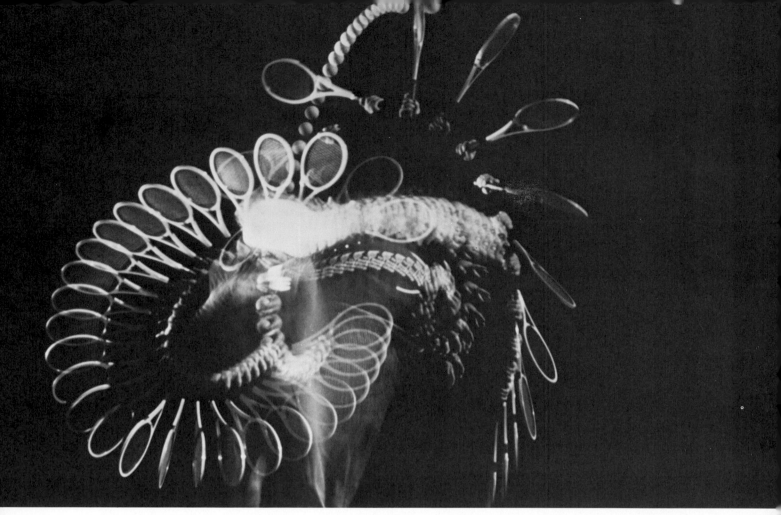

PHOTO BY JOHN G. ZIMMERMAN

In this single photograph of the complete service motion, notice the racket being drawn back starting at waist level while the left hand makes the toss. The racket then disappears behind the body for its loop, comes up and strikes the ball at the peak of the ball's arc, and then completes its follow-through. Observe how far out in front of the original body position the ball is hit, and how the hitting palm pronates (rotates) and faces downward toward the court. Notice also the fluidity of the swing. If the hitter had paused anywhere along the swing, the racket images would have all bunched up on top of one another. Finally, note how close the rackets are on the backswing and then how far apart they become near impact, which shows the tremendous speed being generated by the swing at that point. That's why you never want to break the kinetic-energy chain by pausing at any point during your swing.

Chapter Six

The Serve

WHATEVER YOU HAVE READ or have been told about the serve, reconsider everything in terms of the following physical law: to hit the ball hard, on a straight line, so that it clears the net by one to six inches and lands one inch inside your opponent's service line, the center of your racket must be ten feet in the air. But you must be about 6'6" or 6'7" tall to reach this height. If you want to have any margin of safety, you need to stretch 12 feet — or as high as a tennis court fence. That's why you must visualize yourself as *a midget hitting up on the ball, rather than a giant hitting down,* if you hope to hit the ball with speed *and* placement. You must learn to hit "up and out" with a degree of topspin, never down.

Maybe it's because I've been looking into belly buttons all my life, but I love to tell a guy who stands 6'5" and who tries to bomb his serve without any topspin, "Sorry, pal, you're too short to do that." Of course, he never believes me. For 20 years he's been slugging *down* on his first serve and hitting a line-drive shot that strikes fear in his opponents but rarely goes in. Then on his second serve he has the right idea but the wrong execution. Instead of fighting physical laws, he goes, "Dear God, please let this one go in so we can play the point," and he hits a helium ball that gravity brings down into play. Unfortunately, a smart opponent simply comes in and gives him an early lunch, so he loses either way.

What everybody needs to realize is that the first serve should have the same basic physical properties as the second. They are not two distinct swings. You have to bend the ball over the net to get it in play and there are only two ways to do this: (1) with topspin rotation, which forces the ball to bend with speed, or (2) with gravity, which produces the trusty patty-cake shot.

Another underlying premise is to think of the serve from the standpoint of throwing a baseball, instead of regarding it as a "down, up, down, up, down" motion. Get the feeling of both shoulders working together by rotating your upper body back on a horizontal plane so you never lose the kinetic energy generated by the loop of your hitting shoulder. The principle here is the same as in baseball: if you try to throw a ball without using shoulder rotation, you have only the power of your arm and the ball won't travel very fast.

A third important concept is that you don't have to go through a series of gyrations or a muscular kind of effort to hit the ball hard. The great servers conserve energy and generate all the power they need by synchronizing arm and body movements in a relaxed, flowing motion with a well-timed wrist snap at impact.

What always impressed me most about Pancho Gonzales' serve was not his speed, but the fact that fundamentally he had a flawless stroke that is without peer in the history of the game. He didn't have one hitch or one wasted motion; he never made any muscles work against him. He hit the ball harder than anyone, yet his motion was so fluid that he never had upper arm and shoulder problems. At 18-all in the third set, back in the days before the tie-breaker, he would still be hitting rhythmically and throwing in bombs.

Even when he was 41 years old, Gonzales was still the greatest server in the game because he generated his power with rhythm rather than brute strength. At the old Madison Square Garden, wrestling mats were hooked up in the corridors downstairs and you could find Pancho warming up there before a match, working on his serving motion. He would throw the ball up and just swing nice and easy, trying to make sure there were no hitches in his swing. Sometimes he wouldn't even use a ball; he would almost close his eyes and go through the serving motion, trying to sense the rhythm of his swing rather than the isolated movements of his body.

Out on the court, whatever he did while serving or preparing to serve was calculated to keep himself relaxed. He never bounced the ball hard on the court. He never gave his motion excess gyrations. When he walked to the line he would try to shrug his shoulders and shake his arms loose. He looked so calm you would think, "Why doesn't he get excited?" The first time one of my students, Jeff Austin, faced Gorgo's serve, his motion was so easy that Jeff thought Gorgo was going to take it easy on him 'cause he was just a kid. But when Gorgo uncorked the ball right down the middle, Jeff wasn't ready and it scared the heck out of him.

So remember Gonzales the next time you go to serve — not to try to duplicate his speed, but to copy his loose, flowing motion. You needn't go through a lot of grunting and groaning and weird, twisting gyrations in order to hit a good hard serve. You can generate terrific power with an easy, rhythmical

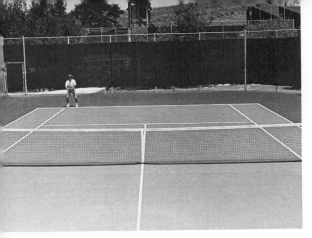

If your racket had eyes, here's what it would see on the serve when contacting the ball *ten* feet above court level. Not much room to hit down on the ball, is there? Most six-foot players, in fact, cannot reach ten feet in the air with the center of their racket face.

swing — *if* you know what you're doing. And that's what we're going to work on in this chapter.

The Grip

Many beginners prefer to use the regular forehand grip to hit a basic "flat" serve. But intermediate and advanced players should use the Continental, halfway between the Eastern forehand and Eastern backhand, in order to facilitate greater ball rotation with less stress on the wrist.

Some pros feel that everybody should start with a Continental, since this is the ultimate goal anyway. I like people to start out right, but I also want to motivate them to stay in the game. The Continental is just too doggone uncomfortable for many beginners because it places the face of the racket in an awkward position that requires a stronger wrist. Very often they can't even get the ball in play and you hear them complaining, "This is a stupid game — we can't even play a point when I serve." So instead of driving these people into another sport by insisting on the Continental, I let them use the forehand grip — but always with the understanding that if they start playing well they are going to have to change to the Continental if they want to remain competitive on their serve.

Whatever your level of play now, try the Continental. But if you can't handle it don't feel guilty. Just shift to the forehand grip and try to gradually move your palm towards the Continental as your wrist gets stronger and you develop a good serving motion. Later in this chapter I'll point out the limitations of the forehand grip and the strengths of the Continental.

The Swing: An Overview

When you begin your service motion, you need to coordinate two simultaneous movements — the ball toss and the action of your racket. For many people this is the single most difficult aspect of tennis technique. But then, the serve is the single most important stroke.

The toss is made by holding the ball near the fingertips, with the palm up, and then releasing the ball upwards with all fingers simultaneously. The ball is tossed to the peak of your racket's reach (some 27 inches out of your outstretched hand), at least one arm's length in front of your body and slightly to the right of your head. Beginners are taught to release the ball straight up, but as I'll point out, this inhibits a smooth, rolling motion by your shoulders. Try instead to rotate your left shoulder back towards the fence, in sync with the racket arm, until your opponent can see the back side of your front shoulder. At this point your ball-toss arm is approximately parallel to the baseline. Now raise this arm upward and out toward your opponent as you release the ball. This motion enables you to maintain a simultaneous rotation with both shoulders.

Meanwhile, the racket arm goes back toward the back fence until it reaches a horizontal position. Then begin rotating both shoulders forward and allow the hitting arm to break naturally at the elbow so that the racket falls to the small of your back. This loop by the racket — *if uninterrupted* — is one of the primary sources of power in your serve. Then stretch up to hit the ball with an upward and forward striking motion while the elbow and wrist snap out through the ball. The feeling you should get is hitting up at the ball or hitting out — but never down. Try to contact the ball approximately two feet in front of your body, off your hitting shoulder, so that your weight — and power — come forward naturally. Let your follow-through carry you into the court, even if you're planning to stay near the baseline.

Keep your chin up throughout the swing to help keep your body from sagging and pulling the ball down into the net, and keep your eyes focused on the ball until it has left the strings. At impact, your racket should be extended to the peak of your reach and the face pointed toward the target. But when you hit with a Continental grip, the racket actually carries out to the right of your target line, and then in an arc down the left side of your body.

Specific Elements

Ready Position

If you are serving from the right side (deuce court), stand as close to the center stripe as possible. This (1) facilitates hitting the ball to your opponent's backhand over the lower portion of the net, and (2) divides the baseline in half so you have less distance to run towards your opponent's return. When serving from the left side (ad court), you may stand about three steps from the center stripe to give yourself a better angle at your opponent's backhand corner. But you now lose the division of the baseline.

As you prepare to serve into the deuce court, stand with your left shoulder pointed out towards the left net post (if you are righthanded), with your feet comfortably spread, hands and racket held at waist level. Make sure you don't have one tense muscle. Have your arms literally go spaghetti. Exhale (biofeedback studies have shown that exhaling decreases the amount of muscular activity while inhaling increases it) and wherever your shoulders fall, leave them there. Tell yourself you're going to have the smoothest swing in the world. Remember, there's very little relationship between the power of your serve and all the pre-serve antics some people like to go through. Jimmy Connors' serve has never been his most powerful weapon, and even when he bounces the ball five or six times as he prepares to serve, he bounces it almost in the same way that he serves — with a rather rigid body.

Adopt a Baseball-Throwing Motion

Ideally, the tennis serve utilizes the basic principles of a baseball pitcher's motion. That's why I've said for many years that in terms of tennis, the PE instructor who teaches girls how to throw a ball properly is worth her weight in gold. Most boys learn how to throw a ball naturally as they grow up, but until recent years most girls were simply not taught the correct way to throw, or were discouraged from learning. Thus, when they turn to tennis as adults they have a lot of trouble coordinating the proper service motion.

A good pitcher gets 270 degrees of shoulder rotation on his delivery by pivoting with both shoulders on a horizontal level. He starts off by turning his back to the batter, and then he uncoils his body in the following sequence as he pitches the ball: his front leg comes forward, followed by his hips, shoulders, elbow, and wrist. This unbroken sequence of body movements (also known as a kinetic energy chain) is what supplies his rhythm and power, and this upper body rotation is exactly what you want on the serve.

From a starting position, take your hitting hand back at about waist level as you turn away from your opponent with a horizontal pivot. But unlike the pitcher, keep your weight evenly distributed and don't rock back. Then, as you turn your hitting shoulder in toward the toss and your hips uncoil, let your elbow break and your hitting wrist relax, and the energy generated by your shoulder turn will form a perfect loop motion with the racket. *No*

(1)

(2)

(3)

(6)

(7)

(8)

(4)

(5)

(9)

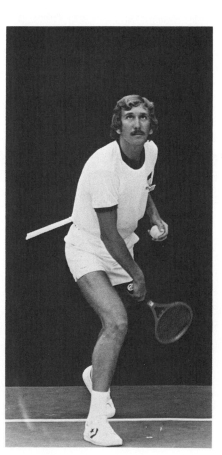

(10)

The Serve

(1) The hitter is relaxed just before activating his service swing. No fancy movements are necessary. His elbows rest comfortably at his sides. The toes of his left foot point to the right net post. His back right foot is parallel to the baseline. The ruler attached to his back will help you recognize the extent of body rotation. (2) The advanced player turns his body and both arms to the right, as if to throw a ball. Instead of rocking back he turns on a horizontal plane, with his weight remaining evenly distributed. (3) This is a profile view of the initial turn. The ball-toss arm is pointed toward the right sideline rather than toward the opponent, which provides the hitter with a greater shoulder-turn and thus more power when he unwinds his body. Some professionals actually gain as much as 90 degrees more body coil. Also notice the ruler: it should not dip significantly off this horizontal level until the hitter stretches up to hit the ball. (4) This is where most servers get into trouble. Instead of starting to unwind their shoulders horizontally when their backswing reaches shoulder level, they wait until the racket drops behind the small of their back. This costs them rhythm and power. To correct this error, stick a tennis ball in a fence at shoulder level. Step away from the fence and start your backswing. When the racket head reaches the ball in the fence, start turning your body forward into the ball. (5) Allow the racket to continue its upward backswing as you release the ball. If your hitting elbow is relaxed, the forward body- and shoulder-turn will automatically enable your arm to produce a perfect loop — and you'll never again have to try to "scratch your back" with the racket. Just allow your entire arm to "go spaghetti" when it reaches the point shown in this photograph. (6) The hitter's right side is rotating forward (notice the horizontal ruler) and the hitting arm is ready to thrust the racket upward and forward. This hitter has the palm of his hitting hand facing upward more than most players. If you wish to put significant spin on the ball, the palm should face more toward the back of your head at this point. (7) The service toss is only a racket's length (27 inches) out of the server's hand and to the right of his head. He keeps his chin up so as not to drag his body down on the serve. (8) A rear view of the proper ball toss to the hitter's right side, with the racket going up to strike the ball as the racket face moves from left to right. (9) Contact is made out in front and on the right side of the hitter's head. (10) The hitter's back foot has stepped across the baseline and the racket follow-through has crossed his left side.

intentional effort should be made to form a loop with your hitting arm. Let it flow naturally, so that your hip rotation and the shoulder roll is followed by the elbow, followed by the wrist. Hip, shoulder, elbow, wrist . . . and then the back foot moving forward into the court, the same as a pitcher. Rosie Casals has this motion and that's why — at 5'2" — she can stand up there and serve as hard as most men.

Serving with this type of motion sounds pretty easy to people until they get out on the court and give it a try. Then they have to overcome either their lack of a natural throwing motion or what they've previously been told or have learned about the serve.

For one thing, you can't use a beginner's toss and expect to develop a continuous motion. By failing to rotate away from the net with your front shoulder, you limit yourself to 180 degrees of rotation — instead of gaining an extra 60 to 90 degrees of rotation with a front-shoulder turn. Players who throw the toss straight up can usually be identified by stiff upper body movements.

Second, most people have been told to start with both arms held high, and then to "go down with both arms . . . up with both arms . . . then get that racket down and scratch your back," at which point they can expect to turn in and unleash this gigantic serve. *But when they swing this way, they're dead.* First of all, they've destroyed the kinetic energy chain, leaving only the power in their arm to salvage any speed on the ball. And second, by forcing their arm down behind their back to form a loop, their arm goes rigid, when the goal is to have it become spaghetti-like.

A similar problem occurs when you drop your hitting elbow as you draw the racket back or while forming the loop. I call this the "chain-puller's syndrome" or the "train-conductor's swing" — pull on the whistle, "toot, toot!" This action destroys the continuous swing that you seek.

The dropped elbow and the down-up-down motion can be traced back in large part to the artist who designed one of the original serving trophies. The model was Les Stoeffen, Sr., who teamed with Don Budge to win the Wimbledon doubles in 1934, and who had absolutely classic form. Unfortunately, the artist didn't know the first thing about tennis and he didn't like the way Stoeffen held his elbow high and his shoulder up on the backswing. So, for artistic reasons, he arbitrarily put Stoeffen's elbow down. It's a beautiful pose, but as a model sitting in trophy cases everywhere, it has done more to ruin good serves over the years than any other thing. If Les Stoeffen had actually served that way he wouldn't have beaten Bertha Finkenbaum.

This player is trying to make an intentional loop behind his back by dropping his elbow in the classic "chain puller's syndrome." Although he forms a beautiful straight line from his left hand down to his right elbow, this isn't how you loop. You must keep the hitting arm on a horizontal plane just before activating the loop, and let the *shoulder-turn* form a natural loop. The elbow should never drop.

The Toss

Since the beginner's toss inhibits a smooth, rolling motion by your shoulders, I like to have people learn the advanced toss as soon as possible — and preferably without ever trying the beginner's toss. Why start with a technique that is so limiting to a good consistent serve, when the advanced toss is really no more difficult to master? Both tosses try to release the ball to the same point out in front, but the advanced toss enables your shoulders to work together and thereby generate considerably more power. The key difference is that beginners are taught to throw the ball straight up from their

A dropped elbow on the forward service swing often results in a "patty-cake" serve in club tennis. Dropping the elbow costs you all your power at that point, which makes it much more difficult to hit a hard serve.

outstretched arm, while advanced players turn their front shoulder and draw the ball back before releasing it up and out.

However you approach the toss, think about standardizing a smooth *arm lift* and just opening the fingers to release the ball. Let your arm do the work, and not your wrist or your palm. The arm won't produce drastic variations in the toss, but a little flick of the wrist can throw the radius off drastically. Nor do you want to have a death clutch on the ball. Just hold it lightly and keep the heel of your hand *raised* to insure that the ball keeps moving up and out. If you let the heel sink, the ball will come back behind you. See for yourself. If you release the ball when your arm is parallel to the ground, the ball should fall back in your hand or slightly in front of it. If the ball comes back too far, then the heel may have been down. To prevent the heel from sinking, keep the arm moving up in a flowing motion; don't let it suddenly stop as the ball is leaving the fingers.

Trying to coordinate a consistent toss with the stroke is the toughest part of the game for many people. In fact, we've had people at the tennis college who are so nervous or confused that they can't even release the ball from their fingers as they bring the racket back. So I tread quietly here because I've learned that once people get the fear of an inadequate ball toss, they have to work extremely hard to overcome it.

Nevertheless, the fact remains: you will never develop a consistent serve until you learn to throw your toss in the same place every time. *It takes a perfect toss to effect a perfect swing.* You can swing beautifully, but if your toss goes in a different place every time, you will have to adjust your swing accordingly to get the racket to hit the ball. Yet people will throw the ball behind their head, then blithely say, "No problem, I'll just make this little adjustment." They have a lot of interesting twists to their stroke but they don't win too many matches because variety kills them. You want to make the same old boring toss to the same spot on every serve so that you can hit the same old boring winner. Ideally, this spot should be slightly to the right of your head, about a racket's length from your outstretched free hand, and as far out in front of your body as possible, without disturbing the rhythm of your service motion.

When you adjust your swing to accommodate a bad toss — instead of devel-

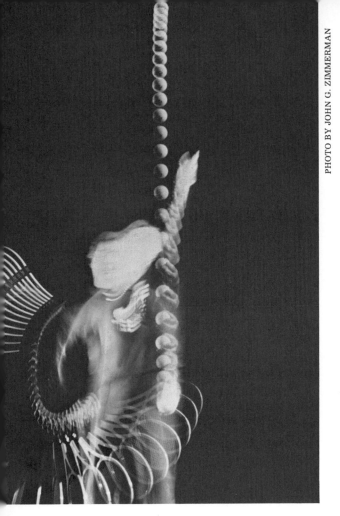

PHOTO BY JOHN G. ZIMMERMAN

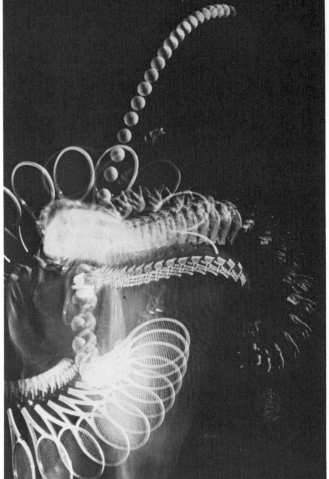

PHOTO BY JOHN G. ZIMMERMAN

this photograph of the beginner's toss, notice how e arm follows the ball up on just about a straight ie. Learning to throw the ball straight up is extreme-difficult, even for advanced players who try to monstrate the toss to beginners.

On the advanced service toss, which requires a ball thrown farther toward the net and increased shoulder rotation, notice how the arm of the throwing hand is up near the head before the hand actually releases the ball, thus shortening the length of the toss and making it more consistent. Observe how the ball arcs out in front of the body so that the hitter can swing up and out and then follow through with a natural and forward movement. Also note that his chain remains *up* throughout the swing.

oping a perfect toss to accommodate the swing — you defeat yourself in three ways:

a. Swinging at a toss that is behind your head or straight out in front of your body will stop your natural shoulder action and prevent a proper follow-through by forcing you to either pull your hitting elbow in, arch your back, or make a severe wrist adjustment.

b. Your hitting arm takes a terrific beating and can develop tennis elbow. If you throw the ball behind your body, your arm must take nearly all the strain without any help from a rotating shoulder.

c. Swinging at a ball that's in a different place every time requires a different set of muscles, and tennis is a muscle-memory sport. You must groove your swing and master a toss to accommodate that swing.

Therefore, if you are serving in a match and you don't like your toss, catch the ball and try again. *Your opponent cannot force you to swing at a bad toss.* There isn't a rule that allows your opponent to say, "I'm giving you

Keep the heel of your throwing hand raised during the toss and you'll seldom throw the ball back behind your head.

159

There's no need to swing at a lousy toss. Let it fall and then start over again.

A ball needs to be thrown only 27 inches from your outstretched hand for a perfect serve.

three tries and then it's a fault." The only rule is that play must be continuous. So if you are playing in a *tournament* and you spend 15 minutes trying to make the right toss, your opponent can call over an official who has the power to tell you, "Play the next ball or it's a fault."

Another myth that helps destroy good serves everywhere is the statement, "Give yourself plenty of time on the toss." This leads people to throw the ball so high that it takes two days to come down; if they play in a high wind they may never see the ball again. But remember, all you need to do is throw the ball 27 inches out of your outstretched hand — to the peak of where you can reach with your racket as you contact the ball. This will give you plenty of time to complete a continuous serving motion. John Newcombe, one of the best servers in history, hits the ball precisely when it stops moving upwards; when his toss reaches its peak, his racket is there to meet it. Roscoe Tanner also tosses the ball to about 27 inches, and he has one of the fastest, most accurate serves in the game.

Why do you want to hit the ball at it's peak? What's wrong with tossing the ball high so that you can marshal your body for a gigantic hitting effort?

When you hit the ball at its peak you dictate a smooth, continuous swing.

A ball tossed directly over your head can cause an awkward wrist and elbow position on the hit. . .

. . . or can force you into a bonebreaking back bend . . .

. . . or can require you to have a wrist as strong as steel.

Each little section of your serve should be part of a kinetic chain that builds up energy and reaches maximum speed where it is really meaningful: at impact. Think of your swing as sounding like a smooth-running motor that starts slowly and then quickly increases speed without any hesitation. Then think of a whirring motor trying to stay in sync with the average player's herky-jerky motion.

When you throw the ball too high you must wait for it to drop, which means that somewhere along the swing you must build in braking motions. You may drop your hitting elbow going back or you may pause with the racket behind your back until you know it's time to go up after the ball. But when your swing stops or slows down in any manner, you must go like crazy and expend more energy just to regain the speed you had built up. You could even *start* your motion with the racket behind your back and serve just as well, if not better. I've had people stand flat-footed at the baseline, facing their target, and hit harder than they ever have in their life, just by swinging with a snappy wrist and a continuous rolling motion by their shoulders — and using no footwork whatsoever.

Theoretically, if you are serving with a continuous motion and you throw the ball higher than the peak of your outstretched racket, you should miss the ball. But most people won't do this. Instead of learning to lower their toss, they continue to stop or slow down their swing. Thus I prefer to have people throw their toss too low rather than too high, because *a low toss forces them to maintain a quick, easy shoulder roll.* Also, you physicists know that an initial one-inch error by your wrist is magnified on a high toss and that the lower the toss, the more inaccurate you can be without paying an awful price.

Tossing the ball out in front of your body, but in line with your hitting shoulder at impact, is crucial in getting the most out of your serve. By keeping the ball out in front you achieve three things: (a) you maintain a natural flowing motion without any fancy "adjustments," (b) you enhance the ball-trajectory angle, because geometrically, the farther inside the court you are, the less chance you have of hitting the tape of the net, and (c) your front shoulder turns naturally and your racket comes down to the left side of your body, so that you are ready to move into position for your opponent's return.

Try to go too far forward on your toss; get the feeling that you're going to fall on your face. By stretching out over the baseline you enable your wrist

161

to snap into the ball ahead of your body, and not straight above your head, where all power is lost.

Initially, don't allow the fear of foot-faulting — touching the playing surface before contact with the ball — to destroy the rhythm you want to develop on your serve. You need to develop respect for the foot-fault rule, but first get your rhythm down. I see beginners all the time who are afraid to even step over the line after they've served. They throw the ball straight up and they do nothing with their shoulders. You can see them thinking, "Don't go across the line," and their whole movement comes to a sudden halt. Their serve is lousy but you hear them saying, "Well, I never foot-fault."

The Racket Arm and Loop

You should take your racket back at the same time you start to make your toss, even though it *feels* like you're not going to have enough time for the racket to complete its loop behind your back and still contact the ball at the peak of its toss. That's why you've always heard, "Throw the ball high and give yourself plenty of time." But I've filmed serves at 10,000 frames a second and the racket can make its loop and go up to strike the ball before the ball has even dropped an inch.

To facilitate the loop, keep your palm *down* as you draw the racket back, and keep your elbow *up* once you begin the forward motion. When your hitting shoulder starts rotating forward, have your arm break at the elbow — sufficiently to squeeze a finger — so that the racket falls naturally behind the small of your back. Don't force the racket down or dwell upon what you are trying to do because this will ruin the looseness you seek. Then turn in and stretch up to strike the ball, with the elbow and wrist snapping in a whiplash-type of motion.

A good drill for practicing the motion I seek is to stick a ball in a fence the exact height of your shoulders. Stand away with your back to the fence and begin your service swing by taking your racket back toward the fence. When your racket reaches the ball in the fence, rotate your shoulders forward and let your arm relax. Your rotating shoulder action will automatically form the loop you seek, *if* your hitting arm is completely relaxed.

Ideally, if you start your swing slowly with a loose, spaghetti-like motion, your racket should be reaching maximum speed as it approaches the ball. Have somebody watch to see if your racket comes into focus as it makes the loop. If it does, then you know you've slowed up and are losing your kinetic

Practice Tip: A Drill for the Toss

If you have a consistent toss, you should be able to point to the spot where the ball reaches its highest point for an imaginary serve. Bobby Riggs would even practice serving blindfolded in order to groove his toss, and he won a lot of bets as a result. But when I ask people at the tennis college, "Where do you throw the ball?" they say, "Somewhere out there." Well, "out there" isn't good enough if you are really serious about consistency. So try this drill to help you find the specific spot where you want to throw your toss on each serve.

Get a friend to stand on the other end of the court as you begin to serve. Have three or four balls with you. Now keep your chin up as you hit and do not look at your friend — just concentrate on where the toss is going, and where you contact it. Purposely throw the first ball straight above your head, but still hit *up* on the ball. Have your friend yell where the ball lands — "It's 40 feet out," or whatever. Then throw the second ball a little farther out in front and hit up through the ball while trying to record where you make contact. Now your friend may yell, "It's 15 feet out." Keep throwing the ball farther out in front until your friend says, "It's in by a foot." Then mark that imaginary spot where you contacted the ball, and start practicing to have your toss end there every time. Don't hit the ball unless you throw it to that spot. If you have a proper swing, that's your spot for the rest of your life.

energy; but if your racket is a blur, then you know you are generating real speed.

You want the racket traveling fast while your muscles take it easy. The job of your biceps, for example, is to flex your arm inward. If you tighten it, straining for more power, you simply oppose your own serve.

Your Head

Think about *hitting up at the ball with the chin up,* because everybody has a tendency to pull down on the serve. For one thing, few people respect how high the net actually is, and for another, when the chin drops, your stomach muscles tend to relax, thus pulling your racket head down. Keeping the chin up also helps keep your eyes focused on the ball. I once climbed up into the rafters to photograph John Newcombe's service motion, and as he made his toss and contacted the ball, his eyes were looking straight up at me, not out at the target.

Impact and Follow-Through

When you go up to contact the ball, try to think of hitting to the sky (or the roof) and let the wrist snap bring the ball down. You want to be aiming up at the ball and swinging up, since you are too short to hit down. If you hold a Continental grip, your racket face will actually go from left to right (inside-out) at contact, while the wrist makes a 180-degree turn.

Experiment with the ball toss and note how your hitting wrist breaks naturally much farther out in front of your body than you might have imagined. Try to contact the ball approximately two feet out in front so that your right foot (if you are righthanded) will come over the baseline to support your body weight as it moves forward and to help keep good balance. Some top players even contact the ball as much as four to five feet in front of them. Physicist Pat Keating did a study which shows that if you can learn to get way out in front on the toss, you will give yourself a chance to swing slightly down on the ball. But if you stand one foot behind the baseline and toss the ball straight up, the center of your racket has to be 12 feet high in order to hit down.

Good servers don't stop with the fall-in step. They take two more steps forward and then bring both feet together with a stutter-step, or check-step. At this point the serve should be on their opponent's racket and they are in position to break in any direction with equal ease to handle the return. John Newcombe moves in farther off his serve than any player I've ever seen. His long strides often take him to within a foot of the service line on his third step, or about six feet ahead of most other players, pros included.

Consequently, therefore, you gain three advantages when you contact the ball in front of your body: (1) you can be shorter and hit the ball harder with greater safety, (2) all of your energy is going into the shot, which gives you a faster first step, and (3) you can take longer strides — and thus get closer to the net on your third step — because you're already on the move.

Understanding Ball Rotation on the Serve

The four variations of the serve all have spin, so what we're really talking about is the angle at which the racket strikes the ball, and the degree of ball rotation. First is the "flat" serve, which has the racket contacting the back side of the ball and continuing forward and slightly to the right of the target line. Second is the "topspin" serve, ideally contacted at about a 45-degree angle, halfway between a full vertical and a horizontal plane. Third is the "slice" serve, which is produced by a racket moving horizontally left to right and brushing the *back side* of the ball; it's a myth that you actually come around the outside of the ball. And fourth is the "American Twist," which is contacted with a severe upward lift that produces almost vertical rotation on the ball. I hate to teach this serve, however, because it places too much strain on your back and the elbow of your hitting arm. The American Twist can make you a hero in Pismo Beach, but it will keep you off the tournament circuit — and you may eventually have to learn to play with your other arm.

The Flat Serve

In reality, the "flat" serve is a misnomer, since nobody can produce a ball that is hit without rotation. But the flat serve is hit with the least amount. Beginners who don't hit hard can make the racket follow straight behind the ball after impact, but for most players the racket strikes the ball going from left to right, imparting a small amount of slice. When this serve is hit with an Eastern forehand grip, you can't make a natural snap of the wrist at impact in order to supply spin, and thus you can never rotate the ball hard

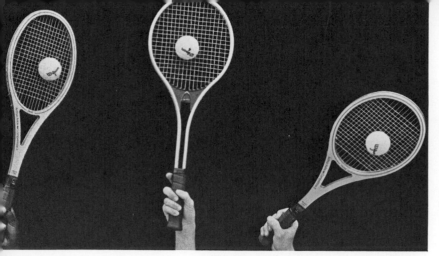

The racket face on the left is moving across the back side of the ball on an almost horizontal plane and will produce sidespin, or "slice." The middle racket is moving forward and striking the back side of the ball, which will produce a "flat" serve. The racket on the right is rising while brushing the ball at a 45-degree angle. This will produce the typical topspin serve.

enough — by brushing up — to ever be very effective. Furthermore, to hit this serve hard and still keep it in play, you have to thread a very fine needle.

The Typical Topspin Serve

Eventually you will want to use the Continental grip so that you can hit your serves with considerable topspin, and thereby slug the ball as hard as you want, while bringing it down in your opponent's service box.

The principle of applying topspin to the serve is basically the same as on the forehand and backhand groundstrokes. You have to swing from low to high and brush the back side of the ball at about a 45-degree angle, with the racket moving from left to right for righthanders. This is why you must use the Continental grip. It gives you greater wrist flexibility and automatically places the racket on the right plane to facilitate increased ball rotation.

Contrary to popular opinion, the racket does not go over the ball at contact but hits the back side. Even top professionals advance the theory that on the advanced serve you want to get the racket to come over the top right side of the ball to impart topspin. The problem with this concept is that you guarantee a double fault. You're not even tall enough to see over the net and yet some pros would now have you put a roof over the ball, forgetting that you can't hit down on the ball and get it in play unless you're as tall as the average pro basketball forward. I'll admit, coming over the ball is the *feeling* you seek. But I teach this only as a sensation to help you produce the correct swing, with the clear understanding that this is not what actually happens. You must hit "up and out," visualizing a dot on the back of the ball rotating from the lower left to the upper right — or from about 8 o'clock to 2 o'clock on an imaginary clock.

If you have been serving with a forehand grip and you switch to the Continental, don't feel like a klutz if you suddenly can't get your serve in play. It's only natural to experience an awkward sensation — you're now brushing up against the ball with very little racket face meeting the surface of the ball. Furthermore, you are turning your palm outward, at a 90-degree angle away from the flight of the ball, whereas the natural tendency is to want to turn your palm in the direction where the ball is going. When you hold a Continental and let your palm turn in the ball's direction, the ball goes to the left fence. If this is your problem, then concentrate on keeping the face of the racket brushing up and across the ball and carrying out to the right.

A strong wrist will help you on the Continental, yet there are people with fairly weak wrists who know how to snap their wrist into the ball and produce a strong serve. And there are players with strong wrists who still feel awkward using the Continental.

The Slice Serve

Like a curveball in baseball, a pure slice serve can be a valuable weapon, *if* you can make the racket strike the center of the back side of the ball while the racket moves across on a horizontal plane. Serving from the deuce (right) court, a righthanded player can break off a ball that drives his opponent off the court and forces a weak, out-of-position return. Since the slice serve has a lower trajectory than topspin, it bounces lower and can be particularly effective against a tall player who hates to bend, or anybody who has slow lateral movement. Jack Kramer, who developed the most notorious slice of any player I've ever seen, could move you to the side fence on a 60-foot-wide court and take you right out of the point, even if you managed to get the ball back.

Still, tempting as the slice serve might appear, it raises dangerous problems for most righthanded players. For example, if you are a righthander serving to a righthander, you must slice the ball to your opponent's forehand, which is normally his stronger return side, since it facilitates a topspin return that bounces at your feet. Thus you should never use the slice unless you are (1) positive your opponent has a weaker forehand than backhand, (2) positive you will ace your opponent, or (3) positive that you will pull him so far out of play — when serving from the deuce court — that he'll hit a weak return and give you an open court for your own return. If you're not positive you can achieve this with your slice serve, then concentrate on serving with more topspin to your opponent's backhand corner. The same principles apply in doubles.

Most people tend to hit a mixture of topspin and slice. When they brush up at the ball, they leave the horizontal plane but they fail to achieve the 45-degree angle needed for proper topspin. Thus, they may spread an opponent fairly wide but the ball has a more horizontal bounce when it hits, which gives their opponent an easier return to handle with their forehand. Similarly, most righthanders have trouble serving the ball to the backhand

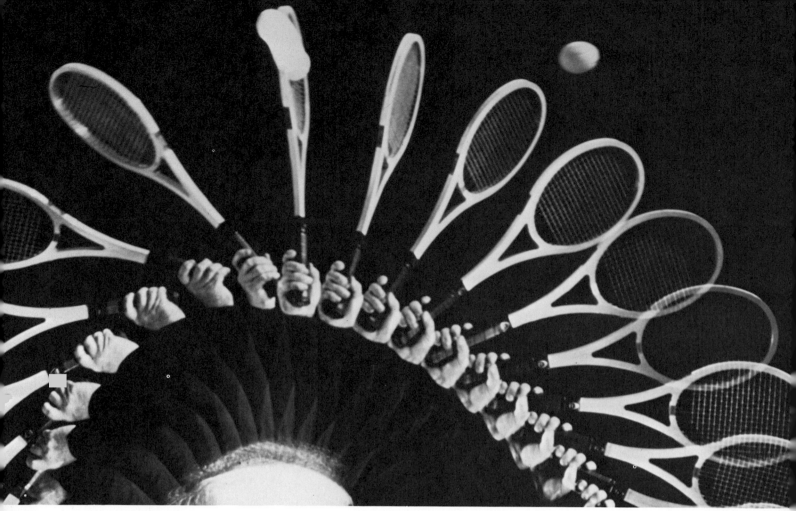

PHOTO BY JOHN G. ZIMMERMAN

This close-up highlights the hitting hand to show the rotation of the palm immediately after contact (notice how the thumb rolls under). Medical doctors who have seen this photograph love the way it shows where the palm begins its downward rotation (pronation) and how much it actually turns. This is where tennis elbow can develop unless you learn to serve with a shoulder roll so that the hitting arm doesn't have to absorb all this stress.

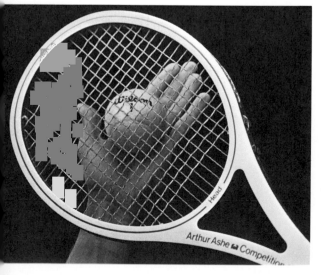

Most beginners and intermediates who hold a Continental grip on the serve have a hard time visualizing the position of their racket face when it contacts the ball, and experiencing that sensation. So try this drill. Hold a ball in your left hand high over your head and hold the racket in a serving position. Place the racket face against the ball and roll the ball up and over the fingers at about a 2-o'clock position. You never actually hit over the ball, but this is exactly the feeling you will experience when hitting a proper topspin serve.

corner from the deuce court because they have some slice to their serve. What they need is a more vertical upward swing so they can break the ball toward their opponent's backhand.

People are always asking me, "Why does a lefthander have a natural slice serve?" They think there's something physiological in the wrist of the left-hander that allows him to throw in a bigger slice. But that isn't the case. It's simply that the lefthander grows up playing primarily against righthanders, and he discovers at an early age that if he can slice his serve, he can spread his righthanded opponent wide to the backhand side. So he starts working earlier on slicing the ball, whereas the righthander is penalized for slicing the ball to another righthander, unless he can break that ball off horizontally.

One advantage of a good slice serve for the righthander comes when he plays an opponent who has a strong forehand and a much weaker backhand. Most people in this situation make the error of trying desperately to serve to that weak backhand side, but their opponent keeps running around and hitting his powerful forehand. Instead, to get the ball to this person's back-hand — serving from the deuce court — here's your strategy:

First stretch him wide to his forehand with a slice serve. That sounds sui-cidal, but remember that very few players in the history of tennis have been able to hit outright winners from the baseline, especially when they're pulled off court. If your opponent gets the ball back, return it sharply to his back-hand and he'll normally be too far out of position to recover with a forehand.

This strategy can backfire, of course, if you hit a weak slice serve that fails to move your opponent far enough off the court. Then he can knock off a big forehand and still protect his weak backhand.

The American Twist Serve

A lot of men have become enamored with this serve, for it can be lethal in intermediate tennis with its high-bouncing kick. But go to a pro tennis tour-nament and see for yourself just how few players actually use this serve. They know that a big kick doesn't bother good players. These players just laugh, step into the ball, and knock your brains out because your serve has lost too much speed.

The main reason I'm against this stroke, however, is that it can lead to ten-nis elbow. Generally, the ball is thrown directly over your head or some de-gree behind you, meaning your body must bend backwards in order to fix the racket on a horizontal plane before it starts its forward and vertical lifting motion. This in turn "freezes" your shoulder rotation and forces you to hit the ball with a sophisticated wrist and elbow snap. By halting your muscular system as you turn in to hit the ball, you have to rely on the strength of your arm to supply all your power. Placing these excessive pressures upon an elbow that is already severely twisted can cause a great deal of damage. Tony Roche used the American Twist and was one of the world's top players for a number of years — until finally he practically ruined his arm.

Strategy and the Serve

Target Areas

Once you can get your serve over the net and in play, start concentrating on at least *aiming* for your opponent's backhand corner. There are three basic reasons for this:

a. Most people have less accuracy and power — not to mention a basic lack of confidence — hitting from their backhand side.

b. You have to react faster on the backhand than on the forehand in order to meet the ball out in front of your body. Lateness is more damaging on the backhand, and most people fail to react fast enough.

c. From the records I kept in pro tennis, the chances are 85 out of 100 that your opponent's backhand will produce a higher ball, because players who are late can only underspin. Thus, if you are attacking the net, a high service return gives you a much easier volley. But if you hit to your opponent's forehand and he produces topspin, the ball may go over and down at your feet and you will be forced to hit from a lifting position, thereby losing your tactical advantage. Maybe you're thinking, "Yeh, Vic, but I like to serve to the forehand to keep my opponent honest." My argument is, "Why let him off the hook? If you are beating his brains out by attacking the backhand, why give him a chance to get his confidence back by letting him hit his forehand?"

The basic principle should be: *always serve to the shot which will produce the highest and weakest ball in return*. Thus, the only times you should try to hit to the forehand are when you're positive you're going to ace your opponent because he's cheating too far to his backhand side, when you're positive his forehand is weaker than his backhand, or when you're positive you're going to pull him so far off the court that you will have an easy put-away volley if he returns your serve.

I talked earlier about how Gonzales could hit with speed, and could also place the ball beautifully and move you far out of court. But what the players of his era remember most is the fact that he got a greater percentage of first serves in play than anybody. That was the real pressure he put on you. He was one of the few guys you had to play hard on the first serve every time because it usually went in, whereas against most players you had a tendency to relax on first serves. In fact, he produced a lot of service-return errors simply because his opponents were so tight and nervous, knowing what was coming.

Yet back in the early 1950s, when Gonzales was winning every tournament on the pro circuit, the other pros managed to convince themselves that they could handle Gonzales if he didn't have the big serve. So they came up with what they thought would neutralize Gorgo's greatest weapon: a one-ball-serve tournament. They figured that with only one serve, Gorgo would have to ease off and hit like the rest of them, and then if they could keep the ball in play they could beat him. Jack March bought the idea and organized the tournament in Cleveland. The other pros were so happy they could hardly wait — they were going to knock off the King.

Well, Gonzales never had such an easy time winning a tournament. He was so sound on his service stroke that he was even *more* effective than everyone else with just one ball. Before the tournament was even dreamed up, he was already in the habit — mentally — of serving only one ball; when he walked up to serve, he never thought about serving two balls. But the rest of the guys were going, "Dear God, I've only got one!" and then hitting the most pitiful serves in the world. They single-faulted the tournament away.

Taking the Net

If you're a typical beginner or intermediate player, you should simply serve and stay back, then wait until you get a short ball before you try to take the net. Most tournament players, however, don't even wait around for a short ball — they serve and attack automatically so that they can volley their opponent's return. They say, "If I don't go, my opponent is coming to the net against me." But the pros are different from you and me. They know that when they go to the net on their serve they are going behind a weapon. Plus they are playing seven days a week and are in good shape. So before you try to emulate them, you need three things:

a. A good first serve. You can't attack behind a helium ball. That's like throwing a hand grenade and running underneath it.

b. A strong volley. This enables you to defend yourself in that no-man's-land between the baseline and the net.

c. A sound heart. If you're not in shape and you try to attack the net on every serve, your friends will be carrying you out prone after five or six games.

If you have the ingredients to play a serve-and-attack game, then your footwork after the follow-through is crucial. Remember the three key steps after you fall in, ending with the little stutter-step as you bring both feet together momentarily in order to prepare for your opponent's return shot. Some people get so stoked up when they serve — "Attack, attack, you little devil!" — that they go barreling in without stopping. Then their opponent hits an angled passing shot and all they can do is salute the ball as it goes by: "Terrific shot, Bertha."

Okay, so you serve and move in three steps, ready to break in any direction. Then what do you do? It's simple: you either move forward on the diagonal to hit an approach volley, or you retreat for a lob. If your opponent drives the ball, break in that direction instantly; don't hesitate or you'll get trapped down around your feet by half-volleys. *Your goal is to get ahead of the service line to make your second play.* If you advance that deep, the chances are enormous that you will hit your second shot while it is in the air, before it bounces (an approach volley). This means you won't get funny hops and you can contact the ball above the level of the net.

When you get to the ball, try to punch the volley to your opponent's weak side (which again is usually the backhand side) and move up to take the net, halfway between the service line and the net, to the side of the center stripe to which you hit the ball. Remembering what I discussed in the previous chapter, if you hit a deep volley your opponent is in serious trouble. He will have only four different options: lob, hit a passing shot straight down the line, hit a short-angled topspin shot to keep it away from your lunge at the net, or hit right at your navel. All of these strokes are tough for most players to execute, with or without pressure.

Whether you're a beginner or an experienced player whose philosophy has always been to serve and stay back, don't be frightened off by the footwork and exertion required to play like the pros. Rushing the net at every opportunity is critical if you want to raise the level of your game, maximize the physical conditioning that tennis offers, and add a new dimension of excitement. You've elected to go for the home run ball because statistics show that you will normally win or lose the point on the very next shot.

Therefore, when practicing — and even during a low-pressure match — try to fall in as you serve and move into your stutter-step position. Then as your serve improves, your footwork will already be ingrained and you won't have to break the habit of automatically staying back.

The Second Serve

Nearly everybody asks me, "How do I keep from choking on my second serve?" They talk like they own a good second serve, if only pressure wouldn't interfere. But I've found over the years that *most people choke simply because they don't have the stroke.* Even without stress they can't get their second serve in play. Furthermore, their first serve isn't very good, so why should their second one be any better?

Another reason most people don't have a good second serve is that they haven't related the first one to the second as identical strokes. Usually they simply think in terms of speed differentiation — "the first one didn't go in, so now I have to ease off on the second" — when actually it's a ball rotation differentiation.

For example, I think the serve should always be an all-out but properly controlled effort on *both* attempts. This is why I like to have people learn to hit with a Continental grip so that they can serve with speed and control under pressure: all they need to know is at what upward angle they should brush the ball to impart topspin.

Let's say your first serve has gone long. If you hit with a Continental, you know that you can swing just as hard on the second serve, except that you want the face of your racket and the stroking pattern to be more vertical so that you can produce greater topspin. This causes the ball to react with a greater arc and brings it down more quickly into play.

That's why you always want to hit your first serve deep. If it goes long, you know precisely the amount of error you made, and you have the confidence to swing just as hard on the second serve as long as you increase the amount of topspin on the ball. (If you hit at the same speed, increasing the number of revolutions per second of the ball increases the spin and thus slows the ball down because you get less ball depression.)

Here's how most people go wrong. If they hit the "flat" serve with a

(1)

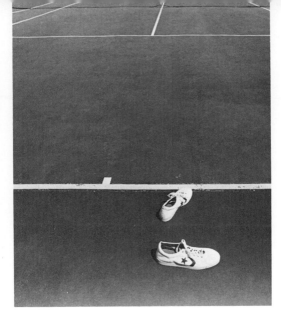

(2)

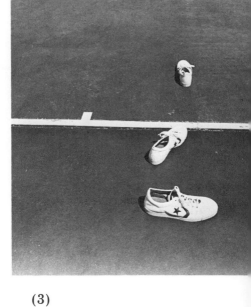

(3)

(5)

Footwork on the Serve

If you serve properly, your follow-through should carry down your left side, and your right foot will step naturally across the baseline (as in the third photograph) — as the hitter has done here. Then you want to keep moving forward: left foot, right foot, and left foot, at which point both feet come together with a "stutter-step." This leaves you ready to break in any direction. Some students tell us that they understand the principle better by seeing only the shoes move. The final shoe is as far as any of the pros can reach before they come to a momentary ready position. But that shoe should be your goal.

(4)

(6)

(7)

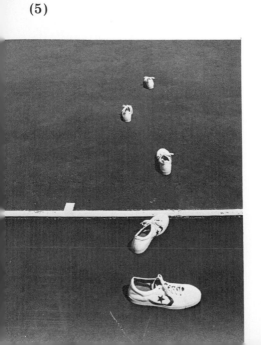

forehand grip, and their first serve goes long, their only alternative is to reduce the speed of their swing. But it's very difficult to gauge speed reduction, especially when you have a choking feeling. It's far safer, I feel, to be able to hit out and hit hard, by just using a system which makes the ball spin faster. Better to throw the ball out in front and hit with excessive topspin — knowing that you can never hit too hard — than to throw the ball straight up and think to yourself, "Dear God, let this go in."

People should take the speed off the ball not by slowing down their swing but by increasing the vertical lift of the racket. Having to swing softly or daintily under pressure, when you really want to hit all-out, is one of the worst feelings in the world. That's why many of the men who play club mixed doubles, as well as pros who play against celebrities, serve so poorly. They don't want to kill anybody, so they try to hit patty-cake serves and end up double-faulting all the time because they reduce the speed of their body and arm motion rather than just increasing the spin on the ball.

A second common problem occurs with those who hit a topspin serve on their first attempt. If the ball goes long, most people have a tremendous fear of also knocking the second serve long. But instead of swinging just as hard, with more of a vertical lift, they turn the palm out and hit their second serve flat. Yet even though they swing slowly, the ball still goes out because the flat serve can't bring the ball down in time.

Tips and Checkpoints

1. When you walk to the line for your first serve, think about serving only one ball. Don't let the second ball be a crutch.

2. Don't think "serve": think of a rhythmical throw. Notice how most pros try to simulate a baseball pitcher's motion.

3. Remember, you are not looking down on your opponent's court — you are looking through the little holes in the net. Thus if you try to hit down on the ball it may go *under* the net. Think "up and out," not down.

4. Take your time. The serve is 100 percent your own stroke and creation. No one can run in and grab your toss.

5. Try to be calm and let everything glide. When you think about your serve up at the line, be more concerned about rhythm than about isolated

movements of your body. Trying to concentrate on each little movement is self-defeating.

6. Learn to start your swing slowly and speed up steadily so that your motion is continuous. Don't start off with a gigantic effort and finish with a cream-puff delivery.

7. The serve is one stroke where you don't want to worry about bending the knees. You don't want anything that promotes a "down-up, down-up" type of motion. Think "around and up," and pivot on a horizontal plane. Strive for a nice easy shoulder roll and work to eliminate the hitches and jerky movements that rob you of rhythm and a natural throwing motion. An Aussie once showed me that you can face the net and still hit the ball 100 miles per hour if you rotate your body and snap your hitting wrist properly; you don't even need footwork.

8. Whether you are attacking the net or not, toss the ball out in front of your body to the right of your head, not straight ahead. And don't fall for the myth that you have to throw the toss high and let it drop so that your racket has time to catch up. Release the ball to the peak of your outstretched racket and the proper swing will make perfect contact.

9. Keep your chin up and eyes on the ball — don't be opponent-oriented.

10. Hit "up and out" and let the snap of your wrist and ball rotation bring the ball down.

11. Don't serve and back up. Tell yourself that you want to be stretched out over the baseline before you hit the ball, so your weight comes forward and you maintain a natural flowing motion.

12. As your serve improves, practice taking three steps forward and bringing your feet together momentarily on the third step, ready to move in any direction for your opponent's return.

13. Establish a psychological pattern that you are always going to try to serve long, and that you're never going to hit the net. When you keep your opponent deep you prevent him from taking the net and you give yourself more time to react to his return.

14. If you make service errors, feel good about going long. Long serves are more easily corrected than those which hit the net, plus you get used to hitting deep.

15. If your serve is going long (and your wrist is breaking properly), your only error is that you are not throwing the ball far enough in front. You can also make the serve fall shorter by brushing up against the ball with a vertical racket head.

16. If your serve is falling too short or going in the net, you have two

possible errors to consider: you are either swinging down on the ball rather than up and forward, or you are throwing the ball too far in front.

17. Serve into your opponent's backhand corner the majority of times. Most backhand returns are weaker and normally at a higher elevation, making it easier for you to hit volleys and groundstrokes.

18. If you've been telling yourself, "I'd be terrific if I just had a second serve," you may be blaming the wrong stroke. Does this mean that you already have a great first serve? If so, then you hardly ever need a second serve.

19. Before you can serve and attack, make sure you have a weapon. Some people beat their serve to the net and they can't understand why they lose. When you get hit in the back of the head with your own serve, you have to stay back.

20. Practice. Get out during the week and try to serve as many balls as possible. Don't settle for 10 to 15 practice serves before your weekly match. When you practice, set up target areas, and always try to hit deep. Even if you're wild, be tickled to death if every ball winds up on the other side of the net.

Chapter Seven

The Service Return

I N GOLF, the long driver can belt the ball all day and if he keeps it in play, there's nothing his opponents can do, short of talking on his backswing. But in tennis, your service return gives you a nice tactical and psychological weapon. If you can take your opponent's best serves and get them back in play, you may demoralize that person in a couple of games, especially if his serve is his pride and joy. He'll try to save face by straining to hit the ball harder and harder, but this generally leads to a loss of rhythm and a succession of double faults — providing you can keep the pressure on by returning the serves that manage to go in.

The service return, in fact, is the second most important shot in the game. If the serve goes in, the return determines where the point goes from there, in every match in the history of the game. Therefore, *when you receive serve you should think of it being your only shot.* Your second, third, and fourth shots become important only if you make an effective return of serve.

Yet how many times have you practiced service returns? Or even given them much thought? Most people regard the service return as simply a forehand or backhand, and not a stroke all in itself, as it must be against good players. So they hit a lot of forehands and backhands when they rally before a match, thinking they're also practicing their service returns. But when they meet an opponent who can serve the ball reasonably hard, with accuracy, they don't know how to get their racket on the ball in time, let alone get it back in play, and thus they're forced to always win their serve just to stay even in the match.

The serve would be much less important than it is if people worked to develop better service returns. Then the game would come down to who had the better groundstrokes. Once you learn to return serves consistently, you force the server to beat you with other strokes; you don't allow him (or her) to win by being a one-shot artist. Good service returns can provide another benefit psychologically. Since you likely spend most of your time

The service receiver normally stands close to the singles sideline on the right court because that's halfway between where a talented righthanded server can hit the ball (as indicated by the sheets of paper).

The service receiver stands closer to the center stripe on the left court because the righthander's serve usually curves to the left, which limits his serving range from the left side. Remember the principle: the receiver calculates the distance a server can move him both right and left, then stands in the middle of that distance.

working on groundstrokes from the baseline, your tension is reduced dramatically if you can get the serve back. You're now ready to play your "comfortable" strokes and you've placed all the pressure on your opponent to make the first mistake.

Jimmy Connors has shown how the service return can actually become a devastating offensive weapon against even the fastest servers in the game. Yet my goal is to first have you learn to return the ball consistently — "Get it back and dig," said Kramer — before you worry about more sophisticated aspects such as placement and varying the pace of the ball.

Preliminaries

The Grip

Hold your regular Eastern forehand or Eastern backhand grip. Against a hard server, where you need to gain every split second possible in order to reach the ball in time, hold a forehand grip in advance so that you only have to switch if it comes to your backhand. Most people fail to hold either grip as they wait and thus must switch no matter where the ball goes. If your opponent is always serving to your backhand, then hold a backhand grip in anticipation.

Also, tighten your third and fourth fingers (ring and little finger) just before impact to insure a firm grip. This will allow you to hit off-center and still make a fairly clean return. But if your grip is loose and you hit off-center, the ball dies. Don't place all the emphasis on your index finger, for this sometimes throws the racket across on the forehand.

Where to Stand

In principle, you should stand halfway between the distance the server can stretch you on the forehand and the backhand. Most top players, for example, will straddle the singles sideline. But in typical club tennis, you can generally stand several steps closer to the center stripe because most people can't break the ball wide and draw you off the court. If you don't have a backhand then I know you like to stand way over by the center stripe, as if to say, "Bertha, anything to my backhand is out." Unfortunately, you can't get away with this against good players. They will slice the ball wide to your forehand and you'll have to call a taxi to get your racket to the ball in time. So stand in the proper position and force yourself to start working on a backhand.

If your opponent is getting his first serve in play, you can usually determine your position fairly early in the match. But ideally you should chart him beforehand (see Chapter Eight) so that you already know how far he can stretch an opponent to either side. Remember, breaking his serve in the first game is as meaningful — and perhaps even more valuable psychologically — as breaking it in the fifth.

Ready Position

There is no universal ready position — only *that position which will get you to the ball the fastest.* However, you should start from a high body position so that your first move is forward, and not up. You can wait for the serve in a low crouch and you don't have to come up before you start forward, but eventually you must straighten up to play better players because they topspin the serve and you often are forced to hit at shoulder height.

Still, I see people all the time who are obsessed with the low crouch. They are trying to imitate the pros they see in tournaments, but they make one crucial mistake: they look away to watch the server, and they fail to see the receiver stand straight up (since most service returns in big-time tennis must be hit at chest or shoulder level). Remembering only the low crouch, the spectator goes out to play and now he gets down with his nose almost touching the court because he wants to play like the pros. But for you to be successful returning serves from that position, your opponent must serve the ball *under* the net.

The Stroke

When you play against a patty-cake server, you will have time to hit your regular forehand and backhand groundstrokes. In which case, concentrate on returning the ball deep in your opponent's territory so that he is forced to hit defensively.

The hitter's right arm typifies a common error on service returns by the average player. Tucking the elbow in against the body takes the racket face off the line of the oncoming ball, and the hitter will have to be pretty talented to meet the ball squarely. Conversely, the left arm is properly positioned, with the elbow high and away from the body so that the racket strings can follow the flight of the ball right into impact.

Against fast serves, most forehand returns are hit with a blocking motion — similar to the volley — which usually produces a relatively flat shot. I prefer the same stroking pattern on the backhand return, but many players prefer to "chip" the ball with severe underspin because they are late and they have no other choice.

On the forehand return, the most common problem against fast serves is that *people try to do too much with their racket.* They lay the racket back and try to take a full swing, only to get caught late every time. You don't need all that motion. Simply fix your racket, maintain a firm wrist, and keep the face of the racket on line with the approaching ball. Your forward body motion — and the server's speed — will supply all the necessary power.

Starting from a ready position that has the racket face up at about eye level, turn your shoulders back the instant you detect the direction of the serve, and try to get a fast first step forward. Keep your hitting elbow up and away from your body as you move into the ball, with the racket face vertical and pointed up at about a 45-degree angle. By leading with a slightly bent elbow, you keep the wrist from laying back — a kiss of death on most shots — and you'll find yourself making returns against even the hardest hitters. Glue your eyes on the ball and think about hitting across a table at shoulder level. Contact the ball out in front of your body, hit through the ball, and then keep the racket moving high so that the ball carries out with depth. *Hitting down on the ball is the sucker play.* The higher the ball bounces, in fact, the more vertical you should try to raise the racket on the follow-through. When you know that you want the racket to finish up — not down — you help yourself develop the proper stroking pattern, and you keep from pulling the ball into the net.

On the backhand return, most pros would prefer to hit with topspin, which requires fewer variables to control than underspin. But they rarely have time to meet the ball properly out in front of their body; thus they tend to settle for a "chipped" return. To produce underspin, I like to emphasize a short, high-to-low-to-high forward motion with a slightly beveled racket face. Visualize an "inverted bow" pattern that brings the racket back up on the follow-through.

Some pros, however, prefer a more severe "chopping" motion in order to produce excessive backspin and a shot they hope will land at the feet of the onrushing server. But this is a tricky shot that deserves careful attention and practice. Not only do you have to calculate — under pressure from a hard serve — how and where you are going to contact the ball, but you also need a strong wrist and a strong arm to maintain racket control.

(1)   (2)   (3)   (4)

The Service Return

(1) The stroking principles on the service return are the same for the forehand and the backhand. The backhand return is shown here. Starting from a high ready position (since most service returns are normally hit at chest level or above anyway), the hitter carries his left elbow high to help shorten the backswing. (2) He contacts the ball with a racket head that is slightly beveled and moving from high to low to high. (3) The racket begins an upward movement immediately after contacting the ball . . . and (4) the hitter finishes with the same old "Air the Armpits" follow-through. The completed stroking pattern should resemble a slight bow.

This backhand stroke is often compared in imagery to a man chopping down a tree with an axe, but this leads people to simply swing down, or chip down, at the ball; then you see them walking up to the net and retrieving their shot. Remember, you must also bring the racket back up on the follow-through so that it goes out toward your target. Try to imagine yourself chopping *into a tree and coming up*, rather than chopping down, and you'll develop a far more reliable stroke.

To prevent wrist layback on the backswing, and to keep the racket perfectly positioned, hold the throat of the racket with the fingers of your left hand and raise your left elbow (if you are righthanded). Lead with this elbow up and away from your body as you take the racket back, and have the left fingers help keep the racket face on line with the ball.

Try to avoid the tendency to watch whether the server is attacking the net or staying back. Rather, attempt to maintain perfect eye contact on the ball, which focuses your attention upon what is more important to you than your opponent. Also, keep your head still as you focus on the point of impact and you will tend to hit much more consistently on the center of the strings.

Footwork

Your speed afoot is not nearly as important as your ability to get a fast first step towards the ball. To do this you must concentrate on the serve, anticipate the direction of the ball, and then react as quickly as you can by telling yourself, "It's a forehand!" or "It's a backhand!" Make your first step go forward; don't automatically go back when the serve comes harder than expected. Do all your backing up *before* the serve has been hit by finding the place where you feel safe enough to move forward into every ball. Get up on your toes as the ball is served so that your weight is forward and you don't settle in on your heels.

A good drill next time you play is to try to move in against every serve, no matter how fast it comes, instead of automatically stepping back and waiting for the ball. You'll be amazed at how many balls you actually get back, and at how much quicker you learn to react and move to the ball. This forces you to concentrate on the serve and prevents you from settling in on your heels. Plus it makes you realize that all you really need is good concentration, a firm grip at impact, and a vertical racket head that makes a clean hit. Your opponent's shot will supply all the speed you need.

Don't be afraid to guess wrong about a fast serve. Break one way or the other because your guesses will later become educated, and at least you'll have a 50–50 chance. Most people simply stand in the middle and do nothing, hoping they can call the ball out.

The "Big Chippers," as they are called, are those who chop down on the ball at a sharp angle to impart severe underspin. Some top doubles players use this motion on the service return, but most intermediates who try it aren't very successful, because the stroke requires strong wrists and control of a large number of variables. Some players believe you should stop your swing where the hitter has in this photo (displaying a severe chip), but I feel you should get in the habit of continuing up and finishing high. This keeps you from making too severe a chip.

Tactics

I've found that if I ask intermediates to hit a particular corner with one of their groundstrokes, they may not hit that corner, but they generally land the ball on that side of the court. Yet when they go to hit service returns, they can't even name a side beforehand. So before you worry about getting fancy with placements, work to get ten out of ten returns back in play. You'll force your opponent to play tennis, and you'll be surprised at how many easy "sitters" he misses. But he'll never get the chance to make that first mistake if you don't get the ball over the net.

Once your game improves to the point where placement becomes important at your level of competition, don't let yourself be fooled. For of all

The balls on the fence represent the course of the stroke on a regular service return (left) and a severe chip (right). The player on the left will follow an "inverted bow" pattern, while the other player will make a severe "chopping" motion.

the shots in the game, you can involve yourself in strategy *less* on the service return. You can talk all you want about chipping the ball down at the server's shoelaces, or underspinning it down the line, but if your opponent hits a hard, deep serve then your only real play is to get it back and scramble. Still, when you do have a chance to "control" your service return, you should have two main objectives:

1. If the server is rushing the net, try to hit the ball at his feet so that he is forced to bend and scoop for his return shot. This reduces the angle at which he can hit and forces him to lift the ball, which of course gives you a much easier shot to return.

2. If your opponent remains at the baseline, return the ball deep so that he can't take the net. Then you start looking for the first short ball to come from your opponent so that *you* can gain the net.

When you scout an opponent before a match, you want to find out whether he comes in behind every serve, and how far he gets. If he takes those three big steps and practically reaches the service line as his opponent is hitting the return, you have a right to feel a little nervous. You're going to have to lay your return in at his feet — either with severe topspin or by taking speed off the ball — or throw up some lobs to keep him off-balance and away from the net. You also want to learn whether he has a tendency — and the control — to throw the serve into a particular corner on certain points. For instance, some players will always try to fool you with a "change-up" at certain scores. Try to determine how well his serve holds up when he gets tired. If he starts to lose a little of his first-serve speed and accuracy when he gets tired, be patient and keep pressing him with your service return because he will have a much greater tendency to "choke" on his serve as he tires.

Remember, too, that the server is generally trying to serve to your backhand. This is normally your weaker side and the tendency is for you to lift the ball high. On the advanced level, in fact, you know that your opponent is going to aim for your backhand, and he knows that you know. Everybody knows. The question is: "Does your opponent have an accurate serve, and do you have a backhand?" It just boils down to who has the strokes under stress. You can be a brilliant strategist but first you need the fundamentals.

A final point: *Just as your poor service return will put real pressure on your own serve, a strong serve will also make your service return more effective.* Pancho Gonzales was a great example of how these two strokes can be closely related. When Gorgo was at his peak, the fact that he always won his serve gave him a great psychological advantage going into a match. He knew the best anybody could do against him was to tie, since he was going to win his serve every time. Thus, when he returned serve he knew he had his own serve as a stopper and he could just stand back there and flail out. If he won the first two points with good returns or he got the score to deuce, then he would fight for the game. But if he fell behind 30-love, he would virtually concede the game, catch his breath, and put all his effort into his next serve. When Gorgo's opponent served again, Gorgo would go all-out early in the game, knowing that he just needed to break serve once each set to win the match. His attitude was: Why beat your brains out in big-time tennis when your chances of breaking your opponent's serve are relatively slight anyway? Better to grab more oxygen and concentrate on your own serve.

Of course, I don't want to encourage you to let up like Gorgo on your service returns, unless your serve is so great that you can get away with it. The average player can be serving and leading 40-love but he tends to make so many errors that you still have a chance to win the game if you're fundamentally sound. When you serve yourself, in most cases you are struggling just as hard to win as when you try to break your opponent's serve. In fact, if you are leading 40-love, you'd still better be fighting your guts out for the ball.

Checkpoints

1. Relax while waiting for the serve. Only strain during the hit. If your body tightens up, you won't move your legs.

2. Start from a high position, especially if you are tall, and work to get a fast first step. You can bend down before the serve, but make sure you come up in plenty of time to take your swing. (Research indicates that you can move faster laterally by using a higher center of gravity.) You don't stay low when you hit a service return.

3. Move forward and into the ball; think aggressively, not defensively.

4. Most players are caught in the middle of a big backswing when returning hard serves. So develop a compact little stroke that enables you to meet the ball out in front of your body with a perfectly positioned racket face. The server will supply all the power you need.

5. Don't let your racket head lay back. Keep the racket face nearly vertical and on line with the ball throughout the stroke.

6. On the forehand backswing, keep the elbow of your racket arm raised and slightly bent. On the backhand, keep the elbow of your non-hitting arm raised as it cradles the throat of the racket going back.

7. Try to watch the ball as long as possible, and then keep your head down and focused on the point of impact until you have followed through.

8. Maintain a firm grip at impact. This will help insure a good return even if the ball hits off-center.

9. Don't let the racket head drop below the level of your wrist, and have the hitting arm and racket finish high on the follow-through.

10. Scramble, get the ball in play — and then work to get it deep.

11. How well you return serve at 30-all or deuce is what will make you famous. This is the pressure point, the one you need to win to force the server into a "choking" situation, the one he desperately wants in order to gain the advantage. So have a friend chart all of your service returns and see how you fare at different points during each game.

Chapter Eight

Singles Strategy

TENNIS STRATEGY PRESENTS an endless challenge to most players who get hooked on the game. Others feel that if they can learn a lot about strategy, this will somehow overcome their lack of strokes. These are the people who say, "Vic, I can't control the ball — but can you give me some strategy?" But let's face it, unless two players are evenly matched in stroke production and thus seeking the winning edge, overall strategy and point-to-point tactics are basically overrated for most people. If you can just get the ball back consistently — with good depth — you're going to be tough to beat without knowing the first thing about "hitting the lines," "opening up the court," and other fancy stratagems. Even at the pro level you must have the basic weapons to win, not a unique theory.

Instead of espousing new horizons in strategy, I'm much more concerned about *delimiting* the number of options that are available to people. Everybody worries about not having enough shots, but in reality there are only about five things you can do with the ball from the baseline: hit to your opponent's left, to his right, over his head, at his feet, or through his navel. You can try 100 different bizarre shots and tactics but they won't make you famous. The winner isn't the one with all the fancy shots, but the one who can keep giving his opponent one more chance to take gas.

Nevertheless, developing your strategy and putting it to intelligent use during a match will make the most of your strokes when you play in tournaments, challenge players on a club ladder, or just try to knock off your neighborhood rival. Strategy also means devising a realistic game plan, which forces you to evaluate your own game and to learn how to scout future opponents. This in turn leads to faster progress, more success, and more fun. Learning about strategy and match-play tactics is also kind of comforting. It's nice to know that what you thought you should be doing on the court really isn't all that complicated.

"Strategy" for the Beginner

It's tough to outline a strategy for those who hit the ball into the net every other shot. Strategy is basically an automatic response to a given set of conditions, and with beginners there are no "givens." The player hitting the ball doesn't know where it's going or why it's going there once it leaves his racket, and his opponent is just as mystified. So they simply try to hit the ball back and forth, giggle a lot, and have a lot of fun. If this is the way you play, you may not care the first thing about strategy. But if you're tired of losing to the same people all the time and you're trying to develop sounder strokes and the right habits, here are some overall thoughts that can make you more successful.

Your first goal is to get the ball back safely, anywhere in your opponent's court. Then, as your shots improve, visualize a five-foot semicircle around the center stripe — at your opponent's baseline — and try to hit every shot there when the two of you are playing from near the baseline. It's hard to keep landing the ball in or around this target area, but "down the middle and deep" gives you an easy system to remember and one that can be trusted against any type of opponent, and on any kind of playing surface. It can help make you a winner in four ways: (1) You keep your opponent hitting from behind the baseline; (2) the net is 5½ inches lower in the middle than at the singles sideline, meaning you have less chance for error; (3) you can concentrate more confidently on the stroke you are taking because you're not gambling by trying for the corners or the sidelines; and (4) by playing the ball straight down the middle, you reduce the length of the diagonal available to your opponent if he wants to hit a cross-court passing shot. He must hit with topspin in order to produce the proper speed and accuracy.

The only trouble with hitting down the middle comes when your opponent has only one strong shot, either a forehand or a backhand, and he can step around and hit from his strength every time. But if you can keep the ball deep enough, nobody's going to hurt you. Besides, once you learn to keep the ball in play and deep, you can adjust your semicircle away from the center stripe toward your opponent's weak side, and just concentrate on hitting to that target.

I talk a lot about hitting only the shots that you "own," and by that I mean hitting a specified target area under stress. By this definition, most players don't even "own" one shot, and thus strategy is almost a contaminant. If these people worry about strategy they now have two problems:

This same photograph appeared earlier, but the concept is so important to what I teach that it is used again here. Remember, strategy is not that complicated. If you're capable of consistently hitting to this five-foot (radius) semicircle in your opponent's backcourt, you'll soon be famous. You can beat almost anyone with this shot — and patience.

(1) they must deal with stroke production, and (2) not having the strokes, they must try to mentally manipulate some tactical variables, such as where they should try to hit the ball if their opponent is at the net. They would be much wiser to forget these mental variables and just try to hit the ball properly.

I'm always amused by the beginners who want to know, "When will I know I'm no longer a D player — that I'm now a C?" I tell them that their peers will let them know. "When you begin to win, they'll start calling you dirty names and avoiding you at the club and making excuses not to play you. Even without a 'ladder' you can consider yourself a C player when you start to lose some friends."

Strategy for the Real Buff

No matter how successful you become in this game, hitting "down the middle and deep" should always remain a fundamental aspect of your strategy. Throw in an adequate serve, two good legs, and a high frustration-tolerance level and this "system" can take you right to the top, as we've seen with Chris Evert. Unfortunately, few of us can hit with this kind of relentless precision and thus we must look for ways to gain an edge on our opponents with the weapons we have.

1. The basic starting point for all intermediate and advanced players should be: *the advanced player will attack the net at every opportunity and the intermediate will wait for the first short ball before going in.* This assumes, of

course, that you know how to hit an approach shot and how to volley, and that you appreciate how important it is to gain control of the net.

The biggest mistake made by intermediates who try to emulate the pros is that they fail to anticipate the first short ball when playing at the baseline. They hit and back up, or hesitate too long, instead of thinking, "The next ball is going to be short," and getting that fast first step forward if it lands in their short ball range. In fact, against most intermediates you should play just *inside* the baseline and start running as soon as the ball is hit because statistically the next ball will be short. *The average player is average because he seldom hits the ball deep, except by accident.*

I don't want you to think you can beat many players by always backing up and digging in at the baseline, unless you have sound groundstrokes and a long fuse. Good tennis is a game of closing out the point and not letting your opponent keep playing. This means you must fight to get to the net — preferably behind a deep shot that keeps your opponent pinned behind the baseline. If you can develop confidence in your approach shot and volley, and force yourself to concentrate on going forward rather than automatically staying back, your opponent is going to feel the pressure. Let him know that you are going to rush the net on the first short ball and you will affect his concentration and the rhythm of his swing as he tries to keep the ball deep.

I'm often asked, "What kind of person should go to the net more often?" In intermediate tennis, it's the person who has the short fuse, who is frustrated by baseline rallies and wants every point to be quickly settled. This type of player should be up on his toes, ready to pounce on the first short ball.

Then people ask, "Well, what if I have a short fuse but I don't volley well?" And I tell them, "Then you're going to lose. If you don't have the patience to stay back and try to win with groundstrokes, you have to learn how to hit an approach shot and to volley."

2. *Strive for consistency by playing the percentages; it's variety that kills you.* The trouble with the "Hit the lines" concept is that very few people can play with that kind of control, and they put too much pressure on themselves in a baseline rally. Kramer was the greatest strategist I've ever seen and he played everything for position and percentages — "deep and safe," he used to say. When he went for the "corners," he usually aimed about four feet inside the baseline and four feet inside the sideline.

The reason you want to simplify your strategy is the fact that there are very few places you — or your opponent — can actually hit the ball. The fancier you try to get, such as by moving your opponent from forehand to backhand to forehand, the more you risk hitting the ball out. Why gamble like this if you can already get the ball back consistently? Statistics show that someone is about to make an error. Better your opponent than you.

3. A corollary to this would be: *never try to hit a shot you don't own.* Temptation shots normally lead to another second-place finish in a field of two, whether you are in control of the point or on the defensive. If you are in trouble, always hit the shot which has a high probability of getting you back out of a hole. Don't look for a miracle shot to win the point. Surprise your opponent by just getting the ball back and he may end up dumping it into the net.

If you have the upper hand, keep hitting the shots that put you there. That's why I hate to see a player try to hit a drop shot under pressure. The pressure is on him to thread the needle and lay the ball just over the net, and if he misses he gives his opponent a big boost.

I once sat with Kramer and Arthur Ashe to watch Gonzales play Laver in Los Angeles about 1965. Gonzales had the service ad in a key game but he tried to drop-shot Laver and Rod came up, got the ball back, and won the point. Kramer turned to Ashe and me and said "Let that be a lesson to you. Never drop-shot on a big point. Why do you want to add pressure on yourself?"

About two years later, when I was with the Davis Cup team in Ecuador, Ashe was playing Pancho Guzman in the second singles match. They were in the fifth set, but Arthur had won the fourth, 6–0, and now led 2–1. He was just one point away from breaking Guzman's serve and Guzman was so choked up he could only hit a little baby serve. Arthur came in, but instead of hitting his approach shot, he tried a drop shot — a shot he didn't "own." The ball went into the net and suddenly Guzman had new life, while Arthur's confidence went skidding down. Guzman went on to win the game, the set, and the match — which enabled Ecuador to knock the United States out of Davis Cup competition by a 3–2 score.

4. *When playing under pressure, don't let the situation dictate your shot. Hit the shot you know you should hit.* When the average player is down set point and faced with an approach shot, he usually thinks, "I just want to play it safe and get out of this alive." So instead of aiming deep to his opponent's backhand and following his shot to the net, he simply tries to get the ball over the net and then retreats to the baseline. But a player like Laver will always say to himself, "Deep and go. If it's out, it's out."

Rod's old rival and friend, Roy Emerson, once told me, "That's why you were never comfortable playing the Rocket. When you got him down match point, that's when you started worrying. You would be thinking about winning the match but you knew he would still try to hit the shot that needed to be hit. He had the guts to make the play, where others would choke. And if he hit the big shot and won the point, you got mad because you had him on the hook and lost him. That's what made him so great."

5. *The moment you are pressed on a ball or your opponent starts to move you around, elevate your next shot 10 or 12 feet over the net in order to buy time and to disrupt his momentum.* People love to stand at the baseline controlling the pace of the match while you scramble all over the court trying to get the ball back. When you find yourself on the run like this, the normal tendency is to want to regain the upper hand by blasting the ball back, hoping for a miraculous placement or an error by your opponent. This usually leads you into more trouble. But if you can return the ball high and deep, you can change the rhythm of the game unbelievably. Your opponent goes crazy waiting for the ball to land while you regain good position. Plus, the ball bounces higher so he can't crack his hips into the shot and you aren't supplying the power.

6. *Try to learn from the dinker.* If you don't like to hit a ball that comes up around your chest — the kind often hit by dinkers — you are not alone. Why don't you offer your opponent the same kind of shot by elevating the ball so that it lands near the baseline and bounces high? This is especially true if you play against a person who you've heard complain, "I don't like to play Bertha — she ruins my rhythm." Bertha, in other words, is giving this person a variety of heights and speeds, when what she wants are low, hard groundstrokes that always set up nice and fat in the same place. People like this have a short fuse and you want to give them plenty of high-bouncing balls so that they can never get in the groove. Instead of trying to blast them off the court with power, use a little finesse, like the clever pitcher who mixes up his pitches.

Throwing off timing is not the only reason you want to bounce the ball high to certain players. I've noticed that the pros are starting to smarten up against the short guys in the game by emphasizing topspin groundstrokes. For example, after losing to Bjorn Borg in the WCT championships in Dallas in 1976, 5'6" Harold Solomon commented that he had to keep reaching up against Borg's high-bouncing shots. "The ball was over my head all the time," said Solomon. "So much topspin means you have to hit the ball very hard to make it go anywhere, and when it comes as high as Bjorn hits it, I can't get any body weight behind it. I am forced to just use my arms."

Remember to hit cross-court when you're getting pushed out of court and your opponent remains at the baseline. One, you'll hit a longer ball, which will give you more time to get back into play. Two, if your opponent wants to hit to your backhand, he will have to hit your cross-court shot down the line, which is one of the most difficult shots in tennis. And three, your opponent will never be able to run you beyond the singles sideline.

7. *Try to overplay your opponent's strong shots and force him to beat you by hitting his weaker shots.* If he can only hit his forehand with confidence, and he prefers to go down the line with this shot, then overplay the court on that side so that he must win the point by going cross-court. Let him know: "You can beat me, but you're going to have to use the weaker of your two shots to do it." Don't let him win with his strength. If he swings on a horizontal level, then overplay to the cross-court side because that's where he's going to pull his shots, unless he purposely swings late — and then you are forcing him to add another variable.

Also remember to move to the side of the court to which you hit the ball when you rush the net. Tempt your opponent to hit what looks like the easier shot — away from you — but which actually is very difficult to execute.

8. *Hit cross-court on sharply angled shots that draw you off the court. Try to return the ball on a diagonal — with a lob or a drive — and don't be tempted to hit straight down the line.* On the forehand, especially, the tendency in singles is to try to hit down the line to your opponent's backhand corner when he is on the baseline. But you are much safer and wiser to go cross-court for the following reasons:

a. The net is lower in the middle than on the sides.

b. If you hit the ball eight to ten feet over the net, you keep the ball in the air longer and you gain time to scramble back into play. You may also bother your opponent's rhythm.

c. The singles court is 78 feet long down the line and 82½ feet on the diagonal, giving you extra length with which to hit.

d. By hitting on the diagonal, you now tempt your opponent with the tougher of two returns — down the line to your backhand. Even if he hits a great forehand, he is threading the needle and he can only move you to the singles sidelines.

For example, let's say you have been run off the court to hit a forehand and you return the ball to your opponent's forehand. If he now tries to hit into your "wide-open" backhand corner he opens himself up to the following problems:

• There's no margin for safety when you go down the line; the ball can only land in play on one side of the singles line.

• The ball is arriving at his racket on a diagonal and it tends to deflect off the racket at a slight angle when he tries to go straight down the line. This helps send it off-target and out of bounds if he doesn't compensate.

• Meanwhile, even though he is hitting to your backhand, the easiest shot in the game is to hit a straight ball cross-court, since most people have a natural tendency to pull across their bodies and hit the ball on the diagonal. You have to be a talented player to hit a straight ball *straight*, anywhere on the court. If you don't believe me, get a friend to rally with you in one of the 4½-foot doubles alleys and see how difficult it is to keep hitting the ball *inside* the alley.

Now, with these thoughts in mind, visualize yourself again running off the court to hit a forehand, only this time you try to go down the line to your opponent's backhand. Not only are you attempting the toughest shot, you are increasing the number of steps your opponent can run you with his own return. First, your momentum may carry you farther off the court when you try to hit down the line. (This also gives you less time to recover for your next shot.) And second, even though your opponent must hit a backhand, he can use his natural pull-across swing and hit it diagonally — to your backhand — which also pulls you off the court on the other side.

Therefore, unless your opponent has a weakness which dictates otherwise (such as a crummy backhand and a powerhouse forehand), always go back on the diagonal when you are being run off the court and you'll be way ahead of the game. Also try to lob the ball high in order to gain more recovery time, unless your opponent can take a lob and really push you around with his overhead. Then you will have to drive the ball back, but only as a last resort.

9. Every hot-dog strategist likes to talk about "opening up the court" with a variety of fancy, high-risk shots that very few players in the world can hit with any consistency. You have to learn to recognize when you really have an open court, but the question is: can you still hit a winning shot? When you get an opponent off the court or in one corner, how often are you able to hit the ball into the other corner for a winner? If your opponent is at the baseline, how often can you really catch him off guard with a short-angle roll shot or a drop shot that barely clears the net, hits, and dies? Realistically speaking, the number of times you win a point outright by hitting into an open court is going to be a lot smaller than the number of times you win a point because your opponent makes an error.

For beginners, worrying about an "open court" is a joke. Their opponent has to be against the fence, and even then the likelihood of a placement is slim. But for more advanced players, my advice would be to keep a purpose in mind for every shot. You can't "open up" a court by always hitting the ball deep; you have to learn to learn to hit the drop shot or the soft diagonal that falls inside the service box and then bounces into the alley, forcing your opponent to race in just to get his racket on the ball. If he makes the play, you have to be prepared to put his shot away before he has an opportunity to recover.

10. *Use the lob to tire your opponent.* Pros have found that one can tire older opponents faster with the lob than with any other stroke. Not only do you exhaust opponents by driving them away from the net to chase the ball, but you make them stretch their stomachs out entirely when they go up to hit an overhead. That's why the younger pros would try to pause on their lob or drive as long as possible so that guys like Segura and Gonzales would crowd the net even more, and leave themselves more vulnerable to the lob.

11. The great offensive players normally have exceptional serves, volleys, approach shots, and overheads. If you do not have these qualifications, then *a great defense is the best offense*: develop your forehand and backhand so that you keep the ball in play — with depth — and provide your opponent with the opportunity to beat himself. Don't give him a helping hand by going for winners when you're out of position.

I see juniors all the time who think the name of the game is to hit the ball as hard as they can, even if they don't have control. They think they're too good to just try and keep it in play. But I'll never forget the time I brought two leading junior players from Argentina to train with me in Palos Verdes, where I was the pro at the Kramer Club. They were very fine players (not too long after that they had a win over Ashe and Grabner) and I wanted Kramer to watch them play. Jack drove 65 miles to do me this favor, but when he arrived they tried to look good by just slugging the ball. They were young and they were going to impress Jack with all their power. But Jack took just one look and got back in his car and left. "Why do I want to watch these clowns?" he said. "They can't keep the ball in play."

Preparing for a Match

Charting

If you are playing in club tournaments, or you're serious about moving up your challenge ladder, don't wait until you rally before a match to start brewing up a game plan. Take the time to scout people you play regularly,

To use the Match Play Recording Chart, sketch a blank court and place the appropriate symbol for each error at the exact spot on the court where the error was committed. For example, the letters *LFccn* placed inside the forehand singles sideline corner would mean the person being charted hit a low forehand (*LF*) cross-court (*cc*), and the shot landed in the net (*n*). Thus recorded are the stroke, the ball direction, and the zone in which the ball landed. Most players chart errors because there are too few placements to be recorded. The *N* and *S* refer to north and south sides of the court. Service, service return, and overhead errors are simply tallied in the boxes provided, since such errors are usually numerous.

or those you are likely to encounter in club tournaments, and pretty soon you will have a "file" on possible opponents that you can draw on before a match.

This is where charting is invaluable. Only by charting can you supply the two key "academic" ingredients necessary to build a winning tennis game: (1) knowing your own strengths and weaknesses, and (2) pinpointing your opponent's strengths and weaknesses. If you can learn to use the Match Recording Chart discussed here, you will be able to quantify match-play data that are far more trustworthy and revealing than your own memory or interpretation of a match. With this information you will know how to best deploy the strokes that you have, and how to attack your opponent's weaknesses.

Charting is like detailed scorekeeping. Whether you are charting a future opponent or having a friend chart you during a match, the idea is to record *errors* — where they occur and with what stroke — since they outnumber placements by a large margin. There are normally so many errors on the overhead, the serve, and the service return that you should keep separate box scores in order to have room on the paper.

Having a friend chart your match provides you with a much clearer idea of which shots actually worked and which ones let you down. This makes you far more objective about your own game, and enables you to go to work on specific weaknesses. For example, if you have a cluster of errors on your forehand approach shot, that's what you need to work on in practice. You may think you have a good serve because you seldom double-fault, but if you discover that only two out of ten first serves are going in, you are putting too much pressure on your second serve. In fact, you don't really have a serve — you have a prayer and a cream puff.

Charting should also clear up misconceptions about your groundstrokes. For instance, you see the following phenomenon happen all the time in club tennis. One player says after a match, "If I just had a backhand, I'd murder the guy, 'cause my forehand is terrific." Well, he doesn't have *either* stroke, but he gets his backhand over the net with a little dink shot that always goes in. He doesn't try anything fancy since he knows he doesn't have the stroke. But when the ball comes to his forehand, he thinks, "Great, this is my weapon," and he slugs the ball as hard as he can — but right into the net. Charting would show him *on paper* that his forehand, and not his backhand, was actually producing the most errors.

Charting your own match requires a friend or a spouse who knows how to chart, but there's no excuse for you not to chart future opponents at the

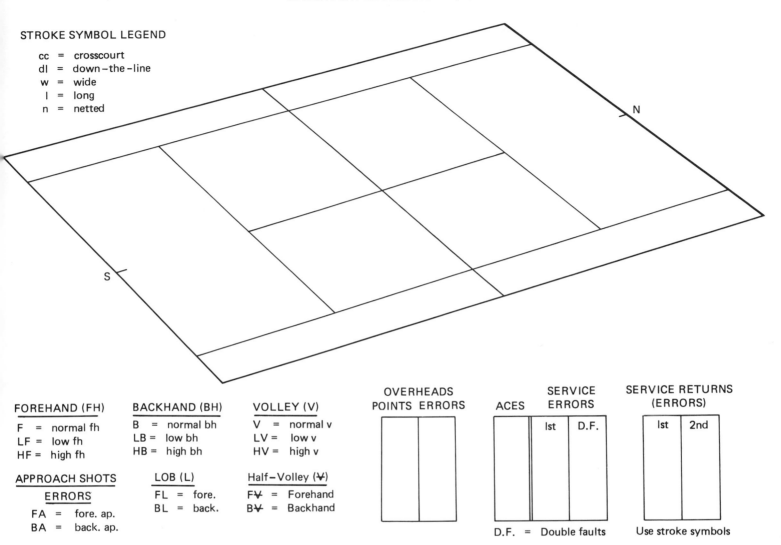

STROKE SYMBOL LEGEND

cc = crosscourt
dl = down – the – line
w = wide
l = long
n = netted

FOREHAND (FH)

F = normal fh
LF = low fh
HF = high fh

BACKHAND (BH)

B = normal bh
LB = low bh
HB = high bh

VOLLEY (V)

V = normal v
LV = low v
HV = high v

APPROACH SHOTS
ERRORS

FA = fore. ap.
BA = back. ap.

LOB (L)

FL = fore.
BL = back.

Half – Volley (V̶)

FV̶ = Forehand
BV̶ = Backhand

OVERHEADS
POINTS ERRORS

ACES

SERVICE
ERRORS

Ist	D.F.

D.F. = Double faults

SERVICE RETURNS
(ERRORS)

Ist	2nd

Use stroke symbols

club. Tournaments themselves can offer an excellent opportunity to observe other players while you kill time waiting for your own match.

When charting, also try to observe such things as: Is the person slow to get his racket back and slow to get into position? Where is the ball when he starts moving? Does he have trouble handling the lob? How quickly does he react and get back? Does he hit his groundstrokes with topspin or with underspin? Does he like to rush the net? If so, how far does he get after his approach shot in order to volley? Does he move in behind his serve? How hard does he hit his second serve? What shots does he rely on most? How does he seem to react to pressure? Does he seem to play harder and concentrate better when the score is 30-all than on the first point? What does he tend to do on important points? Does he seem to have a short fuse, or a lot of patience? Does he play better when he's ahead or when he's behind?

Answers to these questions will obviously help you formulate a realistic strategy for when you play a match — providing, of course, that you have the strokes to capitalize on your opponent's specific weaknesses. If you have some weapons, I've found that good charting stimulates logical tactics on the tennis court. Knowing your own strengths and weaknesses helps keep you from playing recklessly and encourages you to stick with the high-percentage shots — the ones that you "own." This is what produces victories.

Devising a Game Plan

Strategy is defined as your overall game plan, while tactics are those tools which you use to implement this plan. For example, your particular tactic may be to keep the ball low, but your overall strategy is to try to tire your opponent by making him bend down more often. By devising a game plan with these specifics in mind, you can go out on the court with a mind that is free to hit. You can't try to devise your strategy as the match unfolds, experimenting with different tactics and strokes game by game, point by point. Anybody I've seen who has tried to play this way is usually a loser.

Even among the pros there is very little intellectualizing during a tennis match. They just want to be free to hit the ball under pressure. They know that tennis is basically a trained response to a given shot, and that it is played best when played instinctively, assuming your instincts trigger the proper strokes. As Laver once told me, "When I start to think too much on the tennis court, that's when I know I'm going to lose."

Unfortunately, most players do their thinking in the middle of the point because they don't have a game plan. When they run for the ball they're thinking, "Bertha is going to run that way, so I'll hit over here. No, she's running the other way — got her." But the ball rolls off their racket and down their thigh. Another problem is to start arguing tactics as the ball is coming. "I just hit to her forehand, so I'd better go to her backhand. Yeh, but she likes the backhand — maybe I should lob." Debating with yourself like this will simply destroy your ability to anticipate your opponent's shot and to get that fast first step, while inhibiting a rhythmical swing once you do make up your mind.

Before you can develop a realistic strategy, you must have an objective understanding of your own strengths and weaknesses. *The reason most game plans fail is that they're based on some weapons that people don't even own.* For example, you might say, "I'll take every second serve by my opponent and attack." Okay, that's good. But if you don't have an approach shot, you'll end up losing more points than if you simply stay back and rely on your groundstrokes.

Just the fact that you sit down and try to devise a strategy forces you to ask questions about your game that most people tend to avoid. They just play, play, play without ever stopping to analyze their game in an objective way. That's why I've found that stroke production seldom matches the strategic plan outlined by the average player, but that this discrepancy narrows considerably with winners because they are much more objective about themselves.

Even without playing a match you can get a very realistic idea of what shots you "own" and don't own. If you are always losing to people who attack the net on every short ball, go out on the court and place a friend in a volleying position — let's say halfway between the net and the service line, to your backhand side — then just bounce the ball and see if you can hit your backhand past your friend, either down the line, cross-court, or with a lob. If you're not interested in humility yet, take your friend off the court and try to hit your target areas without any visual pressure at all. You'll find that you still can't hit certain shots, with or without stress. This really brings you home fast.

If you then try to draw up a game plan that is based strictly on the shots that you "own," and takes into account your opponent's abilities, you will realize how few options you have under pressure. People tend to think they have 20 or 30 options available, but when they write down the strokes they can rely on under pressure, and their corresponding strategy, they discover there's not much to decide.

A good game plan will also include specific objectives that you want to pursue, depending on your opponent's playing style and the shots you have that you feel can hurt him. In addition, there are certain rules of thumb that can be applicable no matter who you play. Review the following checklist before every match (adding your own reminders, and deleting those which you feel don't apply to your own game) and try to work these points into your subconscious so that you can learn to react and move and stroke the ball under stress automatically:

a. Every shot is important because statistically it may be your last.

b. Work hard not to hit the first short ball. If you keep your opponent behind the baseline, and away from the net, he'll need sound groundstrokes and patience to beat you.

c. Your first instinct at the baseline must be to move forward, not back, unless you have an agreement with your opponent that if he promises not to attack, you won't attack.

d. Beginners and intermediates seldom get beyond the serve or service return before hitting a weak shot, so be ready for the first short ball from your opponent, then move in to hit an approach shot.

e. Get yourself in the frame of mind that you came to play — not to put the ball away. Concentrate on reducing your errors and let your opponent go for broke. Against big hitters, if you can hang tough until they start to miss, they very often will fall apart.

f. Don't spend time worrying about being vulnerable to the extraordinary shot.

g. If your opponent runs you wide, off the court, "buy time" by returning his shot on the diagonal, with a drive or a lob.

h. If your opponent gets you on the run, break up his rhythm by elevating your shots 10 to 12 feet over the net and slowing them down.

i. In a baseline rally, when you're undecided about where to aim, just remember "Down the middle and deep," and let your opponent do the gambling.

j. Remember to keep your feet moving because everybody has a tendency to become a little more lethargic as the match progresses.

k. If your first lob in the match is long, don't choke or overcompensate and hit the next one short. Swing just as hard but elevate the ball a little more.

l. Try to hit every serve deep. You can learn more from a serve that goes long than one that goes into the net, plus you keep more pressure on your opponent when the serve is good.

m. Don't be bashful about even writing yourself little notes to review when you switch sides during a match.

Warming Up before a Match

A close match can actually be decided during the warm-up rally, depending on how thorough your rally, what you detect in your opponent, and what you give away about yourself.

First of all, if you are an intermediate or advanced player, never start a match without attempting every shot you might want to use. People love to hit forehands and backhands from the baseline, but what are the first two strokes in every match? The serve and the service return. So hit at least 20 serves (which enables your opponent to practice his service return), 20 overheads, and 20 lobs, and practice your approach shots, half-volleys, and volleys, in addition to your regular groundstrokes. *You want to be ready to play your best tennis from the first game on.* Here again, most people rally briefly and then one of them steps up to the line, takes a couple of warm-up serves, and says, "First ball in." Well, F.B.I. doesn't go in big-time tennis. Once that match begins you have to have a serve. (Similarly, if your opponent doesn't try any warm-up overheads, then you should lob as soon as possible, before he's ready to crack off winners.)

Second, don't worry about impressing your opponent with your power. Concentrate instead on getting into position and hitting rhythmically. Kramer, for example, would take great pains to see that his strokes were perfect while warming up. He would take his racket back quickly, step forward early, swing easily, and get everything back. Pretty soon his opponents would realize that they were the only ones missing the ball. So they would start to hit harder in order to put a little pressure on Jack and get him to miss a couple of shots. But Jack would just knock the ball back and remain cool and calculating while his opponents were getting out of sync by trying to go beyond their ability level. Thus he gained an obvious psychological edge going into the match. (Another of Kramer's tricks to test for his opponent's weak side was to hit the first warm-up shot right down the middle. Whatever direction his opponent stepped, that was his confidence stroke.)

Third, while warming up (and, naturally, during a match), don't be so worried about yourself and how you look that you fail to detect flaws in your opponent's stroke or footwork. Even if you've never seen him play before, you can pick up some revealing information. If he swings from low to high, on the horizontal, or with a lot of underspin, this will give you an idea of what type of shots to expect and whether or not he can hurt you with particular strokes. Watch to see if he moves better to the right or left, and how quickly he reacts and gets his racket back. If he keeps contacting the ball on the center of the strings, you are in trouble, but if he keeps hitting a lot of "wood" on the backhand, that's a good tip-off to a weak stroke. Try to sense if he is high-strung or relaxed. If he overreacts to everything and seems to like a fast tempo, then think about slowing everything down during the match by varying the pace of your shots.

Remember, *the way a person swings on his first couple of shots in warm-ups is usually how he will swing in the match, under pressure.* At the tennis college, we photograph our students hitting a forehand on the first morning, before they've had a chance to warm up. Then in the evening we give out a large print to each person, just to have a little fun. But occasionally people get a little upset at how they look and they'll complain, "Jeez, I didn't even have time to get warmed up." Yet I've discovered that although people will swing a little better as they loosen up, they often revert to their same old style once the pressure is on. Regression under stress is so strong and the initial response a person makes is so innate that on his very first swing of the day, he's really doing what is natural for him.

Playing a Match

The beautiful thing about tennis is that you can talk a great game in the locker room, and you can tell everybody how terrific you are — but pal, eventually you have to play.

a. *Occasionally, when you win the racket toss, let your opponent serve first if he or she hasn't warmed up sufficiently.* You gain a nice psychological edge if you can break serve in the first game.

b. *Be observant.* How many times have you played an opponent who happens to be lefthanded, and for about five minutes you're thinking to yourself, "Boy, there's something really weird about this person"? When I was the pro at the Kramer Club, a fellow came up to me after losing two sets to Beverly Baker Fleitz, the ambidextrous former playing great who would switch her racket and hit forehands off both sides. "Vic," he said, "you won't believe this but I didn't get the ball to her backhand *one* time. It didn't matter where I hit the ball, she would step around and hit this big forehand." The poor guy never noticed that she had *two* forehands.

Keen observation will help you detect other patterns in your opponent's play. Most people stick with a style of play and seldom deviate. If they react a certain way under stress on a particular shot, they will usually respond the same way when that shot comes up again. You can learn this by charting, but also by observing your opponent while the match progresses. Rod Laver, for example, kept alive his Grand Slam hopes in the 1962 French Open by being willing to gamble on the basis of what he had learned earlier in the match. Laver was serving in the fourth set and was down match point to Marty Mulligan. But Rod had been noticing that Mulligan always tried to hit his backhand returns down the line. So Rod served to Mulligan's backhand and broke for the sideline where, sure enough, he was able to cut off Mulligan's return with a winning volley. From there he rallied to win the match.

c. *Learn to be adaptable.* I've found that one of the similarities of tennis champions is their flexibility and their ability to adapt to new situations that arise during a match. A lot of people remember Gonzales as only a big hitter, but he was a master at keeping the ball in play. In fact, as the point increased in length, his chances of winning the point increased tremendously. He *hated* to lose those long rallies. He had the big game *and* the slow game, and that's what made him great. But when a lot of players lose their rhythm playing the big strokes, they can't adjust, and their game falls apart.

Top players display their adaptability in other important ways. If their opponent is really getting down low on the ball and making the play, they'll start bouncing the ball high with topspin. If their opponent is killing them on the high ball, they'll start hitting with underspin so that the ball bounces low and forces their opponent to bend down. They have their game plan set up beforehand but if they start losing they already have an alternate plan which was worked out in their head before the match. Thus they can shift gears strategically without losing their rhythm or their ability to hit instinctively. Contrast this to the average player, who falls apart if his original plan doesn't work — provided he even has a plan.

Losing the first set is not a reason to automatically junk your game plan. If you are just playing poorly and you feel you need to try new tactics, that's one thing. But if you are playing well and your opponent has just been hitting the cover off the ball and playing over his head, then all you can do is hang in there, keep the ball in play, and hope your opponent will start playing like a human. Not unless you can analyze a match in this way, and keep yourself from panicking when you get behind, can you ever come back after losing the first set.

This is another reason why it's so important to chart and to know your opponent. Some weaknesses don't begin to appear until a player starts to get a little tired or is kept under persistent pressure. He may be an unbelievable hot dog in the first set but he still needs your assistance before he can close out the match.

The way I watch for a person who's choking during a match is to look at the distance between his hitting elbow and his body as he contacts the ball. I talked earlier about how most players have a tendency to allow the ball to get too close to their body — instead of striding out to meet it — because they feel safer, in a Freudian way. This closeness tends to increase as the stress gets greater and the person begins to lose his confidence. But when I see that person hitting out away from his body, then I know he's pretty confident about his stroke. This is especially true on the backhand, where you must contact the ball farther out in front of your body than on the forehand.

d. *Concentrate on the ball and nothing else.* Kramer knew that his success in tennis stemmed from his ability to focus all of his attention on the ball, and on his stroke in relation to the ball. When he got a service break or he fell behind in the match, he would just keep reminding himself, "Watch the ball, watch the ball," or whatever was necessary to keep his attention on the ball. In fact, he never felt comfortable about the outcome of the match until he had touched the locker room door. Even after winning he would stare and be very intent during the trophy ceremonies, as if the match were still in progress. Not until he touched the locker room door would you see him finally breathe a real sigh of relief. Then he knew the match was over, that he had won, and that he could really relax and feel good about winning.

e. *Never give up.* If you run and stretch out for a ball that is seemingly out of reach, you might get it back and still win the point. I've never known a more determined player than Glenn Bassett, my doubles partner a few years back and a former nationally ranked player. He never had a big serve but he won with guts and intuitiveness and a "get back in there and fight and don't give up" spirit. No matter what the score, the game was never over and the match was never over until the final point had been won. When Glenn would be playing in a tournament, let's say against a guy named Jones, you would be on one court and you could hear the umpire on another court saying, "15-Jones . . . 30-Jones . . . 40-Jones . . ." and you'd figure that Glenn didn't have a chance. But before you knew it you'd hear, "Game, Mr. Bassett." Today, as the UCLA tennis coach, Glenn instills that same kind of fight in his players, which I really love to see.

f. It may sound simplistic, but it's important to remind yourself: *every game is important.* Some tennis buffs like to theorize that the seventh or the ninth game of the set is the most important, but this leads people to think subconsciously that the first three or four games are worth less while later games are worth more and they tend to play with corresponding levels of intensity and concentration. The smart player simply concentrates on each shot.

Coping with Different Court Surfaces

I like my students to understand that an individual who has sound strokes is going to be good on any surface, whether it's cement, clay, grass, or artificial carpeting. Individual surfaces, however, will allow people to capitalize on particular strengths or penalize them for specific weaknesses.

For instances, a person with a big serve and hard but erratic groundstrokes should stick to a fast surface, such as grass or cement. It will reward his speed and help him end the point quickly before his groundstrokes betray him. Conversely, when this big hitter gets on slow surfaces against a person who can get the ball back, he's going to have to return a lot more balls to win each point — and the more times the ball goes over the net, the greater his chances of making an error. So the hard hitter should look for a surface that helps end the point quickly, while the steadier player should find a surface such as clay that demands greater stroke production.

Another reason players with a serve-and-volley game favor a surface like cement is that it guarantees sound footing for when they follow their serve to the net. Very few players are able to serve and attack effectively on clay because their feet tend to slip and slide. Only the great servers will attack regularly on clay because they know their serve is so good they're going to produce weak returns. Some of the new synthetic surfaces are so slow that they, too, inhibit an attacking type of game by having the ball hit and "sit up." Thus the average server finds it wiser to stay back and try to win from the baseline.

One of the great virtues of topspin, of course, is that it remains effective on every type of surface. Even on the new Forest Hills surface of composition clay, a topspin groundstroke that lands short will still kick deep and keep most players behind the baseline, whereas underspin hits and dies, allowing players to come in and make their approach shot.

On grass, groundstrokes tend to skid low and stay low longer, making them difficult to handle by some players. But it's a myth that this inhibits or penalizes a topspin game. Physicists tell me that when you really want to topspin the ball, you want it to bounce low so that you can brush up against it with a big lift. And, they say, it's harder to topspin a high-bouncing ball. Therefore, grass surfaces favor topspin, especially on the forehand side where you have a split second longer to contact the ball properly. This also means that players who use a two-handed backhand gain an advantage on low balls because they are actually hitting with two forehands.

I once asked Kramer, "If you had to play Gonzales when you both were in your prime, and if you had the choice of one surface, what would you choose?" I thought that because Jack was the innovator of the big game, he would choose a fast surface. Yet his answer was, "The slowest surface in the world."

"That amazes me," I said. "Why do you say that?"

"Because I had better strokes," he replied. "Gorgo had a couple of weaknesses, and if we played on a slow surface, he would have to hit them sooner or later. I also had a little better concentration span, and Gorgo knew that. So when we would get into a position where those things were evident —

even if we played a five-hour match and it was very close all the way — I would know I was going to win, and he would know I was going to win."

So it only goes to show that the great champions are confident that if they are put under pressure, and they can't pull off the big game, they can still win with their basic fundamentals on any court surface.

Handling the Wind, Heat, and Sun

Smart players always check the wind before they play so that they seldom have to experiment during the match. Unfortunately, most people find out which way the wind is blowing on a key point when they try to throw up a lob. When they miss it they think, "Well, I'll make the right allowances on the next one." But that chance may come at set point against you.

If wind is generally prevalent where you play, take time before your next match to see how it affects lobs hit from both ends of the court. When you have a crosswind, you want to know how far you should lob the ball to the right or the left of the alley so that the ball will come down into the court. Check one side, then check the other. When the wind is blowing in your face, experiment to see how hard you have to hit; against a strong wind I always tried to lob to the back fence. When the wind was at my back, I tried to have my lob land at the net and it would come close to my opponent's baseline. Checking these things out beforehand will give you the confidence that you won't have to experiment at a critical moment in the match.

I've always been fascinated by how much a hat can bring down body temperature in hot, sunny weather. Rod Laver would even put a piece of cabbage inside his old Aussie hat, while other players will use a wet sponge to keep the head cool and to absorb perspiration. I think it's smart to learn to play with some kind of a hat, as long as you can find a hat that fits, and providing you don't try to experiment with a new hat during a crucial match, because it can be distracting. People who try to play with sunglasses should also practice with sunglasses.

Dealing with the Player Who "Cheats"

The best way I know to head off disputes over line calls is not to have a "play it over — take two" system. Instead, players should know beforehand that if they don't see the ball land definitely out, it's automatically in.

Still, you will always come up against people who give you bad calls. Some players just have poor eyesight, but most of them are cheating you, and when they do you have four courses of action. One, if you think he's your friend and he's cheating you — he's *not* your friend, so why keep playing him? Two, if he's your friend and you don't want to challenge his bad calls, then you have to forget them and tell yourself that you're playing for the fun of playing. Three, if your friend is convinced he's making accurate calls (and he even suggests that *your* eyesight might be failing), then you should try to have an impartial person watch a match to see how accurate the calls are. Four, if it's in a tournament, you can call for an umpire.

In the end, however the calls go, you have to keep from getting frustrated and letting it interfere with your concentration and your stroke production. In most matches, the bad calls on both sides tend to even out.

Miscellaneous Shots

Put-away, or "Kill" Shots

I haven't dealt with these shots during the book because very few people can put a ball away in the manner they intend, and when they do, it's because somebody else has made an error by hitting them a short lob or a weak groundstroke.

Drop Shots

This is mostly a strategic shot for clay courts — and for pro players. I haven't seen one-tenth of one percent of the population that can hit an effective drop shot from the baseline. And for that matter, nearly every pro I see who tries to hit a drop shot from the backcourt fails to win the point. The ball either goes into the net, or bounces up and allows the opponent to rush in and hit a winner. Thus, never hit a drop shot unless you *know* you're going to win the point or you're trying to tire your opponent.

How to Beat a Wrist Player

Periodically you are going to come across an opponent who plays with a lot of wrist action. Wrist-snappers are identified by an occasional wild shot that goes into the next county when their timing's off, and if you watch you'll generally see their racket face come behind their body on the backswing as they lay the wrist back; fixed-wrist players rarely go back this far. "Wristy" players also tend to follow through around their neck or their chest, and they're either too early or late contacting the ball.

Wrist-rollers (who like to think of themselves as "finesse" players) survive on touch, rhythm, and concentration. Thus they love it when you hit the ball at one consistent speed — the faster the better. When the ball always arrives with relatively the same pace, they can learn just when to roll the wrist. The trick, therefore, is to *never give "wrist-rollers" the same pace twice in a row.* Hit the ball fast, slow, medium, fast, medium, slow, fast and watch their game unravel. That's why a wrist player will knock off a hard-hitter one day, then lose to the club dinker the next, because the dinker hits it slow and slower, and the wrist player can never learn exactly when to roll his wrist. His only defense is to berate the poor dinker and try to shame him into hitting the ball hard. "You're such a lousy player, you ruin my rhythm," is the general attack, but the dinker just keeps playing smart tennis.

You also want to mix up spins and speed to the player who hits with underspin, which normally occurs on the backhand. He, too, is dependent on touch and you don't want him to get in a comfortable groove. You can usually detect an underspin player by the way his racket head stays high on the backswing, up at shoulder level, and then comes down to contact the ball.

How to Beat the Dinker

We all know that dinkers are despised around the world. I mean, they play the game like a sissy, right? They try nothing new, they never drive a ball hard, and they go up to the net once every spring. But while you're making fun of them, they're winning another trophy. Dinkers are successful because they just keep the ball in play with a minimum of speed and fanfare, and a maximum of high bounces and patience . . . waiting for you to miss. In fact, instead of scorning dinkers, you should realize that they are simply capitalizing on basic physical principles and a keen understanding of psychology.

One reason dinkers produce so much aggravation is that they never give you a ball that lands in the middle of the court, between the net and the baseline. They always throw up helium balls (also known as "moonballs") that land deep and bounce high, forcing you to hit up around your armpits all day. You'd much rather play against Bertha, who hits the ball short and with just the right speed to bring it up around waist level so that you can crack your hips into the shot. Not only is it harder to hit off a high bounce, but you also get tired of slugging the ball from behind the baseline. You think you can push the dinker around the court by hitting the ball hard, but he has plenty of time to get ready.

Psychologically, dinkers have developed more patience and a higher frustration-tolerance threshold than most opponents. They keep stoking your boiling point by giving you one more chance to lose until finally you blow up. You decide to do something fancy to win the point and that's when you knock the ball in the net or send it out of play. The dinker just keeps smiling and getting the ball back until eventually your game breaks down entirely.

Despite having these well-entrenched weapons, the dinker is still vulnerable to a smart counterattack. There are methods you can use to spoil his fun — short of trapping him in a dark alley — but you have to be fundamentally sound.

First, *you have to make the dinker play your game*. You can't try to outlast him by playing from the baseline, unless you enjoy losing. The dinker just loves a long point. If the ball goes over the net ten times, you're going, "I can't stand this guy," but the dinker's smiling and thinking, "This could go to 100!" That's why I warn people: play a dinker for five hours and you're looking for oxygen while he's looking for another match.

Second, *there's one place dinkers hate to be, and that's up near the net*. They're the happiest people alive when they can stand back and play from the baseline. But when you bring them up, and the distance decreases between them and the net, they begin to worry. You can even see their faces contort the closer they get.

Third, *the problem is to bring the dinker to the net with the kind of shot* that puts him on the defensive — either a drop shot that barely clears the net, or a short-angle roll shot that forces him to bend down near a singles sideline. If you hit a short ball that goes too deep or just bounces up nice and high, then he doesn't even have to be a good net player to put you away with a placement.

Okay, let's say you learn to hit the short ball so that you can draw the dinker away from his pillbox. The first time you do this he may come in, hit a good approach shot, and then retreat to the baseline, as if to say, "You're not going to trick me." If you're a typical player you may think, "Ah, nuts, he doesn't fall for it," and you won't try another short ball all day. The smart player, however, will keep bringing the dinker to the net over and over again. The dinker will run up and run back, up and back, until about the sixth shot, when he starts turning blue. Then he'll say to himself, "I think I'll stay at the net and show him I'm a great volleyer."

Now the typical intermediate does another unwise thing. He (or she) tries to pass the dinker down the line, but the dinker stretches and hits a lucky volley that wins the point. The intermediate shakes his head and thinks, "Gee, he can volley too. It's amazing." Instead, what you must do when dinkers come to the net is *try to give them a new navel.* Blast the ball right at them and call their bluff; don't let them get away with lucky chops or lunges. That's how the pros find out who can really volley, for when the ball comes right at your stomach, about 80 or 90 miles an hour, you can only be lucky once; the rest of the time — if you can't volley — you'll be picking fuzz out of your navel and saying, "Nice shot . . . nice shot . . . nice shot. . . ."

Remember, the authentic dinker is one who can only play from the baseline. I point this out because people sometimes complain, "I did what you said, Vic. I brought this dinker up short all day but he kept hitting the approach shot deep, he could volley, and he just killed me." Well, if a person can beat you long and beat you short, he's no dinker — he's Laver in disguise. The only thing left is to get him in the bar.

To summarize, if you hope to beat a dinker you must learn to control the short ball so that he must leave his stronghold to hit approach shots and volleys. You must make him play your game. You can't "outsteady" him by letting him stay back. Yet I see people try to beat dinkers this way all the time.

The average player will spend a year working on his game, obsessed with finally destroying the dinker on his own battleground. This person tells his friends, "I've been waiting to beat this guy for ten years. If he wants to dink, terrific. If he wants to play six hours, fantastic. I've been running five miles a day and hitting thousands of balls and I'm ready." Yet once the match begins, the challenger seldom lasts for much longer than six or seven games. He might have the dinker down 4-0, playing from the baseline, but the dinker knows he has the match in his hip pocket. He knows his opponent will never have the patience — or the shots — to outlast him, and that his opponent will be a loony bird before the match is over, simply because he doesn't have the experience or the temperament to hang in there that long. Sure enough, the challenger finally ends up smashing his racket against a net post and crying, "Take it! You can have the match if that's the way you want to play."

Ideally, therefore, what you're striving for in tennis is to be able to dink from the baseline when you have to dink and to attack the net when you have the first opportunity. You want to be aggressive but you also want the dinker's patience. Most dinkers can't do both — attack as well as stay back — but their patty-cake system helps them beat about 95 percent of the tennis-playing population around the world, until they meet somebody who can match them from the baseline and can bring them up to the net. Why not try to be that person?

Chapter Nine

Tennis and Your Psyche

ALTHOUGH TENNIS STILL comes down to a mastery of the fundamentals, these weapons can literally be tossed away if you're unable to control— if not master — the psychological stress brought on by the sport's "one wins, one loses" syndrome. Tennis is booming, people are having tons of fun playing, and advertisers are using the game to push health and well-being. But nobody can pretend that stress doesn't exist out on that court. In fact, if you just talk to some people about playing a match they suddenly can't even remember their name. They have all the strokes at 1:30 — but the match doesn't start until 2. When their opponent says, "Ready to play?" they panic, and if they have to serve you hear them say shakily, "Dear God, let this go in."

The purpose of this chapter, therefore, is to help you find ways to play with confidence and intensity — and a rhythmical swing — from the very first point in the match. I'll talk about how you can learn to rule out psychological contaminants; how to raise your frustration-tolerance level; how to close out a point when you have the strategic advantage; how to finish off an opponent when you have the lead; how to keep from caving in when you get behind; how to keep from "choking" on second serves, overheads, and other crucial points; and how to recognize and deal with the personality quirks of your opponent, deliberate or ingrained as they may be.

Reducing Stress before a Match

I've found that most stress in tennis is really *self-imposed*, and not the result of antics by your opponent. This pressure can stem from a fear of losing, of being humiliated in front of club members, of looking out of style in your cut-off Levi's, of letting down your doubles partner. Some people even have hidden masochistic tendencies — they enjoy suffering. Thus it's much more important to understand and to learn to cope with your own psychological makeup (as well as your own strokes) before you start worrying about your opponent.

It's difficult — and perhaps not even advisable, in a competitive sense — to go into an important match completely relaxed. Even when you know you have the edge on your opponent, the *anticipation* of victory and thoughts about a possible upset are going to make you nervous. But there are a number of steps you can take prior to the match to establish the correct amount of nervousness. Stress in itself is not bad, as long as you know how much you need to help you perform properly.

1. Learn to think like a winner. This isn't possible if you are already setting up excuses for losing: the weather is bad, the court's not clean, you didn't get enough sleep last night, your knee is hurting, you forgot to wear your lucky sweater. Instead of dwelling on "ego outs," think positive and visualize your strengths.

2. A realistic approach to your problems is a great stress-reduction mechanism. In other words, if you had specific weaknesses a week earlier and you've gone out and practiced hard to erase them, you will come into the match with much more confidence. Most players, however, avoid their weaknesses in practice and thus have the same old problems and the same old frustrations week after week after week.

3. Be in sound physical shape. You give your opponent a great psychological lift when you're breathing heavily after the first set.

4. Know your equipment is in excellent condition. Broken strings can be discouraging.

5. Don't sit in the sun for extensive periods before matches or you'll be tired before you walk on the court.

6. If you have a great deal of energy, "hanging around" the tournament watching other matches may make you even more nervous. Some players solve this problem by appearing for matches 10 to 15 minutes before their match is scheduled to begin.

7. Have an objective game plan. Unrealistic goals and excess ego involvement will only lead to intense frustration. Know your own ability level and tell yourself before you go out to play that the best you can do is to make a strong effort in every department — and have some fun while you're at it.

Knowing your own strengths and weaknesses will help keep you from being psyched out during warm-ups. If you're unsure of yourself to begin with, you can easily be intimidated by the opponent who wears color-coordinated clothes, has all the latest equipment, and who informs you that today he's going to concentrate on his topspin lob and his American Twist serve, while experimenting with his latest theory on power tennis. That gets you to thinking, "Why hasn't my pro been teaching me these things? How can I win with my $10 racket against this guy? What am I doing here?"

I mentioned earlier how most tennis players fail to notice anything important about their opponent before a match. But some people are *too* observant about the *wrong* things. That's why, even before two players have swung a racket, you can sometimes pick out the eventual winner and loser. The winner is concentrating on preparing himself for the match, while the loser is looking at the winner. He's all wrapped up in his opponent and is already going down psychologically. If the winner has a big black satchel, the loser is thinking, "I wonder what's in the satchel?" Then he spots his opponent's shoes. "Wow, I've never seen those before in my life — he must be fast!" If his opponent then makes a big flourish as he sprays his racket strings, the loser walks up to the net and says, "If it's all right with you, I don't feel like playing today."

Match-Play Psychology

Ruling Out External Stimuli

One of the similarities between tennis champions, I've discovered, is not that they can think of so many unique things to do on the court, but that they can stick with the simple fundamentals and rule out external stimuli while they play. Even though top business people are accustomed to working under intense pressure, they rarely can bring that same kind of concentration to tennis. When they play they are bothered by the wind, the sun, comments from spectators, people playing on the adjacent court, etc. A top player, however, can shut off distractions like he had a light switch in his brain.

Sure, Pancho Gonzales was one of the game's most notorious red-necks, but nearly everybody overlooks the fact that he had an amazing flexibility. He had a short fuse; if somebody started heckling him he would storm into the stands. But when he came back down, he would be absolutely calm —

ready to play tennis again. He'd be thinking, "Watch the ball," while the average pro would be so livid he would just fall apart. Gorgo would just go right back to beating your brains out with a 130-mph serve. I don't advocate going into the stands as a way to let off steam, but Gonzales is an example of how all the great champions are able to refocus their attention on the next point immediately after blowing up, without letting the incident affect their play.

The problem is, how do you achieve that icy concentration where you can learn to rule out distractions such as the weather, bad line calls, thoughts about winning or losing, distracting movements by your opponent — while focusing completely on the object that is most important to you: the ball? How do you detach yourself from any kind of personality involvement?

First, *do whatever you can to keep your attention glued on the shot you are making or anticipating.* Pay attention to your breathing or some little checkpoint on your swing that keeps you thinking of the present condition, not the past or the future. If you dwell on a shot you've just hit into the net, or if you're thinking ahead a few shots, of how you're going to set your opponent up for the "kill," then you're not giving enough respect to the shot you're on. But don't get caught in an internal debate, where voices inside you are arguing, "Concentrate, you dummy! Why can't you concentrate?" You can concentrate *too* much and forget about hitting the ball.

It's fascinating to me that people have to fight off these intruding thoughts at every level of the game. There's no real difference between a ten-year-old girl who's thinking, "I've got to win because my folks are in the stands," or a pro like Charles Pasarell, who commented after a victory several years ago, "I hadn't won a match for so long I was really nervous." That also told me that while he was playing he was thinking that he hadn't won a match in a long time. This is one reason why, as a coach, I'm almost afraid to try to "psyche up" a player to win a match. I want him to be detached, unemotional, concentrating on his strokes. He should do his analyzing and worrying during practice sessions and reflective thinking hours, because once he starts thinking during a match, it's usually all over.

Second, *don't lose your energy — or your concentration — getting mad.* Concentrate on the shot you are making and don't brood about the easy overhead you just whiffed, or a bad line call. The bad calls and the crummy shots tend to fall both ways in a close match.

Third, *don't be discouraged by your opponent's unbelievable saves.* In basketball, for instance, you can shoot your very best jump shot and if it goes through the basket nobody can do anything about it. But if you hit a fantastic shot in tennis, your opponent can still lay it back for a winner. This can have a disheartening effect if it happens throughout the match, since you tend to forget your own good shots while only remembering his remarkable saves. All you can really do is dwell on the present and keep making the play.

Learning to Close Out Your Opponent

Every pro will tell you from sad experience: *never let up when you have an opponent in trouble.* Don't relax, don't ease off because you feel sorry for him, don't give him a break on line calls. If he falls and you have a wide-open court, concentrate on hitting a winning shot, then see if he needs any help.

Tell me it's not true that when you let a person off the hook and he gets back in the game, he shows no mercy. If he goes on to beat you, he just says afterwards, "You're getting better." He completely forgets your generosity. So finish the guy off when you have him on the ropes and let him go get a milk and a sandwich. *Never feel guilty about winning, no matter what the score.*

Kramer's feeling, and I agree, is that if your opponent is a friend, do him a favor by beating him fair and square, as fast as you can. When you give people games or you try to be nice to them, you haven't done anything for them. You've let them think that you've played your best and that they're better than they really are. An honest system in a match is to have opponents know that you are always going to play as hard as you can, and that whenever they do win, they'll know that they really earned it.

A rule of thumb closely related to all this is: *if you are winning, never change your style of play to keep your opponent "honest."* If you take a big lead by playing aggressively, don't suddenly turn cautious and conservative when you sense victory. If you're winning two out of three points attacking your opponent's backhand, you're crazy to go to his forehand just for the sake of variety. Why change a winning tactic? Your opponent may have lost all his confidence, but if he knocks off a big forehand winner he might revive and climb back into the match. Momentum is an elusive element and often impossible to retrieve once lost. (If you are *losing*, however, then you should change your strategy, and the point at which you change should be determined prior to the match.)

All this doesn't mean you have to acquire a "killer instinct," whereby you want to destroy your opponent, humiliate him, make him want to quit the game. I've never seen the pros go that way. They want to win, but they have great respect for one another. What it really means to them is, "Look, the rules of this game are that one man wins and one loses, and I'd rather not lose."

Okay, let's say you buy my argument about showing no sympathy when you have break point on your opponent's serve, or set point, or match point. But when you go out to play you still can't hold on to a lead. What are you doing wrong?

I've found that many people — and even young pros who are trying to break into the top level of play — very often have trouble playing well as they come closer to winning. They get emotionally involved and they increase their thought processes. They have a tendency to let their mind wander to victory — "Jeez, I can win now if I can just hold my serve" — and very often that's when they begin to lose. Instead, they must remind themselves, *"I've been winning by concentrating on each shot. If I maintain that system, that's the best I can do. All these other thoughts are contaminants."*

To keep the anticipation of victory from ruining your concentration and making you even more nervous than when you are behind, try to ignore the set score. If you're ahead 5-3 and you're thinking about the next set, then you're failing to take care of each shot as it comes. This is why so many people lose their serve after breaking their opponent's serve. They make a fatal mistake by thinking, "Now I've got her," when they should be saying to themselves, "Chin up, watch the ball . . ." That's one reason why Kramer was so devastating: when he broke your serve at 5-all, you knew he was going to hold his own serve because he concentrated only upon his present stroke.

So when you get the lead — and throughout the match, for that matter — *let the other person do the extra thinking.* Remember, whenever you have the server only one point away from a service break, he or she is worrying more about *that* than a proper service motion. In fact, this is where most players tend to do their greatest amount of thinking. They know they're supposed to win their serve — the service break is like the goal-line fumble in football — and yet they're suddenly down 30–40. These thoughts are negative, and you don't want to let your opponent get an emotional reprieve. So if his next serve lands in, just keep the pressure on by maintaining your winning system.

Whether you have the lead or you're behind, work to maintain a high

frustration-tolerance threshold. *Don't let overconfidence or your eagerness to win ruin your patience.* If the ball goes over the net three or four times, don't think you suddenly have to do something *big* to win the point — you tend to die young when you try to get fancy.

Finally, learn to treat the first point of every game with the same respect as 30-all. This habit will help you play match points with the same confidence as other points, and help you approach every point with the intensity of match point.

This little volleyer has learned to "laugh and hit." Unfortunately, millions of adults have failed to get the message.

Developing a Competitive Ethic

When people who have managed to avoid head-to-head athletic competition finally get into tennis, they can't believe how hard it is to play under that kind of pressure. Many people, in fact, just refuse to play a match — they are lifelong rallyers — because they don't want to be forced into a win-lose situation. This is a sad kind of thing to me because they've missed the competition. That's why I feel that people need to depersonalize the game, and their opponent, by getting wrapped up in *self-improvement* instead of worrying about their won-lost record. They should measure their success and reward themselves based upon their relationship to the ball during a match: the gains they made on a particular stroke, how well they kept the ball in play, their ability to anticipate and react to the first short ball, etc. If people could learn to do that early in life, "winning" would take care of itself, and we would have many more gracious winners and losers.

"Winning is everything" is such a narcissistic viewpoint. What we're saying is that the world is made for a select few. In a 64-man tournament, we commit 63 people to failure. I can't stand the approach. Sure it's a frustrating game when you lose; there are days when you want to kill your opponent — or yourself. But I say, forget about your losses. Laugh and hit. Chances are you'll have more fun and you'll win more often in the long run.

For years I've watched people do this metamorphosis: A youngster starts out in tennis and you try to get him (or her) to have fun. As his strokes improve, he starts playing in tournaments and getting into tough competition. He gets to a point where maybe he's the city champ but when he finds he can't win on the state level, or nationally, very often he drops the game. Not until later, when he's in his 30s or 40s, will he start playing again — free of all those expectations that were made for him by his parents and his coach and himself when he was a teenager. What a tragic thing that once he got hooked on the game he couldn't play all the way through and just enjoy himself, no matter what level of success he attained.

So don't be consumed by a "win-or-else" philosophy. Half the people who play this game every day are losers, but that doesn't mean they can't have fun. Yet so many people who lose consistently just get down on themselves and get so frustrated — "Jeez, I'm such a crummy player" — that they are never going to improve. Champions have flexibility: they can adapt to losing situations, and learn from them. But I find that losers can't hack it — they lose and the whole world is on their shoulders. They live in the past instead of trying to work on their future by improving their strokes in the present. When a champion like Laver would lose an important match, he wouldn't moan about his bad luck or go off sulking. He would just admit the truth: "I didn't play well, I didn't hit the right shots, I missed an easy volley at 3-all in the third. So I've got to get out and work on my strokes. If I hit the ball well I'll win, if I don't hit it well, I'll lose. All it means is that I have to work a little harder." But he wouldn't let this spoil his enjoyment of outside interests.

Personality Types in Tennis

Most people take up tennis as a way to ease tension and to get a little exercise. But they soon discover that the pressure to win and to "look good" can bring to the surface deep emotions that they've been able to submerge in other aspects of adult life. For example, company presidents are able to rationalize daily setbacks by playing with words. They can state that they expected to get 28 percent of the market but "due to a sudden shift of the business climate" they only got 22 percent. Yet when they go out to play tennis it's a very definitive pressure: one wins and one loses; nobody ties, no matter what the climate.

Unlike other sports, where you can also compete against the golf course, the ski mountain, or the ocean, tennis comes down to just you and that person (or persons) across the net. Laying yourself open like this to direct competition is what trips off a lot of crazy behavior as people try desperately to protect their self-esteem. Many people even admit that they are startled at their behavior on the tennis court. They tell me, "Vic, I'm usually reserved but I'm out there calling this person an idiot and accusing him of cheating me."

The fact that tennis can trigger these raw emotions has given me a chance to isolate and observe many distinct personality types and behavior patterns over the years. If you can learn to recognize these traits in your friends and enemies (and perhaps yourself) you should be able to develop effective counter-strategies.

The Unbelievable Dresser

He has everything — sweatbands, headband, "40-love" underwear, a golf glove for his hitting hand, a sun visor, and embroidered tennis rackets on the towel he carefully lays over the net. Everything is immaculate. But I seldom see people who are obsessed with wearing the latest clothes win too many matches. They place too much faith in a new pair of shorts. If they lean against the fence and get their sweater dirty, they're broken up for the day — it's worse than losing the match.

The only time these people gain a psychological edge is when they play somebody who is worried about his own self-image, who is easily intimidated if he feels he is not dressed right. I know I went through this as a teenager, early in my tournament career. My family couldn't afford the very best, so when I played in junior events against kids with fancy sweaters and starched tennis whites, I'd think, "Man, I can't wait to see this guy play." But the moment we started to rally, I realized I could beat him easily — if I didn't let myself be distracted by his clothes.

The Equipment Freak

Show me a club player with four matching rackets and a leather case and I'll usually show you a loser with an expensive hobby. This person has everything except the strokes, but instead of going to work on his weaknesses, he blames all of his trouble on his racket. He misses his shots, loses the match, and immediately runs over to the pro shop and buys a more expensive model.

The Sensualist

The sensual kind of player flits about the court with unbelievable movements, but his pièce de résistance is his service motion. He's picked out some exotic body image that he has tested for hours against a mirror, and all the lessons in the world won't get him to change. Instead, he gives you 30 or 40 weird gyrations until right before impact, at which point he stops and goes "doink!" and hits a marshmallow serve. This kind of "twist" serve is big on the celebrity circuit.

The Trophy Seekers

They're beautiful. Their needs are so great that they look all over the doggone country for tournaments where they might win a trophy, often claiming they are C players when they are really Bs. I even know people who literally stage their own tournaments and buy the trophies so that they can end up winning one for their living room mantel.

The Scorekeepers

They can remember every score and every highlight of every match they've ever played. If you make a great play, they always have a story to top it. "I remember in '38 I was playing Burt Brown and I had him down 4-2, 30-love, when I hit a shot even better than that. . . ."

The Theorist

He's great at theorizing about the game but he fails to take into account one thing: he doesn't have the strokes to carry out his grandiose plans. "Down the middle and deep" doesn't have enough pizzazz for him, so he keeps coming up with a new "winning" strategy to replace the one which helped him lose, 6-0, 6-0. He often hangs out with the Equipment Freak, exchanging rackets and theories.

The Sadist

His only goal is to give people "the new look." Thus he loves doubles, where he can pick on people who are already fearful at the net. He tries to hit the ball as hard as he can right at them, getting sheer delight out of watching their frightened expressions. He starts a lot of fights in mixed doubles by never hesitating to go after the woman across the net — especially if it's his wife.

The Manipulator

He can't tolerate being in a position where he feels as though he's going to be manipulated, so he does everything he can to gain an immediate psychological edge. Opening a can of balls before the match, he'll tell his opponent, "I really shouldn't be playing you, I'm so much higher on the ladder." When play begins he goes for speed and power, trying to overwhelm his opponent. Yet his need to dominate seems to go beyond winning. He usually beats his opponent to the clubhouse, beats him giving the scores, and beats him in rehashing the match to friends.

In a sense, nearly everybody who plays club tennis is a manipulator. They're business executives, lawyers, doctors, or whatever, and they're used to manipulating. But now they run up against other people who manipulate, which leads to some interesting rivalries on the tennis court. This is also why club management is such a tough thing. If you have 450 members, you have 450 people who know, in their own minds, that they could be doing a better job of running the facility than the manager.

The Power-Motivated Type

Some people are so power-motivated that hitting their forehand with speed and feeling the sensation of their serve traveling 100 miles an hour are greater rewards than keeping the ball in play, or even winning. If they lose, they're happy as long as their opponent appreciates their power by saying, "Jeez, you hit the ball so hard you almost gave me a new navel. I could hardly hang on to my racket."

The Recognition Seeker

Other players could care less about winning, or even playing, as long as they are recognized at the club. If Jim Volley comes to the club wearing his tennis sweater and carrying his rackets, and everybody says, "Hi, Jim," and he gives them all a friendly wave, then he's just made his day and he hasn't hit a ball yet.

The Defense Mechanics

Although it's difficult to find defense mechanisms that work around intelligent people, some players will go to desperate lengths to save face. Before the match begins, they will try to set the stage with something like, "I didn't get any sleep last night so I probably won't play well," or "I don't mean to complain but I haven't played much in six months." When play begins, their "ego outs" may have nothing to do with reality. They'll complain, "Why does the sun only shine on my side?" Or, "The wind keeps blowing in my face." Or, "They only washed your side of the court — I can't stand up over here." But the same excuses will go on even after you switch courts.

Meanwhile, notice how they will examine their racket strings after every bad shot, which always amazes me because the ball is round and it goes right where you aim it; ball manufacturers seldom put a square ball into a can.

The Player with "Two-Inch Eyes"

We all run across the player who has unbelievable eyesight. When he calls shots that land close to a line he's always telling you, "Sorry — your shot was out by two inches."

Psychological Ploys

I've always liked what Laver said: "Keep your mouth shut and let your racket do the talking." Yet some players also find that part of the fun in tennis is trying to probe psychological weaknesses in their opponents.

If, for example, you sense that your opponent is fearful of winning — she hasn't beaten you in 12 years — then try to remind her of the score, just to keep the thought of winning in her mind. "Well, Bertha, all you have to do is win this game and you win the match." If she has masochistic tendencies, you want to sink your hooks into every break that goes against her. Comments like, "Tough luck, Bertha, you almost made a great save," or "Jeez, the calls are really going against you," will give her exactly the kind of encouragement she needs to keep losing.

Don't forget, however, that your opponent will also be searching for your weaknesses. So if you're a miserable loser, keep it to yourself because you'll begin to telegraph your fears near the end of a tight match. Conversely, if your opponent knows that you fight for every point — that you've got guts — this will influence his thinking as the match drags on, and he may feel he has to hit high-risk shots in order to win. (The women on the pro tour would always talk about Billie Jean King's "will to win" and how impressed they were with her ability to dominate. Obviously these thoughts helped give her a psychological edge week in and week out. But I always wondered, "Why do they all dwell on her will? Why not work on the strokes that can beat her?")

A primary objective in psychological tennis is that you want to increase the number of variables with which your opponent is dealing. Thus, if you are losing, you have to get your opponent's mind off the things he's using to beat you. Just to have him begin to self-doubt, to worry that he may start to lose his touch, to brood over a couple of bad breaks, may be enough to turn the match around.

Over the years, a great many players have been manipulated by Bobby Riggs, myself included. I once played him in a pro tournament in Cleveland in 1951 and I thought I had him cold. I was playing well and leading 6–5 in the first set when we switched courts. As we toweled off, Bobby said, "Jeez, kid, too bad your backhand's not too good. But if you hang in there it'll get better." Well, I was just *killing* him off the backhand — but that got me thinking. "What's wrong with this guy? Doesn't he realize he can't handle my backhand?" But I was only 21 and Riggs was a big-name player and a very nice guy so I thought he was just trying to help me. Naturally I went out and tried to give my backhand a little extra juice to impress him, and naturally I lost everything. He had said something that wasn't even true but he got me thinking about that, instead of just concentrating on stroke production and sticking with my game plan.

Another way to disrupt your opponent's concentration — if you're losing — is to increase the external stimuli so that he takes his eyes off the ball. Try making a flourish as you follow a shot to the net so that he is more likely to watch you out of the corner of his eye as he makes his hit. Even if you can't volley well, just the fact that you are coming to the net will bother most people. They don't like to be attacked; they want to sit back at the baseline and play chess, for when you come to the net you force them into an immediate win-or-lose situation.

At the University of Toledo one year, I coached the basketball team and then the tennis team. We didn't have many tennis players in school, so I talked most of the basketball players into going out for tennis as an off-season conditioner. Most of them had never played before, and we only had six weeks to get ready, so I concentrated on having them attack the net whenever possible. I wanted their opponents to see those 6' 8" guys charging down on them, and to hear those size 14 feet pounding the court. This strategy worked so well that we won over half our matches.

If you are winning and playing well, you don't want to change your rhythm or the pace of the game. But if you are losing you want to do whatever you can to break up your opponent's tempo. Gonzales would buy time by squatting down and getting up very slowly as you were getting ready to serve, and Riggs' shoe always seemed to come untied when he needed to stall. But the best way to frustrate a short-fused opponent, as I pointed out earlier in the book, is to start slowing down the ball, hitting it over the net with less speed, or just lobbing deep. When you increase the time the ball is in the air, you increase anxiety levels in most players by giving them more time to think about their next shot.

Finally, if you can't beat your opponent physically, you have to beat him mentally. Don't be afraid to go way out if that's your only hope. You might even try my "Last Resort Strategy."

If somebody is beating you 6-0, 5-0 in the second set, you're in deep trouble, right? Whatever you've been doing is wrong, but you want to at least avoid a whitewash and salvage a little self-respect. So on your opponent's next shot, turn and run the *wrong* way and take a perfect swing at an imaginary ball. This should shake him up enough to help you win a game or two because he just won't be able to get that picture of absurdity out of his mind.

A similar trick was played on me in college. I was beating this fellow from Michigan, something like 6-2, 5-0, 40-love, and I was serving. Suddenly he held up his hand and said, "Hold it, hold it." He started walking up to the net and I was thinking, "What's wrong? Is he going to question a line call?"

When he got to the net he looked me square in the eye and said, "Give up?"

I think I lost the next three games, I was laughing so hard.

Chapter Ten

Making Sense out of Doubles

I F YOU'RE NOT HAVING FUN playing doubles, then you should either find a new partner, search out different opponents, or see your shrink. Doubles is a tremendous adventure when you can learn certain key points about strategy and movement, and then play with enthusiasm and a lot of laughs. It certainly doesn't have to be slow and boring, with everybody standing around waiting for the ball to come their way. In fact, *you can never afford to fall asleep in good doubles.* You should be moving all the time — running, stretching, anticipating, and using a far greater variety of strokes than you do in an ordinary game of singles. To be a good doubles partner you need to know how to volley and play the net, how to hit overheads and lobs, how to hit service returns with pinpoint accuracy, how to anticipate your opponent's shot, and how to work as a team with your partner. You'll win together and you'll lose together; if you're playing crummy but your partner is terrific, you can still have a lot of fun. And the longer you play together, the more you will discover how you can manipulate, and literally control, a team that has better players, but no teamwork.

Before talking about who plays where and how, here are the key concepts you should keep in mind about doubles:

1. In top competition, your goal is to gain the proper net position before your opponents — or drive them away from that stronghold — because the team that gains the net *controls* the point 95 out of 100 times. Your team may still lose the point, but this is primarily the result of weak strokes.

2. *Force your opponents to hit up, so that you can hit down and give them an early lunch.* You can't get pushed around by opponents who are always lifting the ball. But if you finally get to the net and they are hitting down, you can get killed.

3. Learn to move *in tandem* with your partner, approximately 11 to 12 feet apart — up, back, and horizontally.

4. Unless you have a certain put-away shot, always try to hit *down the middle.* Don't be fooled by a myth of intermediate doubles: "Watch your

alley." That's an early sign to sharp opponents that you can't really play.

5. *The person closest to the net has priority on any shot that he can reach.* If you want to win, dump a partner who tries to tell you before the match, "See that center stripe? That's your side and this is my side. Never get on my side."

6. The best system in doubles is both players up at the net. The second best system is both players at the baseline. The worst system of all — but the worldwide system in club tennis — is one player up and one player back. You might be saying, "Hey look, we've been playing 'one up and one back' at our club for 20 years and we're always successful." That may be true, but that's why you're still playing at your club, and not out on the tournament circuit. You're playing a system that is relegated to club tennis, and that can succeed only if the other team promises to play it too. If they don't, you die. Not only do you leave a wide gap between you and your partner for a diagonal shot by your opponents, but they will both come to the net, and whoever is up there on your team is going to have a "Wilson two-dot" tattooed onto his or her body.

Court Positions to Start a Point

The Server

When serving from the right (deuce) court, his goal is to stand as far from the center stripe as possible, while still being able to hit into his opponent's backhand corner. Gonzales, in fact, would stand right next to the stripe because he placed his primary emphasis on hitting to the backhand. You can stand a little farther away when serving from the left court.

The Partner of the Server

He should stand in the *middle* of the service court, where the diagonals cross. Most beginning and intermediate players hate to stand that close to the center because they're afraid their partner's serve will hit them in the back of the head. This can lead to gigantic arguments, where the net man turns and says, "You dummy, you hit me in the head," and the server replies, "You toad, you wrecked my best serve." If you're afraid of being

The player closer to the net has priority on the volleys from net post to net post. If you don't like someone taking your volleys, work to get those two steps forward and take your own. When you're where you're supposed to be, no one "steals" your shots.

hit, just bend over so that your head won't be a target. Then if you get hit in the rear end at least you know it's a service fault.

The Service Receiver

A pro will stand on or very near the singles sideline, because this is half-way between where the server can run him to his forehand and to his back-hand. If your opponent can't break his serve that wide to your forehand, then you can stand closer to the center stripe.

The Partner of the Receiver

Players with especially quick hands and reflexes should stand just in front of the service line. Those with slower reactions should stand behind the line. Stand *on* the line if you're undecided, but realize that this may block the view of the line judge in tournament tennis.

The Basic Role of Each Player

The Server

His main goal is to consistently get his first serve in play — deep and

The best system in doubles
— for pros and club players
alike — is to have both players of the same team at the
net together.

The second-best system in
doubles is for both players to
be in the backcourt at the
same time.

The worst system in doubles
— and yet the most common— is
for teammates to play one
up and one back. However,
this system is okay if the opponents will promise to use
the same system.

Note the starting positions for all four players. The server stands near the center stripe so that he can serve to his opponent's backhand. The server's partner is at the net in the center of her service court. The receiver has split the distance that the server can run her from forehand to backhand. The partner of the receiver is halfway — ready to go forward or backward depending upon the success of his partner's return.

Responsibilities at the beginning of this point are identical to those of the previous point. The server, however, may choose to stand a little farther to his left to improve his chances of forcing a righthanded receiver to return serve with a backhand.

hopefully with some pace, so that the service receiver can't take the offensive. Then he works on hitting his opponent's backhand corner. Remember the advantages: (1) most people have weaker backhands than forehands; (2) the tendency is to elevate the backhand, which makes it easier for the other team to hit a put-away volley or an overhead; (3) in the deuce court the receiver must hit inside-out or away from his body — which is opposite the natural outside-in tendency — in order to keep the ball away from the opposing net man (This backhand advantage, however, doesn't apply when serving from the left-hand [ad] court: then the tendency is for the receiver to pull his shot away from the net man); (4) the receiver must contact the ball farther out in front in order to hit a topspin backhand at the server's feet; and (5) because the receiver has to hit farther out in front, he tends to be late and thus usually underspins the ball.

The only times you should aim away from your opponent's backhand are: (1) when your opponent's forehand is weaker than his backhand; (2) when he is overplaying his backhand so much that you are positive you can ace him by hitting to his forehand; or (3) when you are positive you can pull him so far out of court that you produce a weak return. If you hit to your opponent's forehand just to "keep him guessing," then you're also guessing that he won't come up with a big winner.

Just as in singles, you should serve and move forward by taking three steps and then momentarily bringing your feet together, ready to break in any direction to handle the service return. Unlike singles, however, you should move in behind a weak first serve and join your partner *if he is already at the net*. Otherwise he's going to be bombarded by your opponents and he won't look the same by the end of the match. If you hit a cream-puff second serve, the two of you should come back and work on lobs to drive your opponents away from the net.

The Partner of the Server

This person plays a key role in helping his partner hold serve. The last thing he can be is a passive spectator. First, he must learn to study the service receiver's racket in order to anticipate a drive or a lob. If the racket is on the same level as the intended point of impact with the ball, it's normally going to be a drive (nobody is talented enough to suddenly drop the racket and lob) and he will break forward on the diagonal to try to cut off the shot near the net. If he sees his opponent's racket head drop below the

(1)

(2)

(3)

(4)

(1) The server has hit to his opponent's backhand, the ideal target in most cases because of the tendency on the backhand to hit a higher return — a pleasant sight for a volleyer at the net. Also notice how the server brings his feet together on his third step, ready to break in any direction. This split-step can be eliminated in doubles if the server knows exactly where the return is going to land. (2) The receiving team can attack the serving team if the receiver's service return is placed at the feet of the onrushing server. This forces the server to hit up, giving the receiving team a chance to hit down. Notice here that the partner of the receiver is closer to the net and has priority on all volleys. Also, the server's partner has moved over near the center stripe to maintain that 11- to 12-foot distance from her partner. (3) A view from the other side of the net shows the server being forced into a low volley. The partner of the receiver should watch the volleyer's racket face to determine whether he should poach or stand his ground. Remember, he has priority at the net. (4) If, however, the receiver's return is high, both players on the receiving team must retreat . . . or else risk getting a fuzz sandwich.

oncoming ball with a beveled face, then it's going to be a lob and he turns and tries to get three quick steps back.

Second, as he studies his opponent's racket he has just one other thing on his mind: "The next ball that's hit is mine. I don't care where it is — I'm going to get it." He should always be surprised that he can't actually get to the ball, never surprised that he makes the play. *He wants to be thinking that he owns that fortress from net post to net post.* He's not embarrassed about thinking that way, or that he will be accused of being a ball hog. He knows he has the advantage over his partner by being able to hit a much sharper volley, closer to the net. But to gain that edge, the strong volleyer is always concentrating, ready to get that first step forward so that he can hopefully close out the point. Weak volleyers, on the other hand, never think about getting a jump on the ball; they just stay rooted in their ready position until the ball has been hit by the service receiver, hopefully to the server.

Remember, you and your partner have to be determined to play an attacking game — to rush the net *as a team* at every opportunity. If your partner serves and doesn't come to the net to join you, that will limit how far you can advance, but not your dental bills; you'll be pulling wool out of your teeth all day. Your only options are to dump your partner or come back to the baseline as he prepares to serve. If he says indignantly, "What are you doing here?" simply tell him, "I want to live."

The Service Receiver

He has two major goals in good tennis: (1) to hit the ball away from the net man, and (2) to hit at the feet of the onrushing server (which forces him to hit up) or to move him as far laterally as possible in order to open up the court.

If the service receiver can land his shot at the server's feet, he must attack the net with his partner because the server is going to have to play the ball defensively. A ball hit from below the tape of the net is impossible to hit hard and accurately. Yet I'm often asked, "What happens if you go charging in and the server hits a good lob off the half-volley?" My answer is, "I've only seen two or three players in my life who could do that. It's a unique kind of ability, so don't let it keep you from storming the net." If the server does get the ball over your heads, then remember that each player is responsible for his own lane — from the net to the baseline. If each player is always ready to cover anything that goes over his head, then that team is always going to take care of itself on lobs.

The Partner of the Receiver

If the receiver can return the serve away from the net man, everything now depends on the receiver's partner. *He's the one who has a chance to make his team famous, depending on how well he can "read" his opponents and make his move to the ball.* In fact, he should try to emulate the good basketball player who learns to move without the ball — suddenly the pass goes to him and he lays it in for two points.

When the point begins, the first duty of the receiver's partner is to turn enough to see where the serve lands, and to call "out" if it is long or wide. If the ball lands in, he quickly turns back and studies the movements of the other team. If he sees an opponent coming in, going "AHHHaaa! AHHHaaa!" and waving his racket over his head as he prepares to deck the ball, then he knows his partner has hit a lousy return, and it's time to retreat for his life.

However, if either one of his opponents is bending down to hit the ball, then he knows the ball will be coming back up and he can move safely to the net in order to volley down. This is where he earns his keep, by his ability to watch his opponent's racket move on the half-volley. If the racket head is parallel to the net, then he jumps forward to volley; if it is angled cross-court, then he rushes in to his partner's territory. He wants to learn to react instinctively so that he doesn't stay glued to his X trying to make a decision. He knows he must move toward the ball on the very next shot.

Like his rival across the net, the partner of the receiver has priority from net post to net post since he is closer to the net. He is obligated to get anything within his reach, and to try to increase that reach by learning to anticipate and to get a quick jump on the ball — much like Maury Wills gradually lengthening his lead off first base by "reading" the pitcher's move. In fact, I think the day will come when we actually measure the partner of the receiver by his ability to lengthen his range, because he's absolutely lethal up at the net when he does.

Most players have never thought much about their role as the partner of the receiver, let alone broken it down into specific steps. But just knowing these duties or concepts will be meaningless if you don't get out and practice. Work against an opponent who's hitting half-volleys and try to analyze whether he's going down the line or cross-court, then practice cutting off his shot. If you can learn to end the point like this, you will have a tremendous future in doubles. You will be sought out by everybody around because this is really a special talent.

Unfortunately, the role I have just described is not what you see in typical club tennis. The partner of the receiver feels he has nothing to do except watch his partner rally back and forth with the server until one of them makes an error. This is the essence of "one up and one back" doubles, with the server and the receiver playing singles while their partners talk across the net and offer encouragement — "Hang in there, Bertha." The only thing these net persons get is a stiff neck and a suntan on one side of their face; if a shot suddenly comes their way, they dump it — "Oh, I wasn't expecting that one" — because they aren't prepared.

People laugh when I point this out to them, but somebody always says, "Wait a minute, Vic. You're telling us to serve and attack, volley, play the net, run back for lobs — but we can't do all that stuff. We're just happy to be alive."

Don't get me wrong. I'm not knocking "one up and one back" doubles. If that's what everybody at your club plays, and you're having a great time, don't feel guilty. You're supposed to be happy out there. But remember, *"one up and one back" is fun only if the other team promises to play it too.*

Tactics in Good Doubles

Controlling the Net

The net is the battlefield in good doubles. That's where the point is going to be won or lost. Storm the barrier, take over the fortress, and don't let yourself be pushed off except by a great lob. In pro tennis, the first team to gain the net *controls* the point nearly every time. They may miss an overhead or a volley when they get there, but basically they get the *opportunity* to win the point. Intermediates gain the same advantage but their chances of winning the point are about 50–50 because they make so many errors. And beginners rush up there in order to lose at a faster rate.

Intermediates might say, "We can't volley, so we'll just stay back and lob and keep our opponents away from the net." But remember, very few teams can lob well enough from the baseline to beat good net players. Not even the pros can lob deep three times in a row. So going to the net is still your

If the server stays back after he serves, the receiver should hit a deep return to the server and the receiving team should charge the net together.

best shot at winning — providing you also work on the weapons that will get you there. (Although it's a losing proposition, I always encourage beginners to attack the net, since they want to end up playing there eventually. But at their level, if they can just learn to lob, they can win from the baseline against other beginners who take the net.)

Just as in singles, *the reason your team wants to control the net is that you can be crummy volleyers but still win the point.* You can hit down on the ball — which is the natural tendency on the volley anyway — and you can hit at very sharp angles. Even little dinky shots can close out the point. But the farther back you get from the net, the more talent you must have. If you volley halfway between the net and the service line, and you pull down on your volley even slightly, the ball will catch the net. If you hit from the service line, where many intermediates and beginners volley in doubles, you almost have to lift the ball in order to keep it deep and thus maintain distance between you and your opponents. (Also, the closer you get to the net, the more difficult it is for anyone to pass you on any angle, since you are much closer to the line of flight of the ball.)

If your opponents lob successfully and drive you back from the net to the baseline, they should match you step for step and take over the net. In that case you should try to lob right back and regain the fortress, or try to end the point immediately by driving an overhead down the middle. Your odds are better with the lob, but most people begin to balk at this point. "We don't want to go all the way back to the net again," they say. "Then they'll lob over our heads and we'll have to run back and we'll die." But this isn't going to happen because *club players don't lob well two times in a row.* Very often your opponents' second lob — if not the first — will be short and will give you an easy overhead to end the point. So don't be pushed away from the fortress that easily. Try desperately to get it back and let your opponents know they're not going to scare you off with one good lob.

It's that determination to get the net and control the net, and your desperate efforts to get it back should you lose it, that will make you and your partner a great doubles team. If you lob once but stay back, that's a tip-off to your opponents that you're afraid — or too lazy to regain the net. The next time you look up they will be perched at the net, knowing they have nothing to fear but their own errors. Your only hope then of winning from the baseline will be to have a great lob, a lot of patience, and willingness to eat plenty of "fuzz" because the other team is going to be blasting overheads off your weak lobs all day.

Overcoming Fears of the Fuzz Sandwich

When the ball is put into play, two players are already in a position to move quickly to the net — the partner of the server and the partner of the receiver. Both of them should have hot-dog tendencies, eagerly anticipating their chance to make a play at the net that could win the point. Unfortunately, many players only have a feeling of panic mixed with fear: they don't want that kind of pressure placed on their weak volley, and/or they're afraid of getting hurt by the ball. The latter is especially true with women who find themselves in a game of mixed doubles where "everything goes." There are a lot of male chauvinists around who love to try to intimidate the woman at the net with a few hard shots at her navel, all in the guise of giving the woman fair and equal treatment in sports. Thus, it's more important than ever for women to learn to be aggressive at the net and not simply stand there with a racket in front of their face. Moreover, as I point

If your team controls the net, and your opponent looks as though he's going to lob, you and your partner should turn and take three quick steps toward the baseline. Three steps can get you into good position for 90 percent of all lobs.

If your opponent hits a great lob over your head, he and his partner should charge the net while you are scrambling to retrieve the shot.

out in the section on mixed doubles, *the woman — and not the man — is very often the person who makes her team famous since she gets far more shots directed her way.*

I have to be honest with my women readers. Many of you want to play in the big leagues but you don't want anybody to hit the ball at you. You cannot have it both ways. If you don't want anybody deliberately giving you the fuzz sandwich, you have to establish a social relationship with your opponents where this is understood from the very beginning and everybody agrees to it. Then if somebody hits you he's a dirty rat, and he's fair game for your husband or boyfriend. But if there's any kind of competitive effort involved (if you're playing in a tournament, for example), then the sky's the limit. As a matter of fact, trying to produce fear in your opponents is a legitimate part of the game. If you want to play tennis the right way, be prepared to have a ball zeroing in on your body, and don't get mad if it hits you. It's your job to know how to volley or how to scream, one or the other.

Even when women are determined to play the net, I know that fear can still take over and force them — and many men — to do some strange things. I talked earlier about people who run up to the net and catch the ball, when they mean to volley. Very often they will make fantastic mental decisions ("That ball is going to hit me") but have no physical response, and the ball bounces off their forehead. All I can suggest, if you're truly afraid of playing the net, is to keep your racket in front of your body, ready for action. If the ball comes at your head, put the racket in front of your face, then *move your head* to the side. But don't do like some people, who get mixed up and move their racket away instead of their face. The ball hurts, and besides you lose the point.

Protecting the Middle

I've long been fascinated by the intermediates who say, "Watch your alley," while the pros are always talking about protecting the middle. Intermediates are so afraid of their opponents hitting down the line that one of them plays wide to the left side and the other wide to the right. Unfortunately, they're one man short. You could drive a truck between them. They're so intent on guarding their alleys that when a ball is hit down the middle they both automatically turn and say, "Yours."

There are three reasons why, in good doubles, you normally want to try to hit down the middle: (1) the net is lower in the center than it is at the net posts by 5½ inches, (2) you reduce the angle at which opponents can hit back at you over a low net, and (3) there's a chance your opponents will come together and clash rackets.

Conversely, you always want to entice your opponents to try those difficult, low-percentage shots to your outside. Pros will only drive the alleys if they think you are breaking too early for a ball down the center (i.e., poaching) or if they want to keep you from overplaying the middle.

Learning to Anticipate

You can't have an indecisive approach to this game. You have to learn to react instinctively to your opponent's shot, and then break for the ball. Yet the average player can't seem to do this.

One problem, with women especially, is that they immobilize themselves in their ready position as they wait for the point to begin between the server and the service receiver. Instead of staying on her toes, ready to break in any direction, the woman settles down on her heels and gets very comfortable, her rear end stuck out and her racket in front of her face. Hypnosis often sets in and she's not about to move. If the ball goes down the middle she just turns and watches it go by, saying, "Nuts, I should have gone." Then another ball passes nearby and again she doesn't move. So now she really gets stoked up and she's telling herself, "My husband is really getting mad. If I don't try for the next shot I will be an idiot." Then the ball comes and she says, "Yours."

Other players are scared to death of making the wrong move. They may be thinking correctly, asking themselves "Drive or lob? Drive or lob?" as they study their opponent's racket. But they don't want to look bad by starting forward for a drive just as their opponent lobs over their head, so they don't move either way. Suddenly the ball goes over their head and they have to turn and run like crazy to make the play. But they're always too late.

I try to tell all my students: *don't be afraid to make mistakes in judgment.* If you guess wrong, don't get upset. Very often your opponent doesn't even know where the ball is going when he swings. The point of the game is to have some fun, and if you can make yourself experiment and take some chances, you're going to learn to play with the right responses. But first you have to commit yourself one way or the other.

When you're in that momentary ready position near the service line, or halfway between that line and the net, keep telling yourself, "drive or lob, drive or lob," as you study your opponent's racket. At first everybody has trouble judging before impact where the ball might go. Fortunately, tennis balls are round and they travel right where the racket aims them. So if the racket head is tilted up, then the ball is going up, and you can retreat for a lob. If it's tilted down, your opponent will have to hit *under* the net. If the racket face is vertical, and moving straight across, the ball's going on a horizontal level and you want to take off and crowd the net. *The key is to watch your opponent's racket — and don't let yourself be distracted by his body movements.* Prior charting will help give you an even better sense of what he is going to do.

Moving Together as a Team

If you and your partner can learn to move as a team in the direction of the ball, approximately 11 to 12 feet apart, you will rarely be passed, either down the line or between you.

For example, on a 27-foot-wide singles court, it's hard to pass a player who knows how to follow his shot to that side of the center stripe to which he hit, and who knows how to shift with the ball. It's even more difficult in doubles, where the court is 36 feet wide and each player only has to cover 18 feet laterally — if he or she moves in tandem with his or her partner.

Learn to *shift with the ball*: forward and diagonally for a drive, and back for a lob. If you hit the ball to the right side of the court, overload that side to cut off the angle of your opponent's return. If the ball goes down the center, come back to the center, and if it goes to the left side, move to the left — and few teams will get the ball past you on purpose. You may feel you're leaving yourself unprotected on one flank when you shift far to the left. But if you ever find a player who can consistently hit the ball in that narrow target area on the diagonal, I'll show you a player in white robes.

Always maintain that 11- to 12-foot distance apart. If your partner shifts and you fail to move, you obviously leave a gaping hole between the two of you for your opponent's return shot. Get the feeling of being connected to your partner by an invisible rope as you practice shifting together. But don't use a real rope. I once tried this trick with an intermediate tennis team and both persons got rope burns when they tugged — one going east, the other going west.

Communicating out loud with your partner is the best method I know to help coordinate reactions and movements as a team. Both of you should learn to call out, "It's a drive!" or "It's a lob!" while breaking for the ball. At first you may be a little self-conscious, and there will be times when your partner calls out "drive" just as you yell "lob" and you run in different directions. But after you've played together a while you should begin to react instinctively so that when the ball is hit — boom — you're both going as a team. To develop this teamwork, however, neither of you can be reluctant to call out advice or instructions that can help the other partner. This requires a conscious effort. Basketball players think nothing about yelling to a teammate on defense — such as "Switch, I've got this man." But tennis players have somehow gained the impression over the years that they're not supposed to talk to their partner while the point is being played. Thus I see many teams where both players are silent, each of them absorbed in their own game of singles. I've also found that when people forget to even talk to their partner during the point — at least in a strategic or tactical sense — that they each feel less of a responsibility to get that quick jump on the ball. Nor do I give much hope to the team where one player is talking and the other one is quiet. But when both players are yelling and forcing themselves to call out the shot, the player who tends to react later than his partner will start working harder at anticipating a drive or a lob, providing he has the barest sense of teamwork.

Reacting to the Ball

On a drive (any shot that you can volley) your team wants to get that fast first step toward the net. *Attack — don't wait for the ball to come to you.* The closer you can get to the net, the higher above the net you can volley. The ball drops rapidly and if you let it sink below the tape of the net, you place yourself on the defensive and all you can do is try to punch the ball deep. I used to watch Jack Kramer go nuts in the stands when he saw a player with good position hesitate and let the ball fall below the level of the net, then try to hit an offensive volley. Jack has seen few players in the history of the game who could take a low ball and convert it into an offensive volley with any real success.

If you and your partner see a lob coming, turn and run back three steps. *If you can reach the service line before the ball reaches the net, nobody will ever lob over your head successfully.* You will always have good position, either to lob back or to hit an overhead smash out in front of your body.

Net play in doubles should resemble net play in singles. When your opponents are hitting from the middle of the baseline, you and your partner should stand in the center of your service courts, 11 to 12 feet apart.

When your opponents are hitting from their left side, shift with your partner to the right side of your respective service courts.

When your opponents move to the right side of their baseline, shift accordingly, to the left side of your service courts.

Look over your shoulder at the ball as you run, since most people can get back faster that way than by backpedaling. (If you prefer to backpedal, put me to the test. Go out on the court and try both ways to see which is actually faster for you.) Another question I always get is, "What happens if you turn and run too far?" That's never a problem. It's far better to be able to step forward into your overhead smash than it is to be caught with the ball getting behind you. Remember, your goal is to hit an overhead in precisely the same manner as you hit a serve.

Many doubles teams are afraid to react quickly up at the net even if they smell a lob coming. They think their opponent is going to trick them by faking a lob to get them going back, then leveling off, and smacking a drive. Fortunately, people can't hit the two shots with uninterrupted stroke production. If they go to strike the ball in one manner, it's asking too much for them to switch to a second approach all in one swing. Let them *try*, of course, but don't worry about the result.

Good Doubles Is Organized Chaos

Doubles action is pretty slow the way most people play. When a player gets to the net, he says, "Made it!" He's so happy about landing on the X that he's not about to budge. *But in good doubles, if you're standing still for two shots, you've probably committed a serious error.* You should always be moving in unison with your partner — up, back, or laterally — and committing yourself almost automatically.

In fact, at the pro level today there's a trend for a kamikaze type of approach to doubles, where very often the team receiving serve is blindly going to the net because they've discovered that to stay back and try to win from the baseline is a losing proposition. Thus you see all four players attacking each other near the net, and "the first chicken loses." There's a lot of chaos in their exchanges as they rely on quick hands and reflexes.

However, I don't buy the theory that it's impossible to win from a deep position. The "gain the net" system hasn't been tested well enough by two players who have the strokes to really keep the team at the net under constant pressure: by lobbing well consistently, by retrieving overhead smashes and returning them with well-placed lobs, and by hitting strong overheads from behind the baseline. But if a team doesn't have these strokes, then it might as well go kamikaze because to stay back is sheer folly.

Priority and Responsibility on Specific Shots

"Who Has Priority on Shots Down the Middle?"

Intermediates around the world have never been able to resolve the question of who takes the ball down the middle. Thus you either see both of them saying, "I've got it," and then crashing into each other, or both of them saying, "Yours," and then looking at each other with a blank stare as the ball passes between them.

Smart teams, however, can work out this decision before the match by basing it on two fundamental considerations: (1) which player is closer to the net, and (2) who has the stronger shot down the center?

When your team is at the net, the player closer to the net always has priority. He should have the freedom to run right in front of his partner to volley because his angle is better and he can end the point quicker. The player who's deep has a greater chance of missing his volley and he can't hit volleys on as sharp an angle.

If both players are the same distance from the net, then the person with the stronger volley down the middle should make the play. It's not automatic that the forehand volleyer takes the shot, since some players actually have a better backhand volley than their partner's forehand volley. Ken Rosewall, for instance, has such a fantastic backhand that you wouldn't dream of getting in his way.

The best way to prevent confusion and hesitation when the ball comes down the middle is to work out a $\frac{5}{8}$-$\frac{3}{8}$ system with your partner. Decide ahead of time — objectively — who has the best volley at the net and near the service line, and the best groundstroke at the baseline. Then that person will take any ball within $\frac{5}{8}$ of the distance between you if you are playing side by side. If you both have crummy volleys, then flip a coin to decide, but never feel guilty about negotiating over who has the stronger volley and the stronger groundstroke. It isn't simply that you might let a ball get between you, but that the slightest bit of timidity by the player going for the ball can result in a weaker volley. This person needs to go after the ball with all the confidence in the world, his mind free to really crunch a volley without worrying about clashing rackets or getting cracked in the head by his partner's racket. This kind of mix-up can create unbelievable fear and hesitation the next time a ball comes down the middle, so try to eliminate the confusion beforehand.

"What Are You Doing on My Side of the Court?"

One of the most common arguments in tennis starts with the accusation, "Hey, you took my shot." This stems from the predominant understanding in doubles the world over: "This is my side and that's your side. Don't get on my side." But if you have a partner who wants to play this way — and you want to win — then you'd better dump this person fast. If it's your mom, then try to have her realize that the player closer to the net has priority.

There's no such thing as "my side, your side" in big-time tennis. It's zoom, zoom, crossing back and forth in front of one another. If a player is caught back, he *wants* his partner to jump across and take away his volley at the net. He knows that his partner has priority from net post to net post if he can make the play.

You can never get mad at your partner for running in front to steal your shot. Basically he is hitting the volley where you were supposed to have been if your tail had been in gear. Plus your team has a better chance of winning the point. In fact, the person who takes the volley up close should turn around and say to his lagging partner, "Get your rear end up to the net and take your own shots — I'm getting tired of this."

I used to play some doubles around Southern California with Louise Brough, who was U.S. National doubles champion 12 times, and I know what it's like to have your partner keep handling your case. When we first started playing together, Louise had a faster first step than I did, and thus she would beat me to every volley between us. She was better than me, but it still hurt my ego to see a skirt run in front and say, "Mine, mine," while I just went, "Terrific, terrific," all day long. I literally had to get out on the court early in the morning before a match just to practice my first step so that I could learn to hold my own.

Another warning: when you cross the center stripe on the dead run, you now own that side and your partner is obligated to take your side of the court. Don't cross the line and suddenly think, "Oh, oh, I shouldn't have gone," and then jump back, because you'll leave your partner in the lurch. You made a decision to go for the ball, and now you're responsible.

"Who Takes the Lobs?"

Some players think that when their team is at the net and a lob goes over one partner's head, his partner should run back and try to make the play. That is wrong. *In every category of doubles, you are responsible for your own side of the court from net to baseline when a ball goes over your head.* Don't automatically turn around and say "yours," because your partner may be saying the same thing. You must both retreat together and you should make the play unless for some reason you are completely out of position.

Think of yourself as being responsible for a sidewalk that is exactly 18 feet wide and 39 feet long. Your primary responsibility starts there. The only time your partner should come into that area is when he has priority on the shot, or you have lunged for a ball and haven't recovered your balance yet.

"What Side Should the Lefty Play?"

I get this question all the time from righthanders. The key factor is to understand who you're playing. If your opponents are intermediates who always try to hit down the alley, then the lefthander should be on the left side so that you have forehands down each alley. But against good players, who are always trying to hit down the middle, the lefthander may play the right side, which gives your team two forehands down the center. Also, the lefthander can swing across with his backhand on the service return and pull the ball away from the net man.

Tips to Keep You Alive

1. Never try to watch your partner serve. Not only is it dangerous, it contaminates your reactions and movements at the net. Besides, you can tell exactly where the serve has gone by simply watching the receiver.

2. When your partner is behind you and is going to hit an overhead smash, don't turn around to watch him. He may mishit and give *you* the fuzz sandwich.

3. In fact, it's unnecessary to see what your partner is doing — you don't play your partner. Concentrate instead on studying your opponents and learn to sense what type of shot they're going to hit.

4. If your opponent is winding up to deck an overhead, and you're at the

net, don't be a hot dog by standing in front and trying to fake him out or return his shot. That's a good way to risk serious injury. It's *your* responsibility to get out of the way or to turn your back as a sign of submission. Your opponent does not have to try to hit around you and thus risk missing his shot, unless you turn away. Then his job is to simply try to hit a clean winner away from your body. If he still accidentally hits you, he will hold up his hand when you turn around, meaning that he's sorry for the accident. You have to accept that. But if his hand isn't up when you turn around, then it's war — and the next time *you* have an overhead near the net, your opponent's first move will be to take off in the opposite direction.

Other Playing Tips

1. People who have trouble in doubles are those who hero-worship their partner or who are dependent thinkers. They're always thinking, "My partner will get it." But if you want to help form a winning team, you must be ready for every situation that occurs. Your only thought should be, "I'm going to get the next ball." If your partner gets it, fine, but already you're anticipating the very next shot.

2. In good doubles everywhere, the point is going to end very quickly. The ball will seldom cross the net more than two or three times, so take good care of the shot you're on, because statistically it's your last. You can rest between points.

3. Just because you are playing doubles, *don't forget good volleying form*. Work on having fast hands and quick feet so that you can contact the ball properly off your front shoulder. Keep your racket head *up* as you go for the ball and finish with a high follow-through to keep from chopping down. Remember that most volleys in doubles, especially on quick exchanges, wind up in the net because people under pressure tend to face the net and pull down, instead of keeping their side to the net, hitting through the ball, and carrying it out deep. Even if you're angling the ball sharply, don't try to make a little play with the racket head or you will dump your shot into the net or beyond the sidelines. Wherever you volley on the court, *work to be aggressive* in getting to the ball and then making your hit.

Even if you're a raw beginner, volleying is obviously crucial in doubles, since you're at the net half the match. Some people, in fact, have good volleys but weak groundstrokes, so developing sound groundstrokes doesn't necessarily lead to a good volley, nor must groundstrokes come first.

4. Think about your different responsibilities and *practice* them; get them ingrained in your mind so you don't have to think during a point. Each little concept that's important in doubles must be practiced, yet most people tell me, "Jeez, I don't have time to practice — I'll think about it at home and then just do it in the match." But you're not going to pull it off in the match without some prior rehearsal on the court. If you wait to try out all of your new tricks when you're playing a big match, you're going to run out of partners.

Now don't get me wrong. You never want to be afraid to experiment and make mistakes as you play; you want to learn something from every match. But first set up a practice session where you have specific goals in mind. For instance, "Today I will practice taking balls down the center and I will work on getting close to the net. I'm going to keep my feet moving. I'm going to work on anticipating my opponent's shot. I'm going to keep my eyes down on the ball when I make my hit, and try to block out my opponents. Then I am going to work on getting my first serve in play so that my partner won't have to wear a helmet."

5. Psychologically, always try to enhance your partner's position by making him (or her) feel good, not lousy. Your partner's not a masochist and hopefully you're not a sadist, although it's a great combination if you also have the strokes. Great players always try to talk positively to their partners; they have respect for one another and they know they win or lose *as a team*. You should take the same approach. Sure it's frustrating to see your partner play poorly or dump crucial shots, but once a person starts feeling that he (or she) is the weak link on the team — and is constantly reminded of that fact — he can't do anything right.

Tennis is supposed to be fun, and nobody should be having a miserable time. So if your partner is getting down on you all the time and destroying all your fun — or vice versa — then dump that person, or give him the chance to find a more congenial partner. If you say, "Well, I can't — it's my husband," then the two of you should just try to be realistic. If you have a clear understanding of each other's strengths and weaknesses, and your objectives are well known, then this tends to prevent hostile feelings from building up.

Poaching

Poaching means to intentionally enter your partner's territory, normally when your partner is serving and you are at the net. This enables you to cut off your opponent's service return if it heads for your partner. If the ball goes into your former side of the court, your partner moves over to make the play. A second objective is to distract the service receiver by your movement at the net and thus force him into errors.

Most people don't realize how valuable, and how much fun, poaching can be. But it adds three important ingredients to your strategy: (1) By increasing the external stimuli, you make it more difficult for your opponents to focus attention on key fundamentals, such as "eyes on the ball" and "head down through impact." (2) It establishes you immediately as the offensive team. (3) You can literally control your opponents by forcing them to hit in the direction you have preselected, by your ability to poach or fake a poach.

Let's say that your opponents are always returning serve at your partner's feet when he rushes the net, which forces him to bend down and hit weak half-volleys. This in turn enables your opponents to bombard you at the net. You finally get tired of taking that kind of punishment, so poaching becomes your means of retaliation.

You have hand signals worked out ahead of time with your partner and now you hide your hand behind your back and signal your intentions just before the first serve. Many secret signals can be used, but normally one finger means you're going to cut across the court on the first serve only, two fingers mean you're going on the second serve only, a clenched fist means you're not going on either serve, and an open hand means "We've been partners for 11 years and I'm not getting any action up here — I'm going on anything that lands in."

Experience in playing together will help you overcome two common problems in poaching. The first is that while you are busy signaling, your partner is so wrapped up in his own serve ("Dear God, let this go in") that he doesn't even notice your signals. Second, some people forget that they must conceal their intention to poach. Thus you see them turn around, with their signal still in place behind their back, and say, "Did you get that, Bertha?"

Once your signaling is coordinated, then the instant your partner's serve crosses the net, take off across the center stripe to intercept your opponent's

The net man is signaling his serving partner that he intends to poach. Many secret signals can be used, but normally they are as follows: One finger behind the back means the net man is going to cut across the court into the server's territory if the first serve lands in — but he will poach only on the first serve. Two fingers means "I'm only poaching on the second serve." An open hand means "I'm going on any serve that lands in." And a clenched fist means "I'm not going anywhere." This is often used just to worry opponents.

return, while your partner rushes in to cover your old territory. However, make sure that the service receiver is committed to hit in the direction you want before you make your break. Even if you break when the ball crosses the net toward him, there might be enough time for the receiver to actually change the direction of the ball.

The same ruling applies to the server. He must wait until both direct and peripheral vision have been taken off of him by the receiver — when it's too late for the receiver to change his swing — before he breaks and takes the opposite court. He should actually take his two or three steps forward after his follow-through, and then run cross-court. If he's too eager to get to the other side, he will tip off the poach by taking just one step forward and then breaking across.

When the receiver detects a poach, he doesn't have to panic. He can hit a fairly soft return toward the net man's vacated position (where the server is heading) — or he can lob, since both opponents are moving, and in awkward positions. Yet to show you the real value of poaching, even when many service receivers "read" the poach, they're still so bothered that they miss their shot. Similarly, you might poach and miss your own shot, but you will worry your opponents on future shots. *By always threatening to poach — instead of just camping at the net on every serve — you make your team infinitely more effective.* In a sport where few players keep their eyes focused on the ball to begin with, any distraction you can throw at people to force them to start looking your way will increase the number of stimuli with which they are dealing, and thus improve your chances of winning. But when you assume the same ready position at the net that you've had since '38, then you *decrease* your opponents' anxiety because they know right away you're never going to poach.

Learn to poach effectively and you'll see how easily you can manipulate people mentally. You can make a person hit the ball where you want, and even get him so bugged that if you just give a little knee movement or a shoulder fake, he'll drop his racket. But to learn how to poach, you have to practice. Play one match where you poach on every point, or on all the odd points, or all the even points, and you'll be amazed at how many more balls you get to hit up at the net, and how much more fun you have.

To defend against poaching when you see it coming, try to lob, go down the middle as the two players are shifting, or hit behind the poacher down the alley. But *pick your shot and hit it* — don't suddenly second-guess yourself. Know how far the poacher can come across before he is vulnerable to a passing shot behind him. When I try to anticipate poaching by my

254

opponents, I don't watch for head or shoulder movements — they can be fakes. I watch the belt buckle, because a man never runs without his pants. If a woman is poaching, I try to find another piece of clothing.

Mixed Doubles

If you're the woman in mixed doubles, and you know how to volley, you're going to make your partner famous — if his ego doesn't interfere.

Yet we all know what happens on the typical husband-and-wife team when the man goes to serve. He takes his wife up to the net and says, "Darling, big match today, right? If we win, we'll be king and queen of Pismo Beach. You are so valuable and you volley so well that I'm going to put you in this all-time important spot" — a four-foot cubicle in the alley, right in front of the net. When he walks away he says, "And don't forget, hold the racket up in front of your face." Subconsciously, what he is really saying to her is: "Look, I can play these guys alone. If I could, I would put you on the bench but it wouldn't look too good to our neighbors."

Women, believe me, don't fall for this approach by your partner, no matter how long you've been told that the woman is the weaker player and that she doesn't have a big role at the net. The fact of the matter is, *you are much more important to your team than the man.* He thinks he's going to make you famous by running all over the court to save every point, but an interesting thing happens: he starts running out of oxygen while you keep getting all the shots. If you can volley, crowd the net, react quickly, and feel free to cross the center stripe for shots where you have the priority, you will put fantastic pressure on the other team. They will now have to treat your team *as a team*, rather than intimidating you into inaction at the net while they run your partner into the ground.

So women, don't let men push you off to the side and make you so fearful to move and cover your shots that you simply settle into that classic ready position, racket held in front of your face like a gun sight. Neither can you leave the volleying to your partner and still win in good mixed doubles competition. The name of the game is for *both players* to have the freedom to make the play, based on the fundamental principle: *the player closer to the net has priority.* Thus, if you have position on your male partner — and the quickness — jump right in front and take his volley. Don't let him scare you off by saying, "You're a skirt — stay on your side," because that's a

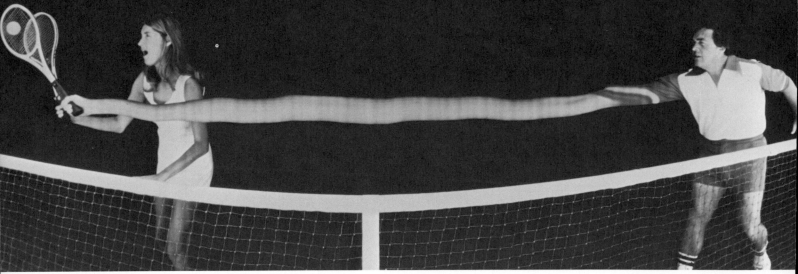

PHOTO BY JOHN G. ZIMMERMAN

Court hogs kill a good doubles team.

losing syndrome right off the bat. What he's really saying is, "Look, darling, the closer you come to my side, the more our chances of losing increase."

Of course, to hold your own with men, you women must learn how to volley, how to react quickly, and how to overcome your fears up at the net — three requirements that are closely intertwined. Not until you learn to defend yourself — and to attack — with an adequate volley will you develop the confidence to react instinctively, and either crowd the net, lunge for a passing shot, or retreat for a lob. Knowing how to volley will also help you cope with the psychological conflicts which inhibit the quick reactions you seek. Tennis is one of the few sports where men and women can compete together — if not always harmoniously. The physical strength aspects encourage many male partners to always try to crowd and take your shots, while chauvinistic opponents work out subconscious hostilities by trying to give you a new navel. Thus it's only natural to fear getting hit by the ball. I'm afraid it's your responsibility to get out of the way, but a strong volley is the best method I know to even the score — by winning the point.

Developing a strong backhand volley requires you to also strengthen the extensor muscles on your hitting arm (see drill, page 107), so that you can keep the ball deep. For example, smart players will test your strength immediately by hitting high to your backhand volley; if you don't have a strong arm you'll hit the ball short and give them an easy put-away shot. But if you can "muscle" that ball and keep the head of your racket up so that the volley goes deep, then your opponents will know they are in trouble.

Positioning

When it comes to deciding who plays on which side of the court, the man very often perpetuates another myth. He plays an unfair role by trying to convince the woman that he's giving her the easier of the two sides. If they are both righthanded, he will say, "Look, darling, I'm giving you the easy

Ever since mixed doubles play began, the man has placed his female partner close to the net and in the alley. Basically, he's trying to get her out of his way — he's really saying, "Look, darling, I think I can play this match alone." In recent years I've noticed more and more women placing the man in the alley. But regardless, if someone wants you to play there, start looking for a new partner.

right side to receive serve and I'll take that tough left side." *This is a lie,* but the woman usually falls for it. When she plays the right court — especially in good tennis — she is in deep trouble. She invariably receives serve to the backhand side, and she must be able to hit inside-out in order to keep the ball away from the net man. Her partner, however, never sees it this way.

Let's say play begins and the opposing team serves to the woman's backhand. The tendency by nearly everybody is to swing across on the backhand, and the woman is no exception: she pulls her shot right to the net man and he gives her husband the fuzz sandwich. The husband then turns around and says, "Dummy, I've told you for 15 years — keep the ball away from the net man. Now look, I'm going to show you one more time how to do this." He goes back to receive serve, it comes to his backhand, and he swings the exact same way as the woman. Except that when he swings across, the ball goes *away* from the net man and right at the server. *The man looks great only because he happens to be on the side which facilitates making a nice shot with his weakness.* So women, don't let the man get away with being an imposter. Remember, the great doubles teams in history have been made by a right-court player who can return serve. This is the pressure point — at 30-all and deuce — and if the woman can get the serve back and help win the point here, then all the pressure goes on the server to hold serve, and her partner can relax.

In club tennis, if the woman has a decent backhand, then it pays to have her play the right court — providing her partner understands the situation. First, the man is faster poaching from left to right across the net. Second, he can move from left to right to chase down a lob over his partner's head. (Although the ideal is for each player to cover his own lane, from net to baseline, the reality is that most women are slower getting back on lobs.) Third, the man is hitting forehand volleys down the middle, which helps compensate for the fact that most women don't have the strong extensor muscles needed to attack the high backhand volley.

When the man arbitrarily puts the woman in the right court, a check-and-balance system fortunately exists that helps the woman get even at the end of the day. When she serves, the man loves to poach at the net and he wins lots of points, which helps her hold serve. But when the man serves, the woman normally doesn't like to volley and she's afraid to poach, so her partner usually loses his serve. Now they're driving home and they start having a gigantic argument about who was to blame for their loss. But the woman flattens the man immediately. "Don't look at me," she says. "I won every serve."

257

Chapter Eleven

Improving Your Game through Conditioning, Lessons, and Practice

WHETHER YOUR GOAL is the singles title in Pismo Beach — or the finals at Wimbledon — I've emphasized throughout this book that your game must be built upon basic stroke production and the mental and physical tenacity to keep getting the ball back over the net. Then you can start worrying about match-play psychology, strategy, fancy shots, and how to jump over the net without breaking your leg.

However, building a sound tennis game assumes a dedication greater than simply playing once or twice a week. You must devote time to physical conditioning, you have to learn how to practice your strokes, and you must have the ability to break comfortable old stroking habits and groove what are at first uncomfortable but proper new habits — with or without the aid of a good teaching pro.

Remember, there's a learning sequence in tennis, as in any other sport, and you have to master certain skills before you can move up to higher playing levels. Nearly all players can reach a certain level of proficiency where they can keep the ball in play well enough to be identified as "tennis players." But when they get about halfway to their goal of being *good* players (on the "B" ladder, let's say) they tend to peel off because they fail to realize that *good tennis is built on the shot you hit prior to the one you are hitting.* Thus, you'll be a much better volleyer if you have a good approach shot that keeps your opponent deep, but you won't get the first approach shot if you fail to hit a deep groundstroke that keeps your opponent away from the net.

Think about what a little improvement can mean to your game: *If you can improve by one ball over the net per point, you'll beat nearly everybody you play today.* We all tend to play people near us in ability, and statistics show that the ball fails to cross the net more than four times on most points. So if you can improve your average by one ball per point, you stand to increase your chances of winning that point by 25 percent. Unfortunately, this improvement is easy to talk about, tough to execute — but that's why tennis is such a fascinating challenge.

Physical Conditioning

A superbly fit tennis player is considered to be that individual who can play aggressive and defensive tennis on a continuous basis from 90 to 120 minutes on a daily workout program. On the other end of the spectrum are those players who take three trips around the ice box and then need a nap. How then to make that quantum leap to physical respectability, whatever your age, occupation, or ability level?

Everybody can start by trying to play the game correctly, once or twice a week. Instead of camping on the baseline and working on your tan, try to chase down every shot and move quickly into hitting position so that you can swing easily once you get there. Then concentrate on playing with your *body* instead of standing flat-footed and "arming" the ball. By lowering your body properly on every groundstroke, and lifting up and stretching out toward your intended target, you give your thighs and stomach muscles a real workout. Add a lot of hustle and you won't find yourself complaining, "I played two sets of tennis and I gained a pound."

Although a set or two of good, vigorous tennis can be a conditioner in itself, you also need to devise a program of general conditioning exercises and specific drills that will help develop the muscles and reflexes you need to play the game right. But before you set out to whip your body into playing shape, remember that proper conditioning is a slow process that demands intelligent planning. If you are over 35, then you should have a physical examination *under stress conditions*, which may turn up special warning signs about the heart. Exercise physiologists such as Jack Wilmore and Paul Vodak also point out that it's better to exercise 15 minutes a day — every day — than to have only one or two long workouts on the weekend. You cannot make up for lost time with body conditioning by adding workout hours at the end of the week.

Arm and Back Muscles

a. Traditional push-ups strengthen back and arm muscles used in practically every stroke. Doing the push-ups on your fingertips will help your wrists and forearms, but this takes strong fingers.

b. Although I've argued during the book that the strength of your arm is unimportant to good strokes if you learn to use the power in your body, strong *forearm* muscles will help give you a more solid stroke. The ball-in-the-racket-cover drill (page 107) is excellent for developing the extensor muscles that are crucial on the backhand. Another popular exercise device can be built and used at home. Take a cut-off broom handle, drill a hole in the middle, and attach a piece of four-foot rope or cord with a small weight (one or two pounds) tied to the end. Hold the stick straight out from your body and *slowly* roll the weight up, then roll it back down. This slow rolling action creates the most continuous exertion on the forearms.

Stomach Muscles

Jack Kramer placed much of his conditioning emphasis upon developing strong stomach muscles. He felt that in lifting up as he stroked the ball, his stomach was as important as his thighs. Thus he would work with a medicine ball, and do a lot of sit-ups, although exercise physiologists tell us today that sit-ups are not the most practical exercise you can do for the stomach.

Thigh Muscles

Personally, I feel the "sit-and-hit" chair drill (page 60) can be one of the most valuable exercises in tennis. Not only does it develop the muscles actually used on proper groundstrokes — particularly the thighs — it enables you to practice the stroking patterns which I seek.

Deep knee bends are good for the thighs, providing you go only halfway down. When you try to bend all the way down, you risk knee injuries (especially in adults) by placing excess demands on undeveloped muscles and ligaments around the knee.

Developing Good Footwork, Quickness, and Stamina

Most people forget about their feet as they play, and very few players practice moving to the ball and covering the court. They just get out and hit the ball. Yet even without natural speed afoot, you'll have time to get into proper hitting position for nearly every shot if you will work on several specific drills — and your concentration.

First of all, remind yourself that *thinking* about good footwork will improve your footwork. Learn to anticipate your opponent's shot and get that fast first step the instant you detect where the ball is going. This alone will give you nearly all the "quickness" you've been told you need to play this game properly. But don't let me mislead you: it's tough to learn to play with this degree of intensity. You have to work at it constantly.

Second, the following exercises should help you prepare for the stop-and-go type of action in tennis:

a. Shadow tennis, as devised by former Davis Cup Captain Dennis Ralston, is the single best drill I know to get your body ready for a match while giving your heart, lungs, and legs an excellent workout — all in five minutes or less. What you want to do is "shadowbox" an imaginary point on an empty court, without actually hitting a ball. (You can even do this at home if you have a piece of lawn half as long — 39 feet — as a tennis court.) Work out your own sequence of strokes, but concentrate on the shots you need in order to beat an opponent by working your way up to the net. For example, serve and fall in, take your three steps forward, and stop momentarily with your stutter-step. Then break left or right for an approach volley or bend down for a half-volley, but keep moving forward as you hit. Stretch out for an imaginary volley at the net, then retreat quickly for a lob. Reach up and hit an overhead back near the baseline, then run in again for a low forehand approach shot or a high backhand volley, before racing back again for another lob. Always keep your feet moving, and bend low, lift up, and stretch out exactly as you would in a match. If you think this all sounds easy, try playing an imaginary point for *one minute* and see how exhausted you become. "Do it two or three times a week," says Ralston, "and I guarantee, you'll improve your quickness and your conditioning."

If you regard yourself as a "baseline player" and you think this drill is worthless to your game, consider these two points: (1) You're a baseline player only as long as you play intermediates. But when you go up against somebody who knows how to play, that person will force you to volley and come to the net. (2) Even from the baseline you have to run left and right for low and high backhands and forehands; you have to serve, and hit service returns, lobs, and overheads. "Shadowbox" a sequence of these strokes, but always come back to the center stripe after each shot, and see how quickly you become winded.

b. Rope jumping will improve your footwork as well as your stamina. The drill I like best is to simulate a boxing match by jumping rope for three minutes, resting for one minute, then jumping again for another three minutes. Go slowly at first, one or two rounds a day, but as your "wind" improves, see how many rounds you can last. Kramer used this drill, and when he could go 15 rounds and still feel fresh enough to play, he knew he was ready for Wimbledon.

c. I believe in practicing pretty much as you must perform. Thus the "coin footwork" drill, on the court or in your living room, can help you develop the proper footwork on your groundstrokes while making you more agile on your feet. Toss a coin out in front of you, then run to the coin and make your back foot always land right on it, with your side to the imaginary or actual net. This enables the front foot to step toward your target. More than likely you will have to take little skipping steps as you get closer to the coin in order to land on it with the back foot, but these skip-steps will keep you from hitting off the "wrong foot."

Warming-up Exercises

I talked earlier in the book about the importance of hitting all of your possible shots while warming up. One reason, of course, is that you want to be ready to play your best tennis from the first point on. But more important is the fact that most people get hurt during a match by doing things they haven't done in practice. On the serve, especially, they can pull a shoulder muscle by failing to warm up sufficiently. Or take the low volley. Very often people will be forced to hit their first low backhand volley in the middle of a key point. As a result, they haven't stretched the muscles they need for that shot, and they're awkward and uncomfortable trying to make the play.

That's why, in my opinion, Ralston's "shadowboxing" drill is the best way I know to get your body — and your strokes — ready for a match. By taking every stroke you can imagine and rehearsing each as you run to the right, to the left, diagonally forward, and then back to the baseline, you'll be puffing hard and you'll be properly loosened up.

Another excellent tune-up drill is Kramer's old trick of never letting yourself be out of proper hitting position for any ball during the warm-up. This requires you to be up on your toes, watching your opponent like a hawk to anticipate the direction of his next shot, and then running — sometimes sprinting — so that you reach the ball in plenty of time for the first bounce.

Finding a Teaching Pro

It's difficult for anybody to learn to play tennis, or to make significant improvement, by operating in a vacuum. The self-evaluation techniques I've described in this book can certainly be helpful, but you still need another person to periodically analyze your swing and point out problems. Unfortunately, most people don't know what to look for; their eyes aren't trained to study technique. They can notice that *something* is wrong with your swing but they're not sure what.

Therefore, unless you can basically teach yourself, or unless you have friends with knowledgeable eyes for good tennis technique, you should rely on a series of lessons with a qualified teaching pro or periodic crash-course instruction at a tennis college or camp. Having worked both sides of the net — as a teaching pro and, since 1971, as director of the Vic Braden Tennis College in southern California — I know what each route can offer to players at every ability level.

The Tennis College Approach

The reason that a tennis college was so important to me was that I was frustrated by the limitations of weekly half-hour and hour-long lessons. I knew that tennis, under stress, was much more of a muscle-memory problem than an intellectual functioning process. Yet a lesson would be over just as an individual's muscles were beginning to learn the correct stroking sensations, and unless that person would practice these sensations during the week, we would have to start over again at the next lesson. Furthermore, I never had a concentrated period of time where I could give a student all the strokes while tying them together with my overview of the game and my approach to strategy and tactics. I had always felt — and still do — that most individuals could make large learning gains by seeing the total picture as much as possible. Conversely, people who learned particular strokes in isolation, without knowing *why* the stroke was important or how it contributed to an overall pattern of play, would very often lack any real enthusiasm for the game.

The tennis college concept (in weekend and five-day doses) solved these problems by giving me the chance to take a group of tennis buffs and close out all other distractions as my staff and I went to work on the correct strokes and appropriate strategy. I've also discovered since 1971 that a good tennis college or tennis camp should also give you a better perspective on the teaching pro you might eventually select, and the value you gain from subsequent lessons.

Evaluating the Pro before Signing Up for Lessons

Qualified teaching pros should welcome the chance to have you sit near the court and evaluate their instruction during an actual lesson — before you commit your own money. Many pros feel that prior inspection is an insult to their teaching ability, but if your prospective pro appears threatened in this way, keep searching for the instructor with the right self-confidence.

Watching a pro give a lesson should help you realize if the chemistry would be right between the two of you; perhaps there's something about the pro's coaching patter, his manner, or his approach to technique that strikes you wrong. Reading this book, in fact, should help you understand whether or not the pro is teaching according to the physical laws and realities which rule the game at every level of play. Remember, *talented pros never offer their students a get-rich-quick approach to the game.* They know that good strokes are built on fundamentals. Similarly, you want a pro whose primary concern is with *proper stroking form,* and who shows that he's not influenced by where the ball lands. He knows that once you develop good stroking patterns, then direction and distance will come easily.

You also want to discover, either in prior conversations with the pro or as you observe one of his lessons, whether or not he makes sense. If, deep inside, you really don't believe what he has to say about technique, then you won't try to work on his suggestions once the lesson is over. He might say, "You're starting to improve. I can see you're trying to make the right changes in your swing." But the moment you begin to play a match, you look over your shoulder to see if the pro is around, and you're thinking, "I know what Vic said, but I've got this little shot that I can beat Bertha with every time." Some people go so far as to tell their pro, in effect: "That's terrific what you teach, I really like you, and here's your fifteen bucks. But don't horse around with my strokes."

Taking Lessons

I think we'll see the day when you don't even hit a ball at the first lesson. Instead, the pro will give you his (or her) overview of the game and what he feels are the important principles of good technique. He'll try to learn something about your athletic background, any fears you might have about the game, or persistent problems you are trying to work out with your strokes. He'll want to know how you learn best. Are you a kinesthetic learner, where you like to have the instructor guide you through the proper stroking movements to give you a feel for the proper sensations? Or do you learn best by imitation? Knowledge like this can save valuable time once you go out on the court, yet many unqualified pros don't even get to know their students until after four or five lessons.

At this first meeting, the pro would explain and demonstrate the proper stroking patterns for the backhand and forehand, plus reasons why (ideally) he is teaching the loop swing rather than "straight back." He could demonstrate the "sit-and-hit" chair drill so that you could practice at home before the first real lesson. If you'd been playing the game competitively, he might also explain how to chart so that you could have a friend chart one of your matches before the next lesson. This would give both you and the pro an objective understanding of your strengths and weaknesses.

Once the on-court instruction begins, you *want* an instructor who judges you by your swing, and not the results of that swing. Don't let yourself — or the pro — be ball-direction oriented. If you have a lousy swing and the pro tries to suggest a correction, the tendency is to answer, "Yeh, but that ball landed in." A confident pro, however, won't weaken. His objective will always be to keep you from repeating — and thus reinforcing — an incorrect stroke, even if the ball lands in play occasionally.

A good pro tries to get you into rhythmical patterns as you swing, but he also knows that anxiety can sap out any rhythm you might have. So he'll try to *reduce* your anxiety level by taking a positive approach to instruction.

If he has to slug you with a concept that's hard for you to accept or to grasp, he'll throw support your way for the trying. He'll always reward your willingness to experiment with new — and correct — stroking sensations, even if the ball keeps going out. I like to start people out the way I want them to finish (grips, basic stroke patterns, etc.) but I won't push so hard for "correct" technique that I drive them into bowling or badminton.

Another sign of good instruction is the coach who doesn't want any shot to be wasted during the lesson. Students will sometimes complain, "Coach, I don't want to run for that volley — it's going out anyway." But so what? You can still stretch for the ball, try to keep your racket head up, and then punch the shot deep. You'll squeeze everything possible out of a lesson by taking this approach to every shot.

In Defense of Ball Machines

Many teaching pros are opposed to ball machines. They argue that nothing can replace the live "feel" of hitting against a coach, and that a person who learns off a ball machine will be thrown off in an actual match when every ball is hit with different pace and bounce. However, I feel that ball machines are of great value — if properly used. No machine can replace the good coach, but if the goal is to standardize a proper stroke, no coach can replace a machine.

First of all, grooving a swing requires thousands of repetitions along the proper stroking pattern. The more often you take the right swing, the less chance there is of returning to the old incorrect one. Thus, when a machine is firing a ball at the student every four seconds, the coach can stand nearby and concentrate completely on the student's stroke.

Second, when the coach is hitting the balls himself from across the net, the student becomes coach-oriented rather than ball-oriented. The machine, being inanimate, makes it easier to concentrate on the ball.

Third, people learn by hearing, feeling, or seeing. So the pro who insists on hitting every ball over the net to the student limits his opportunities to demonstrate proper strokes to that student. Or, if the student learns best by kinesthesia, then it's impossible for the coach to be close to guide the student through a particular movement.

The Role of Muscle-Memory

The pro's basic job is to help you understand the physical laws which rule the game, and to tell you what it is you're doing in relation to those laws. He'll try to provide you with an idea of what the correct sensation should be, and he'll help you recognize what you are doing wrong. But ultimately *you* are the one responsible for improving your tennis game. Even the most dedicated pro can't help you reach a higher playing level if you refuse to break comfortable old bad habits.

As I discussed earlier in the book, it's doggone hard — physically and psychologically — to break away from these habits as you try to effect the proper stroking pattern. For one thing, everybody has a tendency to re-vert back to what he's always done. Even when a person has played only two or three times, and has been unsuccessful, I've found that when he starts to take lessons he insists on swinging the way that is comfortable, yet un-successful. Second, you're tampering with motor movements which have been "grooved" by months or years of improper play. You may tell your-self, "Dummy, don't lay the wrist back," but muscle-memory keeps laying the wrist back, especially when you get under stress.

Therefore, when a qualified pro introduces you to some uncomfortable, awkward feelings, that's exactly what you want. Remember these sensa-tions as you repeat the swing, and try to exaggerate; don't be embarrassed by going beyond the correct movement and then working back. Nearly every-body wants to make only a *tiny* change, but I've never seen players really im-prove this way. They'll tell themselves, "I know Vic says to bend my knees. I usually bend a quarter of an inch, so now I'm going to bend a whole inch." But I want people to lower their body and try to go too far so that they really understand what the sensation is like. Little kids aren't afraid to go way out. If the pro tells them, "You're not bending your knees. You have to get down lower, like you're sitting in a chair," most of them will bend down and literally sit in a chair. But adults will look around. They want to make sure that nobody is looking, or that they don't look funny. But believe me: *feeling good about feeling terrible is the breakthrough you need to make to acquire better strokes.* (Ultimately, however, if the pain and frustration of making changes is just too great for you, and you would rather keep losing with your old comfortable swing, then you should stop taking lessons. Why keep paying money to be frustrated when you apparently lack the temper-ament to improve anyway?)

A related problem that inhibits learning — especially by adults — is that very often they have an image of themselves which is very different from reality. They don't look the way they think they look when they swing and they can get pretty defensive when the pro points this out. That's why video taping can be so effective if people will give it a chance. The television screen shows you exactly what the pro is seeing, and there's no hiding from that reality. So no matter how high your self-esteem, remember to have an open mind when it comes to your tennis swing.

The following are other reminders to help you learn to improve your game at a faster rate, with or without a teaching pro:

a. Be objective about your strengths and weaknesses. Chart your matches and put your different strokes to the test so that you'll have a realistic idea of what you can actually do out on the court. This will keep you from attacking the pro for giving you the bad news about your tennis game.

b. Don't get anxious out there, and don't be afraid to look bad as you work on new strokes, since fear can inhibit proper or desired physical responses.

c. Remember that tennis is a mistake center for everybody. Enjoy learning what your mistakes are and discovering appropriate cures. Your goal should be to strive for improvement; winning matches will follow in a natural sequence.

d. You have a tendency to perform whatever you visualize, so try to develop a positive mental image of yourself playing the game right — even if you haven't yet developed the correct strokes. Most people try so hard not to look bad that they visualize — and thus reinforce — what it is they do wrong, rather than visualize what is right. Billie Jean King once told me that when she goes to the net to volley, "All I imagine is the ball going right through my opponent." She never imagines herself missing or even coming close to missing — only that she makes the successful play.

e. We always have people going through the tennis college who dearly enjoy learning, while others struggle and fight back and work very hard *not to learn*. That's why I stress a philosophy that learning to play a better game of tennis can be fun, not drudgery, and that when you enjoy playing, you have more incentive to improve your strokes. This increases your chances of winning, which increases your enjoyment level, so it's a beautiful circle. If, however, the game is providing more stress than relaxation, then you've got the wrong sport, or the wrong teaching pro.

Many people try to blame the pro for their lack of improvement. They go from lesson to lesson without really listening to the pro or working on making specific corrections in their swing, and yet they complain, "Gee, the pro isn't very good," or "This pro can't coach me." Perhaps the pro is an ineffective teacher, but oftentimes people are simply shopping around for a pro who will tell them what they want to hear.

Every pro, therefore, should develop an evaluative technique *on paper* that will objectively outline the student's specific improvements and the old problems that still exist. The pro can say, "We've been together a month and here's what I've told you (checklist, checklist) and here's what you're doing (checklist, checklist). You've improved here, here, and here, but you're still making the same mistakes here and here. Maybe it's my fault, maybe it's yours, or maybe it's both of us. Perhaps we should change my approach a little." Another of my suggestions to teaching pros is that they videotape their student's strokes at the first lesson — and then again in three months or six months or whatever. The pro should try to see what improvements have been made, and ask himself, "Was this instruction really worth $500?" Some pros would say, "It's worth $500 just to be with me every week," but I doubt if they're going to last long in this business.

Getting the Most out of Practice

Everybody can tell you, "Jeez, I was better before I took lessons." And very often it's true, for when you're trying to break muscle-memory patterns, the tendency is to retrogress before you finally begin to improve. Unfortunately, most people lack the patience or the willingness to keep concentrating on key changes in their swing while their ego takes a beating, and thus when they find themselves under stress they invariably revert to what's comfortable, even if it's a losing style of play.

That's why I urge you to avoid competition when you are working to change your technique, unless you can block out your desire to win as you concentrate on effecting your new or adjusted swing. But whenever your ego interferes, remove the stress by simply rallying with people until you feel comfortable with the changes you have made. If you need to play six points to keep yourself from getting sloppy or to make practice more fun, then don't keep a cumulative score. Serve, receive, and play out the point to get your adrenaline flowing, but don't fall in the trap of seeing who can win ten points first.

I realize it's hard to find people who are willing to be your backboard and your ball machine for an hour; they'd rather play two sets. But a good club pro will always know members who simply want to work on their game in a non-competitive situation and what these people are looking for in a practice partner. For example, Joe Jones only wants to work on ground-strokes, or John Smith is working on his service return and wants somebody to hit serves. To practice your overhead, find the person who wants to practice his lobs.

Try to avoid rallying with somebody who just wants to slug the ball; instead of relaxing and working on your own strokes, you'll worry more about matching this person's power. Better to seek out a dinker who just keeps the ball in play. Even if the ball is hit softly, get your racket back and move into position quickly, then practice swinging easy. Don't try to power the ball back — you're working on your stroke, not the speed of your shot.

However, you practice, *always have a purpose in mind for every shot.* Know your weak strokes and where you are making your errors on the court, then get out and practice these shots; don't simply hone your strengths. Try to isolate what the pro told you at your previous lesson so that you can actually *improve* between lessons. If you have specific weaknesses during a match, practice before you play again and concentrate on your errors. Whenever Jack Kramer had trouble with a particular stroke — such as his low backhand volley — he would go out on a practice court immediately after the match and hit that shot 100 or 150 times . . . or until he knew he could sleep well that night. Contrast this to the average player, who simply takes a shower after a match and thinks, "Maybe next week I'll play a little better."

To get the most out of practice, *learn to become target-oriented on every shot,* since targets point out weaknesses faster than any other method. You'll be frustrated by the fact that you seldom land the ball where you are aiming, but this will help you become much more objective about your game, and what really needs work. For example, to improve the depth on your ground-strokes, stretch a piece of cord across the court five feet inside the baseline, and try to land every shot inside that area. This will give you a graphic reminder of just how short most of your shots land. To work on approach shots, set up a four-foot square inside your opponent's backhand corner and

Practice Tip: Using a Backboard to Good Advantage

Most people fail to take advantage of the backboard as a useful practice companion, or to review their strokes before a match. They use the backboard to either get a fast workout by pounding the ball back, or to pass the time until they play — "I hope somebody comes soon because I'm getting tired of slugging this thing against the wall." Either way, they simply ingrain bad habits by failing to pay attention to what they're doing.

The real value of a backboard is that it gives you the chance to individualize your own instruction without being distracted by your opponent. By concentrating on one concept at a time, you can check out your forehand and backhand groundstrokes, work on timing and synchronization problems, practice your serve, and improve your reactions and footwork on the volley.

When you hit against a backboard — even if it is 39 feet away (the distance from the baseline to the net) — *let every ball bounce twice* so that you have time to check out your rhythm. One reason people end up slugging the ball is that backboards are built improperly; instead of being slanted back 15 degrees so that the ball hits and comes back naturally, backboards are vertical, and thus the angle of deflection brings the ball down. This forces people to keep moving closer to the board as they try to return the ball on the first bounce, and thus they never have a chance to check what they are doing on their swing. But when you let the ball bounce twice, and get into that slower-paced rhythm, you have the time to analyze key elements in your forehand and backhand, such as: Is your front foot stepping toward the board? Are you coming through with your body, and not simply "arming" the ball? Are you staying over the ball through contact? Are you remembering to follow through properly? Are the knuckles on your backhand and the palm on your forehand going out toward the intended target?

If you have 39 feet to play with, your eyes should remain fixed on the point of impact until you hear the ball pop against the backboard. You'll still have plenty of time to reach the ball on the second bounce. This 39-foot distance will also enable you to work on your serve. Have a piece of chalk along so that you can draw target circles one to two feet above the net; if the backboard hasn't been marked with a net, draw in the center stripe and a net line three feet above the ground at that point. To practice serving to your opponent's backhand corner from the right side of the court, place your target circle just to the left of the center stripe and above the net line, and then stand just to the right of the stripe, 39 feet from the backboard.

When you go to practice your volley, do so at close range — unlike your groundstrokes. Try to keep hitting the board without letting the ball bounce and this will force you to learn how to change grips quickly, while sharpening your reactions, anticipation, and eye contact on the ball.

Although the backboard will never replace a court for warming up before a match, it can certainly help you review the key fundamentals of your swing before you get absorbed in rallying with your opponent. But keep in mind that you're not trying to beat the backboard; you only want to check out the strokes you hope will beat your opponent.

try to punch every approach shot there. For the serve, place one or two tennis ball cans in your opponent's backhand corner and see if you can knock them over. On service returns, aim for cans that are set up down the sideline, and others which are set up cross-court, away from the onrushing server.

If you are rallying without specific targets, envision a target area and don't be satisfied with your stroke unless you can produce a shot that lands within three feet of that target. Another way to improve your accuracy from the baseline is to imagine that you're playing in a 4½-foot alley (which is the width of the doubles alley) and that you want to land every groundstroke inside this alley. Strive to keep the ball down the middle and deep at first and then, with experience, you can shift your "alley" down-the-line or cross-court.

You may think that playing tennis with targets in mind — rather than concentrating on just keeping the ball in play — will give you too much to think about ("Who can think and hit at the same time?"). But I've found over the years that when you fail to become target-oriented as you move into a shot, you tend to do your thinking in the middle of your stroke.

A final reminder about practicing: *Everybody needs it to improve.* Some people think that simply playing a lot of tennis will improve their game because they'll gain a better "feel" for their strokes. But if you have improper strokes, playing all the time can only help you reach a certain level — and one that isn't too high. Of course, if your only goal is to just play five days a week without really worrying about improving, then I'm with you all the way. The idea is to enjoy yourself out there. But if you've also set improvement as your goal and you don't improve (because you refuse to take lessons and/or you fail to practice) then you're going to be pretty frustrated because playing five times a week, you get more chances than the average player to recognize your failure.

In the end, I like to measure tennis players not by how many matches they win, but by how hard they work to improve their game. The top playing pros set a good example by using stroke production to judge their progress, while the average player only sees progress in terms of competition: "I won, so I'm playing well . . . I lost, so I'm playing lousy." Therefore, when you're practicing with a friend — or instead of playing a match — try drills in which you compete, but where the reward is not based upon winning the point. For example, gather up all the balls and serve until you're tired, while your friend practices service returns. Then have your friend serve until he's tired while you work on returning the ball. Instead of keeping track of who wins the most points, see who can get the best percentage of first serves in play, or who can return the most serves. You'll still have fun, and you'll improve.

People often challenge me when I talk about winning not being the only thing in tennis — or any sport, for that matter. They say, "What else really counts?" And I tell them: "It's the *striving* to win and *striving* to improve that's important. Learn to judge yourself by your own improvement during a match — and between matches. That's the real reward. No matter what your level of play, give it your best shot, have some fun, and you'll enjoy this great game for a lifetime."